STUMPWORK
Butterflies & Moths

To all who have shared this journey
with me over the past twenty years
— thank you.

STUMPWORK
Butterflies
& Moths

Jane Nicholas

SALLY MILNER
PUBLISHING

First published in 2013 by
Sally Milner Publishing Pty Ltd
734 Woodville Road
Binda NSW 2583 AUSTRALIA

© Jane Nicholas 2013

Design: Caroline Verity
Editing: Anne Savage
llustrations: Wendy Gorton, Bruce Rankin
Photography: Tim Connolly
Printed in China

National Library of Australia Cataloguing-in-Publication data:

Author:	Nicholas, Jane, author.
Title:	Stumpwork butterflies & moths / Jane Nicholas.
ISBN:	9781863514521 (hardback)
Series:	Milner craft series.
Notes:	Includes bibliographical references.
Subjects:	Embroidery--Patterns.
	Stump work.
	Embroidery.
	Decoration and ornament--Animal forms.
	Butterflies in art.
	Moths in art.
Dewey Number:	746.44

10 9 8 7 6 5 4 3 2 1

Contents

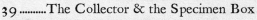

Introduction

Butterflies and moths, with their glorious colours and harmless appearance, are one of the most popular of all insects. From earliest times, the butterfly form has been celebrated in the art and literature of many different cultures.

As symbols of immortality and the human soul, butterfly legends and beliefs have become assimilated into the folk-lore of many countries. Collecting insects, and displaying them, has been the delight of the enthusiast since the early sixteenth century. In the nineteenth century, collecting butterflies and moths as serried rows in specimen boxes, or as decorative patterns in framed pictures, was a popular pursuit.

A specimen box is the perfect way to 'collect' stumpwork insects—it provides for the fascination of research, the challenge of interpretation and the joy of stitching. While I cannot claim to have experienced quite the level of enthusiasm as Alfred Wallace, on catching his birdwing butterfly, *Ornithoptera croesus,* the 'collecting' of moths and butterflies for this specimen box has been a fascinating one. Following Stumpwork Dragonflies and Stumpwork Beetles, the Moth

and Butterfly Specimen Box is the third in a series of stumpwork insect boxes.

This box contains eighteen specimens—ten moths and eight butterflies—from the Order Lepidoptera. The selection was no easy task, considering that there are around 200,000 species in this diverse group of insects. My aim was to produce a specimen box of 'jewels', with complete disregard for size and proportion; to select moth and butterfly specimens for interest and colour—not the most familiar; and to use a wide assortment of materials to interpret these insects. This brief provided me with the opportunity to employ a variety of techniques to work the detached wings, from surface embroidery in lustrous silks for the Indian Moon Moth, to hand-dyed silk fabric for the Purple Fuchsia Butterfly, and even to try stitching clear plastic for the Glasswing Butterfly!

Detailed information and instructions have been provided for each of the eighteen specimens. Four projects are also offered—all including a moth or butterfly. Two of these feature the life-cycle of the butterfly or moth—egg, caterpillar, pupa and adult—the wonder of metamorphosis—the source of much of the symbolism attached to these creatures. Most of these lepidopterans are not difficult to work; some are more challenging; all are fun.

With their beautiful shapes, appealing symmetry and jewel-like colouration, it is not surprising that butterflies have inspired artisans for centuries. They have been depicted in burial chambers, paintings and illuminated manuscripts; porcelain, ceramics and glass; metalwork, wood carvings and wall paper; textiles and embroidery; jewellery, buttons and postage stamps. They are even popular in tattoos.

I have been collecting moth- and butterfly-related material for years—my ideas journals, folders and boxes are overflowing with drawings, photocopies, postcards and magazine cuttings.

Most of these lepidopterans are not difficult to work; some are more challenging; *all are fun.*

When I assembled all the information that I had collected for the Butterfly as Ornament section of the book, I was completely overwhelmed by the quantity—there was enough material for a whole book! With ruthless culling, I have managed to share but a glimpse of the exquisite treasures—illuminated manuscripts, illustrated books of natural history, embroidered butterflies, painted, printed and stencilled butterflies—held in the collections of museums and galleries around the world.

I found it to be as I had expected, a
perfectly new and most magnificent
species, and one of the most gorgeously coloured
butterflies in the world. Fine specimens of the
male are more than seven inches across the
wings, which are velvety black and fiery
orange, the latter colour replacing the green of
the allied species.

The beauty and brilliancy of this insect are
indescribable, and none but a naturalist
can understand the intense excitement I
experienced when I at length captured it.
On taking it out of my net and opening
the glorious wings, my heart began to beat
violently, the blood rushed to my head, and
I felt much more like fainting than I have
done when in apprehension of immediate
death. I had a headache the rest of the
day, so great was the excitement produced
by what will appear to most people a very
inadequate cause.

Alfred Russel Wallace,
The Malay Archipelago, 1869

It has been twenty years since I started teaching stumpwork embroidery—a time of much pleasure, research and challenge—and the making of many friends. My aim, whether through workshops or books, is to share the joy of embroidery and the knowledge of techniques, in the hope that they will be used to inspire people to create their own designs.

Last year, for the first time, I offered a *'Design Your Own Stumpwork Embroidery'* class, to be conducted over three meetings spaced throughout the year. Fifteen people took up the challenge. We met early in the year, armed with our 'ideas' journals, drawings and cuttings—many having been tucked away for years, waiting for the 'right time'. This was a very stimulating session—we discussed our proposals as a group, then went away to draw our designs, ready for the next class. Armed with an array of threads and fabrics, and our design ideas, we met a month later, when we discussed the drawing of a skeleton outline of the chosen designs, and the selection of threads.

The enthusiasm was contagious, with everyone contributing ideas and suggestions, and sharing materials. Several months later, we met to check on progress and resolve any engineering issues that may have arisen—so far so good. When we convened at the end of the year, there was a buzz of excitement in the air. The results—many finished, the others almost there—were splendid! For me, these embroideries encapsulated the reason for doing what I do!

I would like to dedicate this book to all the embroiderers, both here and throughout the world, who have shared (and continue to share) this stumpwork journey with me. It has been a joy and a pleasure.

Thank you.

Part 1

NATURAL HISTORY
OF THE
Butterfly
& Moth

The first primitive moths appeared well over 100 million years ago, in the time of the dinosaurs; the earliest butterflies appeared about 40 million years ago, in step with the rise of flowering plants. All members of this group of insects develop from egg to adult through the process known as metamorphosis.

Order Lepidoptera

With their glorious colours and harmless appearance, butterflies and moths are the most popular and familiar of all insects. Together, the two groups make up the large Order of insects known as Lepidoptera (from the Greek *lepis*, scale, and *pteron*, wing), containing almost 200,000 known species, of which about 10 per cent are butterflies. The order is divided into families of moths and butterflies—there are over 100 families of moths, while butterflies are usually grouped into five families.

From fossils we can tell that the first primitive moths lived between 100 and 190 million years ago, during the age of dinosaurs. Butterflies evolved much later—about 40 million years ago, probably evolving alongside flowering plants. By the time the first people appeared, about five million years ago, lepidopterans (butterflies and moths) were like those we see today.

Because butterflies and moths are so skilled in flight they have achieved an almost worldwide distribution. The greatest variety is found in the shelter of tropical rainforests, where the warm, humid conditions provide a range of food sources—however, butterflies and moths survive in nearly all habitats, from hot dry deserts to the frozen Arctic tundra.

Opposite: A vintage illustration of the life cycle of the Red Admiral or Vanessa atalanta; *Above: Vintage engraved illustration of the Lesser Purple Emperor,* Apatura ilia, *both from* The Dictionary of Words & Things, *Larive and Fleury, 1895.*

The division of Lepidoptera into butterflies and moths is an artificial one, although based on a number of observable differences. For example, most butterflies fly by day and most moths are nocturnal; many butterflies are brightly coloured and many moths are dull coloured; most butterflies hold their wings upright over their backs, while most moths rest with their wings flat; butterfly antennae are clubbed at the tip but moth antennae are either feather-like or tapered. Despite these rules, there is not one single feature that separates all butterflies from all moths, and exceptions abound—there are many colourful day-flying moths, for example, some of which even have clubbed antennae.

Like all insects, adult moths and butterflies possess a head, thorax and abdomen, six legs and one pair of antennae. Most species also have two pairs of wings, which are either hooked or held together in flight. They can be distinguished from other insects by their long hollow feeding tube (proboscis) and by the thousands of delicate scales covering every part of their body, from their wings to their feet. From the giant Atlas moths, to the brilliant blue Morpho butterflies and the tiny micro-moths, these insects display an incredible variety in shape, size and colour.

Vintage engraved illustrations: **left**, *The Large White,* Pieris brassicae, *also called Cabbage Butterfly, Cabbage White, or in India the Large Cabbage White;* **right**, *unidentified moth.*

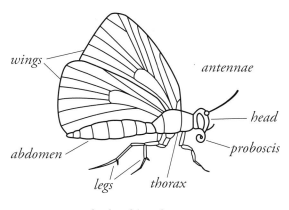

body of lepidopteran

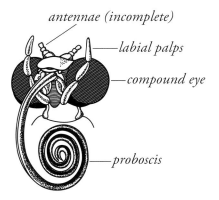

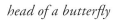

head of a butterfly

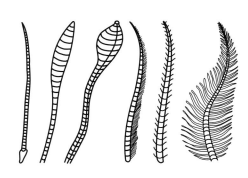

various types of anntennae

THE HEAD

The head is a small spherical capsule which bears two jointed sensory organs
called antennae, used for smelling and touch; two large compound eyes
which are sensitive not only to movement, but also to the colour patterns of
flowers and other butterflies; and a specialised, coiled, hollow feeding tube, or
proboscis, that uncoils when the insect wishes to feed. Adult butterflies feed
mainly on sweet flower nectars, decaying fruit, moist dung or the juices of
carrion. The length of the proboscis varies from species to species, according
to the flowers on which the insect feeds. It is during this process of 'probing'
that pollen is picked up and transferred from flower to flower.

THE THORAX

The thorax is the powerhouse of the body, where both the legs and wings are located. It is composed of three segments and each carries a pair of legs adapted both for walking and clinging. The two pairs of wings belong to the second and third thoracic segments. The delicate wings consist of an upper and lower membrane with a framework of hollow tubes between the layers. These supporting tubes, called veins, are arranged in a very precise way, the pattern being an important tool in identifying a particular species. The upper and under surfaces of the wings are covered with overlapping rows of scales which give the butterfly its colour and pattern. Each wing scale is one colour (there may be 200 to 600 scales per square millimetre of wing). The larger pattern is a mosaic of these. The colour can come from pigments in the scale, from its structural architecture, from the effect of overlapping scales or from a combination of all three. Some moths and butterflies have fewer scales, resulting in transparent wings. Wings are coloured and patterned to help moths and butterflies blend with their surroundings, regulate their body temperature, drive away predators, and attract mates.

THE ABDOMEN

The abdomen is much softer than the head and thorax and consists of ten rings or segments, of which only seven or eight can be easily seen. The abdomen houses most of the digestive system, with the end segments being specialised for reproductive purposes. The most important events in the lives of moths and butterflies are mating and the laying of eggs. When ready to mate, the adult has to find a mate of the same species. Butterflies and moths must usually look, feel and smell right to each other before mating can take place. They are attracted by the particular colours and patterns of their own species, and by scented chemical substances called pheromones, which are released when they are ready to mate.

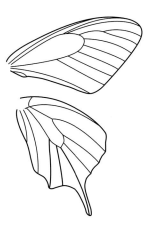

Cassidae (wood moth) wings

Papilionidae (swallowtail butterfly) wings

LIFE CYCLE

The life cycle of the butterfly or moth is no less remarkable than the beauty of the adult. The transformation of the frequently ugly and often bizarre caterpillar into an elegant butterfly or moth is one of the regularly performed miracles of nature. There are four distinct stages in the life cycle—ovum (egg), larva (caterpillar), chrysalis (pupa) and imago (adult). This process of complete change is called metamorphosis. Depending on the species and the climate, the length of a life cycle can vary from three weeks (in the tropics), to several months or more in colder environments.

XXIII

A

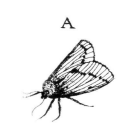

Moths, Caterpillars and Pupae. Copper engravings making up four of the small pages of Johannes Goedart's Metamorphosis et Historia Insectorum, *1663. Note the human faces that Goedart has given to two of the pupae.*

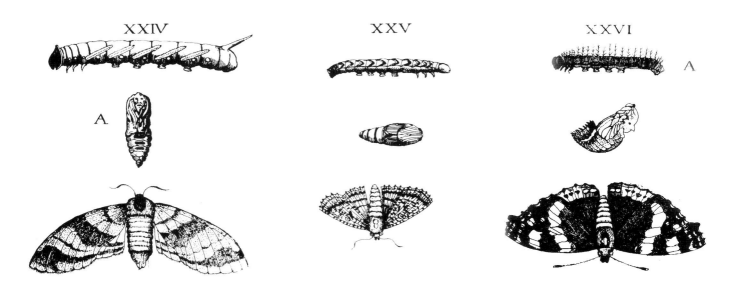

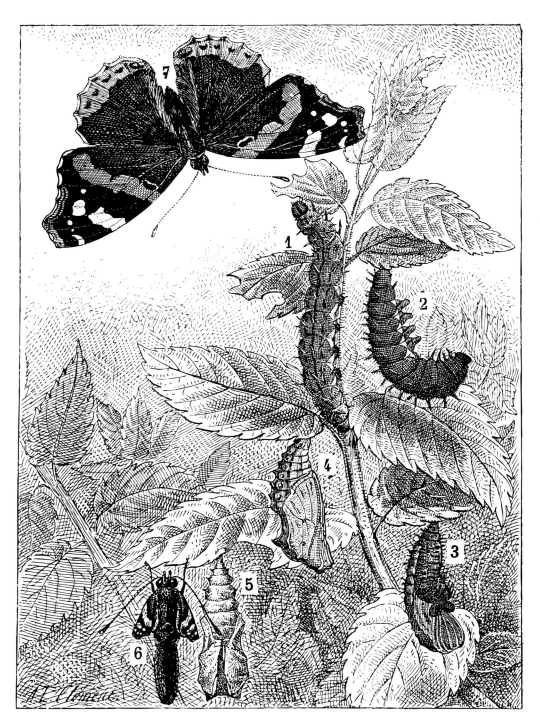

A vintage illustration of the life cycle of the Red Admiral or Vanessa atalanta*:*
(1) Early Instar, (2) Late Instar (3) Pupa (4) Chrysalis (5,6) Nymph, and (6) Imago.

Ovum (egg)

Eggs the size of pinheads are usually laid singly or in clusters on or near to the plant on which the caterpillar will feed. The shape of the egg varies in different species and may be spherical or oval and flattened. Butterfly eggs are commonly white, yellow or green in colour although they may darken just before hatching.

Larva (caterpillar)

Example of lepidopteran larva

The young caterpillar gnaws its way through the eggshell then, after consuming the shell, which contains valuable nutrients, continues to eat voraciously, devouring the plant on which the egg was laid. During this stage, a caterpillar feeds and grows rapidly. As it grows, the caterpillar entirely fills its skin, which becomes very tight. It sheds its restrictive skin, exposing a new and larger one which has formed beneath it. This shedding of the skin is known as moulting and usually takes place four or five times before the larva is fully grown.

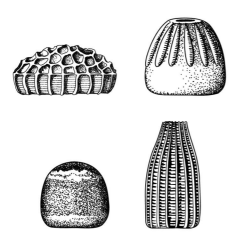

Examples of different shapes of lepidopteran eggs

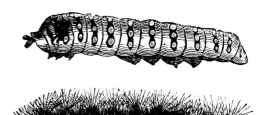

Caterpillars of the Indian Moon moth (top), Brush-footed butterfly (centre), and Geometer moth (bottom).

Example of a lepidopteran pupa

Vintage engravings from Trousset Encyclopedia (1886 - 1891). **Below:** *two transformation stages of the chrysalis into a butterfly.*
Right: *Black Swallowtail Butterfly,* Papilio polyxenes, *larva, pupa and imago.*

CHRYSALIS (PUPA)

The end of larval life is marked by a final moult which gives rise to a pupa or chrysalis. Fully grown larva often select special sites to undergo this transformation and may leave their food plant and enter the soil. Since the pupa is immobile it is particularly vulnerable to attack. The colour and shape of a butterfly pupa is adapted to blend with its surroundings. The naked pupa is attached to the plant by means of a small silken pad, and in some cases is supported by a silken girdle. Moth pupae are often protected within a silken cocoon. This may take the form of a hollow of earth lined with silk, or a roll of leaves fastened together with silk threads. The pupa is a remarkable stage of development, during which tremendous transformations take place. Within the hard, protective case of the pupa, the former larval tissues are broken down, and the new tissues of the future imago are formed.

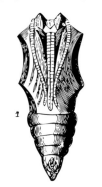

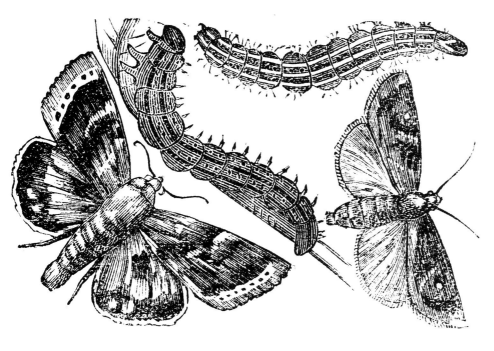

IMAGO (ADULT MOTH OR BUTTERFLY)

The time it takes for the transformation to take place varies from a few weeks to months, depending on the climate and the species. When the imago first emerges from the pupa, its wings are soft and crumpled. It moves to a place where the wings can hang downwards, and sits still while blood pumps through the veins to stiffen and flatten the wings. Once they have reached their full size, the insect holds the wings apart until they are completely dry and hardened, then flies off in search of a mate. A vital role of the adult is to mate and disperse it eggs to ensure the survival of the species. Adults do not grow, and if they feed, it is only to replace the energy they have used up by flying around.

Vintage engraved illustrations. **above**: *larva & imago of the Owlet moth, Family Noctuidae, and* **below**: *The Red Admiral (Vanessa atalanta).*

Part 2

The Butterfly as
Ornament

From earliest times, the butterfly form has been celebrated in the art
and literature of many different cultures. Representations of butterflies are to
be seen in Egyptian frescoes at Thebes (from 3500 years ago) and on objects
produced by the ancient Minoan, Chinese and Japanese civilisations.

ANCIENT SOURCE OF INSPIRATION

Butterfly beliefs and legends have become assimilated into the folklore of many countries. The ancient Greeks believed the emergence of the adult butterfly from its pupa represented a personification of the human soul. So strongly did the Greeks identify with this notion that they used the word *psyche* for both butterfly and soul. When the Hindu god, Brahma, watched the caterpillars in his garden change into pupae and then into butterflies, he conceived the idea of reincarnation: perfection through rebirth. Paintings on ancient Egyptian tombs and sarcophagi show butterflies surrounding the dead. In later Christian art, the metamorphosis of the butterfly became a symbol of the Resurrection. In Ireland, in 1680, a law forbade the killing of white butterflies because they were the souls of children. Long and widely held has been the belief that the butterfly represents a human soul.

With their beautiful shapes, appealing symmetry and jewel-like colouration, it is not surprising that butterflies have inspired artisans for centuries. They have been depicted in burial chambers, paintings and illuminated manuscripts; porcelain, ceramics and glass; metalwork, wood carvings and wallpaper; textiles and embroidery; jewellery, buttons and postage stamps. They are even popular as tattoos. The following examples are but a glimpse of 'the butterfly as ornament.'

Above:** Art Nouveau butterfly motif.* ***Opposite: *Japanese paper stencils, called* katagami, *are exquisitely rendered textile motifs, carefully cut from delicate paper and used for printing designs on cloth. The graceful butterfly is a traditional motif.*

ILLUMINATED MANUSCRIPTS & BOOKS OF NATURAL HISTORY

Exquisitely painted butterflies and flowers, meticulously wrought on parchment or vellum and embellished with gold leaf, adorned the pages of *Books of Hours*—prayer books for noblemen and noblewomen—and illuminated manuscripts, from the fourteenth to sixteenth centuries. Two of the foremost illuminators of this era were the French court artist, Jean Bourdichon, who created several exquisite Books of Hours for Queen Anne of Brittany, including *Les Grandes Heures d'Anne Bretagne* (1500–1508), and the Flemish miniaturist and imperial court artist, Joris Hoefnagel, who added the magnificent illuminations to *Mira calligraphiae monumenta* (1561–62), the monumental work of preeminent scribe Georg Bocskay.

With the development of the printing press in the fifteenth century, butterflies began to appear as woodcuts and engravings in the first natural history publications. The first illustrated work on zoology, *Historia Animalium*, published in 1551 by Swiss scholar Conrad Gessner, was liberally embellished with bold woodcuts of animals. One of the earliest books devoted to the study of insects was Thomas Mouffet's *Insectorum Theatrum*, published in 1634. Still valued as a pioneering entomological work, it contains many charming, thumbnail-size woodcuts of insects, including butterflies. The published engravings may be compared with the original drawings from which the engraver worked (the originals are preserved in the British Library). These illustrations appear to be portraying real insects, unlike some other seventeenth-century examples. In the frontispiece to his book on insects, *Historiae Naturalis De Insectis*, published in 1653, Johannes Jonston reveals his difficulty in distinguishing between the creatures haunting the misty regions of his imagination and those roaming the uncharted regions of the real world.

A great interest in natural history publications flourished in Holland in the second half of the seventeenth century. Among the most gloriously illustrated of

Woodcut of a butterfly by Conrad Gessner.

Opposite:
Joris Hoefnagel: Horntail caterpillar, pear and Marbled White butterfly.

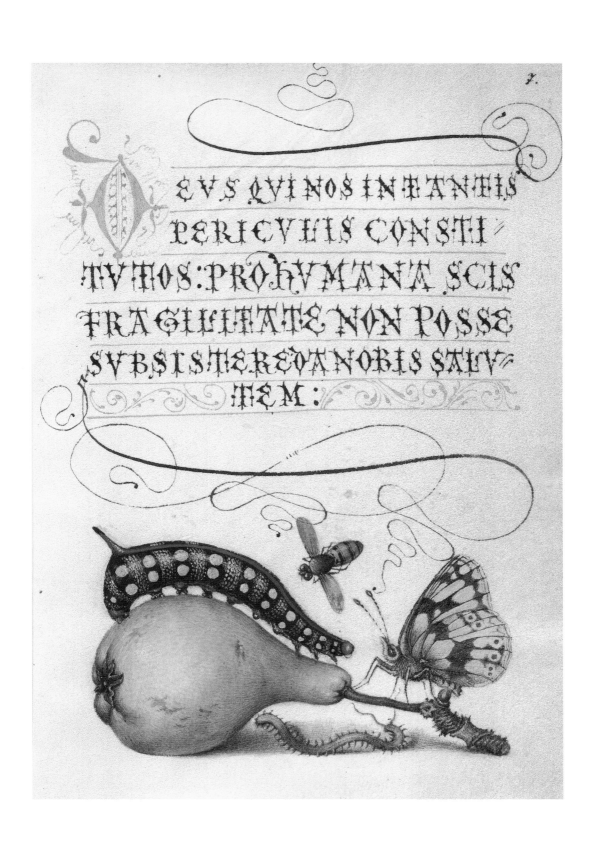

DE

WONDEREN

GODS

in de

minſt geachtste

SCHEPSELEN.

these early entomological works was that of artist and naturalist Maria Sibylla Merian. One of the most remarkable women of her day, her paintings and hand-coloured copper engravings of butterflies show outstanding attention to detail. Her drawings of caterpillars, pupae, butterflies and their food plants, made during her travels in the Dutch colony of Surinam between 1698 and 1701, were engraved for her major work, *Metamorphosis insectorum Surinamensium*, which contained 71 plates coloured by hand (the only way of reproducing colour plates in books in the eighteenth century).

One of the most famous series of engravings of moths and butterflies, published in the eighteenth century, were those of Christian Sepp—a great entomologist, even greater artist and highly successful publisher—and his son, Jan Christiaan Sepp. Born in Germany in 1700, Christian Sepp settled in Amsterdam before his son was born in 1739. The younger Sepp was renowned for his knowledge of Dutch insects and the excellent drawings which he engraved for his masterpiece, *De Nederlandsche Insecten*, published in 1762. The illustrations are of breathtaking beauty and are drawn with a scientific accuracy rarely achieved since.

Maria Sibylla Merian, 'Two Butterflies'. Watercolour on parchment, 1706.

Opposite: *An original title page from the series on Dutch insects by Christian Sepp.*

THE EMBROIDERED BUTTERFLY
· ·

The butterfly has been a popular motif in embroidery throughout the centuries—with examples to be found in medieval ecclesiastical embroidery, Elizabethan embroidery, including crewel work, canvas work and blackwork, seventeenth century raised work, and the samplers of the eighteenth and nineteenth centuries. The twentieth century finds butterflies in the work of Grace Christie, the first teacher of embroidery at the Royal College of Art, and also in the world of French *haute couture*.

Apart from the beauty of its form, the butterfly has often been chosen for its symbolism, with the various stages of its life cycle—a caterpillar, a chrysalis and a butterfly—representing the stages of man's life on earth and the hereafter. In antiquity, the image of the butterfly emerging from its chrysalis represented the soul leaving the body at death, and in medieval ecclesiastical embroidery, the butterfly symbolised immortality and the Resurrection. The butterfly has also been regarded as a metaphor for playfulness, joy and pleasure.

The butterfly and caterpillar were prevalent in Elizabethan embroideries, frequently appearing on clothing and home furnishings, such as cushions and bed-hangings. In an era that eschewed empty spaces, an extraordinary variety of insects was used to fill any unoccupied spaces in designs, with little regard being paid to scale or proportion. These needleworkers sourced their insect motifs from the woodcuts and engravings that illustrated the natural history works of the day, such as those of Hoefnagel and Mouffet. These publications contained finely detailed line-drawings of insects and butterflies which readily translated into designs for embroidery.

Some of the canvas work panels worked by Mary Queen of Scots, on the famous Oxburgh Hangings, were copied from the woodcuts of Conrad Gessner. One of the panels contains three butterflies resting on flowers, with the initials MR worked in red. Being aware of the significance of the butterfly, Mary may have worked them as a symbol of her Christian faith.

Details of embroidered panel designed and worked by Grace Christie, c.1914. Worked in silks on a linen ground.

It was in the seventeenth century that the embroidered butterfly lifted its wings from the surface, as if in flight, with the emergence of raised embroidery (now known as stumpwork) around 1650. The wings of the butterfly were worked with a wire edge—as detached wings. The wire, bent into a wing shape, could either be filled with closely worked rows of a detached buttonhole stitch, or stitched onto fine linen, the wing surface being embroidered before the careful cutting out of the wing, close to the wire edge. The wire tails of the detached wings would be inserted through the background fabric, often shadowing wings that had been embroidered on the background. In this period of great political upheaval (England being under the rule of the Commonwealth, led by Oliver Cromwell), the use of caterpillar and butterfly motifs in these embroideries could be interpreted as symbols showing support for the Restoration of Charles II.

Detail of embroidered panel designed and worked by Grace Christie, c.1914.

The twentieth century also finds butterflies in the exquisite work of Grace Christie. Her glorious panel, completed in 1914, is embroidered in coloured silks on a linen ground, with a wide variety of stitches including satin, long and short, buttonhole, laid and couched work, and interlacing. The design is based on a diamond-shaped lattice, enclosing birds, plants, flowers, berries and butterflies, all within a particularly beautiful wide border. The butterfly has also graced garments and accessories in the world of French *haute couture*.

THE BUTTERFLY AS A DESIGN SOURCE

Nature has always been a sourcebook for artists and designers, but never more so than in the nineteenth century, where the fascination with the natural world was evident in all aspects of life. In the 1830s, there was an intensified search for new motifs to decorate the products of industrialisation, such as wallpapers, fabrics, carpets, linoleum, ceramics, cast iron and furniture. George Phillips, who published *Rudiments of Curvilinear Design* in 1838, was one of the first to suggest insects, including butterflies, as sources of inspiration for the ornamental designer. Scottish designer Bruce J. Talbert, although best known as a furniture designer, featured the butterfly in designs for wallpaper and fabrics, probably in the mid-1870s.

The butterfly, with its elegant curves and intricate vein patterns, was adored by designers in the Art Nouveau movement (1890–1910). A style of art, architecture and applied art, inspired by natural forms, flowers and plants, Art Nouveau designs were characterised by flowing, curved lines, with naturalistic motifs. Art Nouveau designs, some featuring the butterfly, could be found painted, drawn and printed on wallpapers, linoleum and fabrics throughout the period.

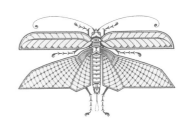

The late nineteenth and early twentieth centuries also saw a revival in the use of the stencil to decorate walls, floors, furniture and fabrics. The stencil, a method of applying a design by brushing or spongeing paint through a cutout overlay placed on the surface, often took the place of wallpaper. The structure of the body and wings of insects, particularly the butterfly, is well adapted to the requirements of the stencil template, as shown by these charming observations made by W. G. Sutherland, in a 1925 publication, *Stencilling for Craftsmen*:

The butterfly in Art Nouveau designs.

Stencil designs for moths and butterflies. Top & below: Art Nouveau designs.

The veining of the wing suggests a regular system of ties which hold the plate well together without any straining of the design, and the wonderful symmetry and balance of each member of the insect tribe provides the decorator with a ready-made series of motifs which, simply repeated, become really satisfying patterns.

He also makes a delightful observation regarding the colour combinations to be found in moths and butterflies:

To the colourist, the butterfly tribe offers a practically limitless opportunity, for there is not a harmonious combination of glowing, sober, or even violently contrasted colour that cannot, if necessary to the completion of a given scheme, be quite legitimately introduced into the wings of a moth. Black and gold, black and red, blue and gold, purple and pale yellow, and a host of other brilliant effects. The range is limitless; only the interpreter is needed.

The French artist and designer, Eugene Séguy, created numerous colour portfolios of visual ideas for artists, illustrators and designers in the 1920s. Included in his *Butterflies* and *Insectes* portfolios are several striking examples of butterflies, each species drawn with scrupulous accuracy of form and colour. He then provides decorative compositions with these insects, as a source of ideas for textiles, wallpapers, mosaics, stained glass and many other areas of design.

Art Deco artists created bold, simple designs suitable for mass production. Designers working in the Art Deco style, like the brilliant Séguy, changed the direction and history of modern design. Séguy's *Butterflies*, published in 1928, demonstrates a master's skill at rendering a realistic composition through strong primary colours and sharp tonal contrasts.

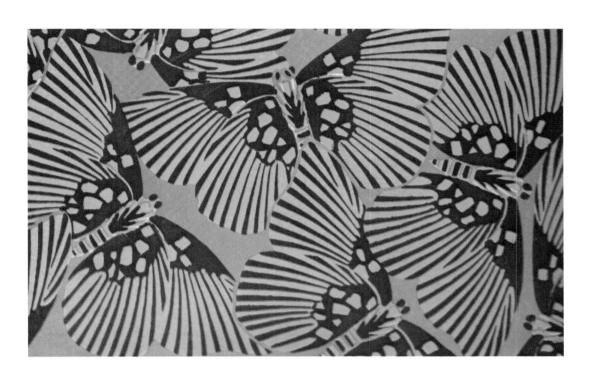

Séguy's Butterflies,
Plates 8 & 16.

THE BUTTERFLY IN JEWELLERY

While the earliest pieces of jewellery may well have played a dual role as both adornment and amulet, there is no doubt that humans have always experienced the urge for self-adornment, taking inspiration from natural forms, and using nature's bounty—from shells and bones to precious stones and gold.

Silver butterfly pendant

Realistically rendered insects, such as butterflies, dragonflies and beetles, have been a recurrent theme in all the decorative arts, particularly in the realm of jewellery. Until the nineteenth century, the use of insects in jewellery was largely symbolic, with noble families occasionally taking insects like grasshoppers, beetles and butterflies as their symbol—Napoleon adopted the bee, a symbol of determination and industry, as his emblem. However, the nineteenth century's obsession with nature encouraged jewellers to interpret insects as brooches, rings, lockets and necklaces, resulting in myriad bejewelled dragonflies, wasps, butterflies, bees, earwigs, flies, beetles and spiders emerging in the 1860s. Since the Renaissance, the butterfly, with its beautiful form and associated symbolism, has always been the most popular subject for insect jewellery.

The Order Lepidoptera continues to inspire contemporary jewellery designers, among them Georg Jensen and the house of Cartier, with butterflies appearing in a range of materials, from pure gold and silver, to the modern plastics.

Silver butterfly brooch, c.1942. Georg Jensen, designed by Arno Malinowski. This bold and elegant design of stylised butterflies perched on flowers is typical of Art Deco jewellery.

Seventeenth century engraved illustration of enamelled brooch embellished with pearls and diamonds

Collection of detachable butterfly buttons and pin. Silver and blue enamel, c.1900.

Designing from the Butterfly

Simple steps in the design process from butterfly to finished design for a brooch. The main lines of the ribs, radiating into the wings, make an excellent study for symmetry.

A. Careful drawing of butterfly

B. Section of upper wing

C. Simplified section

D. More stylised representation

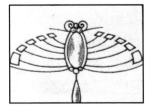

E. Design emerges with more ribs

F. Design for a brooch

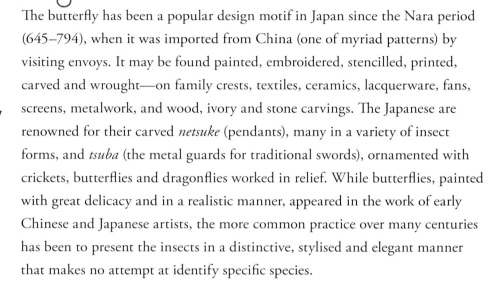

THE BUTTERFLY IN CHINA & JAPAN

The butterfly has been a popular design motif in Japan since the Nara period (645–794), when it was imported from China (one of myriad patterns) by visiting envoys. It may be found painted, embroidered, stencilled, printed, carved and wrought—on family crests, textiles, ceramics, lacquerware, fans, screens, metalwork, and wood, ivory and stone carvings. The Japanese are renowned for their carved *netsuke* (pendants), many in a variety of insect forms, and *tsuba* (the metal guards for traditional swords), ornamented with crickets, butterflies and dragonflies worked in relief. While butterflies, painted with great delicacy and in a realistic manner, appeared in the work of early Chinese and Japanese artists, the more common practice over many centuries has been to present the insects in a distinctive, stylised and elegant manner that makes no attempt at identify specific species.

Viewed as the souls of the living and the dead, by Chinese and Japanese alike, butterflies (*chocho*) were also symbols of joy and longevity, and thought to offer protection against evil spirits. Later, during the Kamakura era (1185–1333), the butterfly decorated helmets and suits of armour—a symbol of good fortune, prosperity and rebirth.

Traditional Chinese butterfly motifs.

Above: *Traditional Japanese butterfly motifs.*

Butterflies—painted, printed, stencilled, or exquisitely embroidered, in smooth, flat silks and fine gold thread—were a popular motif on both Chinese and Japanese textiles, where they symbolised summer, beauty, marital happiness and long life.

The stencil was a favoured method for transferring motifs to fabric and paper, and the vast number of butterfly designs from the eighteenth and nineteenth centuries attests to the popularity of this insect as a design source. Both the Chinese and the Japanese were masters of the stencil. From as early as the eighth century, they were cutting intricate paper stencils to decorate cloth, paper and ceramics, and to create embroidery patterns. The Japanese developed *katazome*, a form of reverse stencilling, and also perfected a method of cutting multiple stencils from mulberry bark. By the nineteenth century, Japanese artists were astounding Western artists with the delicacy and refinement of their stencils.

Above: *Traditional Chinese butterfly motifs.*
Below: *Japanese family crest designs.*

The family crest, or *mon*, epitomises the genius of the Japanese for refined and elegant designs. Mon are highly stylised patterns based on geometrical, floral or animal forms, and have always been admired for their superb design, their ingenuity and wit. With their origin in the eleventh century, when they served as a family emblem or crest, displayed on costumes on formal occasions, mon have also been used in Japan as trademarks, and for decorating a variety of items such as the kimono, lacquerware and door hangings. These circular, often symmetrical motifs, which can also fit within a square, have developed into one of the richest graphic art traditions in the world. Butterflies, with their elegant form, lend themselves perfectly to pattern making within this tradition.

  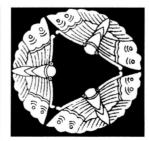 

THE BOX OF CURIOSITIES

In 2011, I was invited to part of an exhibition, *Fantasy World*, held at Goulburn Regional Art Gallery. I exhibited a selection of embroideries, and artists boxes and books - my other love. One of my handmade boxes, *Box of Curiosities II: Butterfly,* was inspired by butterflies, and contains two of the stumpwork moths and butterflies featured in the Specimen Box.

Dong calendered cotton, vintage wallpaper, box board, concertina book, bamboo paper, Reville's Coronation Velvet Butterfly (King George VI and Queen Elizabeth, 1937), paste, paper, packaged butterfly wings, butterfly specimens, beetle specimen, buttons, embroidered butterflies (silk and gold threads on silk) and stumpwork butterflies (silk, chenille and metallic threads, organdie, plastic, suede, gilt metal purl, spangles and wire on silk).

Part 3

THE COLLECTOR & THE SPECIMEN BOX

Collecting insect specimens, and mounting them in specimen boxes, has been the delight of the enthusiast since the sixteenth century. This was an age of wonder. With the discoveries of foreign lands, and the excitement of finding new things in the world, there developed a passion for collecting and displaying wondrous objects in 'cabinets of curiosity'. Within these cabinets, the earliest and most basic system of classification was to assemble 'like' objects:

naturalia, such as minerals, stuffed animals, plants, ethnographic artefacts, and fossils, and *artificialia,* with a special fondness for paintings, weapons, scientific instruments, and mechanical marvels such as clocks and automata.*

In time, classifications became more detailed, and more specialised cabinets emerged, with the collecting of natural history specimens becoming the passionate pursuit of the wealthy in the seventeenth century. The advent of the microscope in the mid-seventeenth century led to an increased interest in insects, and many discoveries about their anatomy (Linnaeus classified insects into genera and species in 1758).

In the nineteenth century, with improvements in education, communications and travel, the study of natural history became a truly popular movement, encompassing all classes of society, from schoolchildren to 'gentleman collectors'.

Russell W. Belk, On Collecting, *Routledge, London, 1995, p. 32. Opposite photograph actual size*

THE
Butterfly & Moth
Specimen Box

Butterflies and moths, in serried rows in specimen boxes, or arranged in decorative patterns in framed pictures, were common features on the walls of many homes. Throughout the world, explorers and collectors were accumulating extensive collections of Lepidoptera, many forming the foundation for the great natural history museums.

Above: *A modern museum butterfly collection display.* **Opposite**: *F.P. Dodd,* Moths–The Butterflies of the Night, *c.1918. The pastel pink, green and blue species in this large case are rare ghost moths of the genus Aenetus. The large specimen in the centre is the Giant Fruit-sucking Moth (*Phyllodes imperialis*).*
The muted pastel shades of many of the nocturnal moths appealed to Dodd.

The Butterfly Man of Kuranda

From 1895 until his death in 1937, Queensland entomologist, Frederick Parkhurst Dodd applied himself to the exploration of Australia's then unknown tropical insects with a passion.

He supplied tens of thousands of perfect specimens to the great museums of the world and to the wealthy private collectors of the Victorian era. Almost one hundred new species that he discovered were named in his honour.

In his later years, F. P. Dodd became a personality of national prominence as 'The Butterfly Man of Kuranda' when he toured his spectacular show collection of insects to the southern states in 1918 and 1923.

Dodd painstakingly spelled out this verse from Longfellow in tiny pyralid moths, while Longfellow's signature is in metallic green beetles. 'SHE' is Mother Nature, and by this quotation Dodd indicated the personal strength and inspiration he continually derived from his insect studies.

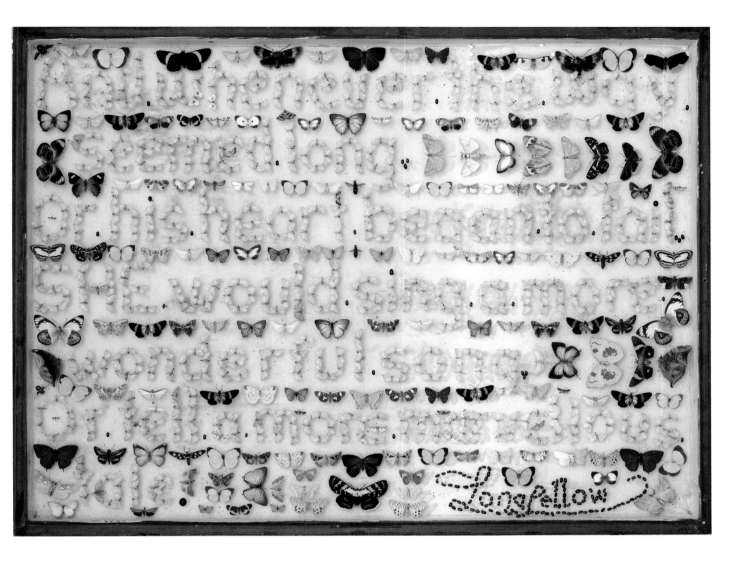

F. P. Dodd, Poem Case, c.1918.

And whenever the way seemed long

Or his heart began to fail

SHE would sing a more wonderful song

Or tell a more marvellous tale.

A specimen box is a perfect way to 'collect' stumpwork insects. It provides for the fascination of research, the challenge of interpretation and the joy of stitching. The *Butterfly & Moth Specimen Box*. overleaf, is the third in my series of stumpwork insect boxes, (the others feature dragonflies and beetles). This box contains eighteen specimens from the Order *Lepidoptera*—the selection was no easy task, considering that there are nearly 200,000 known species. My aim was produce a specimen box of 'jewels', with complete disregard for size and proportion; to select moth and butterfly specimens for interest and colour—not the most familiar—and to use a wide variety of techniques and materials to interpret these insects.

The moths and butterflies in the specimen box were embroidered for pleasure, often with treasures from many years of collecting and experimenting. Detailed instructions accompany each insect, but you are encouraged to experiment and make them your own. Most of these lepidopterans are not difficult to work; some are more challenging; all are fun.

F.P. Dodd, Splendid Ghost Moth, *Aenetus mirabilis. The Splendid Ghost Moth male has pastel aqua-green forewings and shiny white hind wings which attract the brownish females as he flies at dusk.*

Glasswing Butterfly

Brimstone Butterfly

Scarlet Tiger Moth

White Ermine Moth

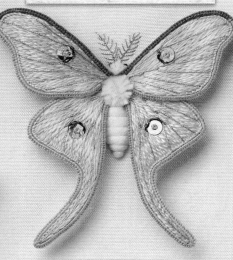

Indian Moon Moth

Swallowtail Butterfly

Blue Morpho Butterfly

Camberwell Beauty

Purple Fuchsia Butterfly

Large Emerald Moth

Large Yellow Underwing Moth

Elephant Hawkmoth

Splendid Ghost Moth

Hornet Moth

Longhorn Moth

Chalkhill Blue Butterfly

Six-spot Burnet Moth

Purple-shot Copper
Butterfly

THE BUTTERFLY & MOTH
SPECIMEN BOX KEY

COLUMN 1
Glasswing Butterfly
Cithaerias aurorina
Family: Satyridae

White Ermine Moth
Spilosoma lubricipeda
Family: Arctiidae

Blue Morpho Butterfly
Morpho rhetenor
Family: Morphidae

Large Emerald Moth
Geometra papilionaria
Family: Geometridae

Large Yellow Underwing Moth
Noctua pronuba
Family: Noctuidae

COLUMN 2
Brimstone Butterfly
Gonepteryx rhamni
Family: Pieridae

Indian Moon Moth
Actias selene
Family: Saturniidae

Camberwell Beauty
Nymphalis antiopa
Family: Nymphalidae

Elephant Hawkmoth
Deilephila elpenor
Family: Sphingidae

COLUMN 3
Scarlet Tiger Moth
Callimorpha dominula
Family: Arctiidae

Swallowtail Butterfly
Papilio machaon
Family: Papilionidae

Purple Fuchsia Butterfly
Anaea tyrianthina
Family: Nymphalidae

Splendid Ghost Moth
Aenetus mirabilis
Family: Hepialidae

COLUMN 4
Hornet Moth
Sesia apiformis
Family: Sesiidae

Longhorn Moth
Adela reaumurella
Family: Incurvariidae

Chalkhill Blue Butterfly
Lysandra coridon
Family: Lycaenidae

Six-spot Burnet Moth
Zygaena filipendulae
Family: Zygaenidae

Purple-shot Copper Butterfly
Lycaena alciphron
Family: Lycaenidae

Photograph not actual size

BEFORE YOU BEGIN

A stumpwork butterfly can be applied to almost any type of background fabric: silk, satin, linen, cotton, velvet and suede. Whether you are working a single butterfly or a box of three, nine or eighteen specimens, the following information may be helpful:

- The background fabric of the specimen box, a very finely textured silk, was chosen to represent parchment. The backing fabric is muslin or fine calico.

- The detached wing and abdomen outlines, and wing and abdomen placement diagrams are actual working size—the drawings illustrating the instructions may not be.

- The insects are as 'entomologically accurate' as the limitations of materials will allow.

The challenge is to interpret the various parts of the anatomy in fabrics, threads and beads. I set myself a brief to use as many different techniques and materials as possible.

The moths and butterflies in the specimen box are not true to size—the actual wingspan of the Moon Moth ranges from 75 to 105 mm, while the wingspan of the tiny Longhorn Moth ranges from 14 to 18 mm.

All the embroidery is worked with one strand of thread, unless specified otherwise.

Read the section on equipment and general techniques before you start.

Families & Species
represented in the Specimen Box

The Order Lepidoptera is made up of many moth and butterfly families, fifteen of which are represented in this specimen box. The families are set out below in alphabetical order, according to their scientific family name. As some families have two representatives, each insect is referred to by its common name.

Family Arctiidae: Scarlet Tiger Moth, White Ermine Moth

Family Geometridae: Large Emerald Moth

Family Hepialidae: Splendid Ghost Moth

Family Incurvariidae: Longhorn Moth

Family Lycaenidae: Chalkhill Blue Butterfly, Purple-shot Copper Butterfly

Family Morphidae: Blue Morpho Butterfly

Family Noctuidae: Large Yellow Underwing Moth

Family Nymphalidae: Camberwell Beauty Butterfly, Purple Fuchsia Butterfly

Family Papilionidae: Swallowtail Butterfly

Family Pieridae: Brimstone Butterfly

Family Saturniidae: Indian Moon Moth

Family Satyridae: Glasswing Butterfly

Family Sesiidae: Hornet Moth

Family Sphingidae: Elephant Hawkmoth

Family Zygaenidae: Six-spot Burnet Moth

Tiger Moths, Footmen, Lichen Moths and Wasp Moths

This large and diverse family of moths includes tiger moths, footmen, lichen moths and wasp moths. Most tiger moths are brightly coloured, a characteristic that often leads them to be mistaken for butterflies when their wings are spread. Two members of the family are included in the specimen box, the Scarlet Tiger Moth, Callimorpha dominula, and the White Ermine Moth, Spilosoma lubricipeda.

The Scarlet Tiger Moth, Callimorpha dominula, a vividly coloured, day-flying member of the family, frequents damp meadows, wooded valleys and the banks of streams. During summer it flies at night as well. Its black fore wings have a metallic-green sheen, and cream and orange spots that may vary greatly in shape. The hind wings, often hidden beneath the fore wings, are a vivid scarlet with black blotches. It has pectinate (comb-like) antennae and the scarlet abdomen has a central black stripe. The markings on its wings are very variable, and in some individuals the hind wings are not red, but bright yellow, with dark spots. At rest and when feeding, this tiger moth is almost invisible among the vegetation, its outline disguised by the pattern of the black and cream marks (tiger-like stripes) on the fore wings. If disturbed by a predatory bird, it spreads its fore wings, revealing the bright scarlet hind wings to startle the bird as it makes its escape.

Scarlet Tiger Moth, *Callimorpha dominula.*

Some colourful tiger moths, including the Scarlet Tiger, synthesise their own poisons. On the ground, it can defend itself from predators, such as lizards, by secreting two blobs of poisonous, bright yellow liquid from behind its head.

Scarlet Tiger Moth

Callimorpha dominula   Order: *Lepidoptera*   Family: *Arctiidae*

Diagrams Actual Size

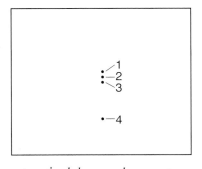

wing & abdomen placement

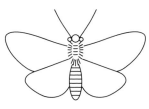

skeleton outline

fore wing

hind wing

detached wing outlines

REQUIREMENTS

quilter's muslin: 20 cm (8 in) square

10 cm (4 in) embroidery hoop

needles

crewel/embroidery size 10

sharps size 12

milliners/straw size 9

chenille size 18

sharp yarn darner sizes 14–18

beads & wire

3 mm bronze/purple bead

Mill Hill petite beads 42014 *(black)*

33 gauge white covered wire:

four 12 cm (4½ in) lengths

(colour wire red and dark navy/purple
if desired: Copic R17 Lipstick Orange,
Copic BV08 Blue Violet)

thread

dark navy or black stranded thread:
Soie d'Alger 165 or Noir or DMC 310

scarlet stranded thread:
Soie d'Alger 636 or DMC 349

dark gold stranded thread:
Soie d'Alger 2526 or DMC 783

cream stranded thread:
Soie d'Alger 2522 or DMC 3823

rust stranded thread:
Soie d'Alger 2636 or DMC 919

black metallic thread:
Kreinik Cord 005c

red metallic thread:
Kreinik Cord 003c

gold/bronze metallic thread:
Madeira Metallic No. 40 col. 482

variegated gold/black chenille thread:
col. Fire

nylon clear thread:
Madeira Monofil 60 col. 1001

METHOD

·················

Transfer the wing and abdomen placement dots to the background fabric.

WINGS

1. Mount the muslin into a small hoop and trace four wing outlines (including the inside wing markings)—a right and a left fore wing and a right and a left hind wing.

2. Using tweezers, shape a length of wire around the wing outline diagram, leaving two tails of wire at the base of the wing. Shape a right and a left fore wing and a right and a left hind wing. If desired, colour sections of the wires red and dark navy using the diagram as a guide (leave the dark gold section of the fore wing uncoloured).

Fore Wings

1. Using one strand of dark navy thread in a crewel needle, couch the shaped wire around the traced fore wing outline, working a couching stitch on either side of the dark gold marking on the lower edge of the wing. Buttonhole stitch the wire to the muslin, working the lower marking with dark gold thread, and the rest of the wing with dark navy.

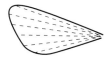

cream   *dark gold*

dark navy   *dark gold*

forewing marking placement

stitch direction

The wings are embroidered, with one strand of thread, in a combination of buttonhole stitch and long and short stitch (for the background of the wings), and satin stitch (for the spots). To help achieve a smooth surface, work all stitches in the direction of imaginary lines, radiating from the base of the wings to the outer edge.

2. Embroider the spots in the wings, with either cream or dark gold thread, as follows:

- Outline the spot in back stitch and work some padding stitches inside the outline (if the spot is large).
- Embroider the spot in satin stitch, enclosing the outline, taking care with the direction of the stitches.

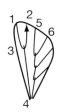

completed fore wing

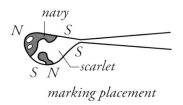

marking placement

completed hind wing

3. Using dark navy thread, embroider the outer edge of the wing (inside the wire) with a row of long and short buttonhole stitch, varying the length of the stitches to work to the edge of the spots as required. Embroider the remainder of the wing surface (between the spots) in long and short stitch.

4. With black metallic thread in a milliners needle, work the veins with fly and single feather stitches, using the diagram as a guide.

Hind Wings

1. Using one strand of scarlet thread, couch the shaped wire around the traced hind wing outline, working the couching stitches to correspond with the colour change markers at the edge of the wing. Buttonhole stitch the wire to the muslin, in either dark navy or scarlet, according to the edge markings.

2. Using scarlet thread, outline the two red spots (at the outer corners) in back stitch then embroider in satin stitch, enclosing the outline.

3. Outline the remaining internal lines in back stitch with dark navy thread, then embroider these areas in satin stitch (enclosing the outline), taking care with the direction of the stitches.

4. Starting at the edge of the wing, embroider the remainder of the wing surface (between the spots) in long and short stitch, using scarlet thread.

5. With red metallic thread in a milliners needle, work the veins with three fly stitches, using the diagram as a guide.

To Complete the Moth

1. To pad the abdomen, make one stitch from 3 to 4, with 14 strands of rust thread in a chenille needle (7 strands doubled). Cross the tails of padding thread behind the stitch (at the back), and hold each end with masking tape.

2. With one strand of rust thread in a size 10 crewel needle, work five evenly spaced couching stitches over the padding, catching in the tails of padding thread behind the abdomen (the tails will be trimmed later). The abdomen will be embroidered in raised stem stitch over these couching stitches so they need to be snug but not too tight.

3. With one strand of thread in a tapestry needle, work seven rows of raised stem stitch—three rows in rust, the centre row in dark navy, then three more rows in rust, working each row towards the tail.

4. Carefully cut out the wings and apply by inserting the wire tails through the upper two dots, using a large yarn darner. Apply the hind wings first, inserting the wire tails through 2, then the fore wings at 1 (the wings will slightly overlap). Bend the wire tails under the wings and secure to the backing fabric with tiny stitches using cream thread, making sure that the stitches do not protrude beyond the wingspan. Trim the wire tails when the moth is finished.

5. The thorax is worked with three straight stitches across the centre of the wings (from 1 to 3), using chenille thread in the largest yarn darner (to prevent the chenille shredding). Using variegated chenille, select a dark yellow section of thread and work two stitches side by side. Select a section of black chenille and work a stitch on top/between the dark yellow to form a centre stripe (for maximum control of the chenille, all stitches can be made with separate lengths of thread, all inserted from the front). Make sure the chenille does not twist and adjust the tension of the stitches (thus the fluffiness of the thorax), as desired. Secure the tails of chenille with nylon thread after the head is applied (to allow for final adjustments).

6. Using nylon thread in a sharps needle, stitch a 3 mm bead close to the top of the thorax, for the head (keeping the hole in the bead parallel to the top of the thorax). Bring the needle through to the front and stitch a black petite bead on either side of the head bead for the eyes, taking the needle through the hole of the bead several times so that the eyes are suspended on either side.

7. With one strand of gold/bronze metallic thread in a sharps needle, make a stitch on either side of the head bead for the antennae (taking the needle through the head bead if desired).

abdomen placement

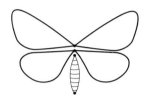

wing placement

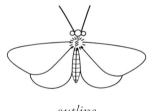

outline

*finished moth
actual size*

Order: Lepidoptera Family: Arctiidae

Tiger Moths, Footmen, Lichen Moths and Wasp Moths

This large and diverse family of moths includes tiger moths, footmen, lichen moths and wasp moths. While most tiger moths are brightly coloured, the **White Ermine Moth,** Spilosoma lubricipeda, is one of the most common of the white tiger moths (ermines). This moth, with pure white wings sprinkled with dark spots, derives its name from the ermine (or stoat), whose white winter fur is used to decorate the robes of peers and royalty.

White Ermine Moth,
Spilosoma lubricipeda

The wings vary greatly in their pattern and number of spots, some of which may be fused or absent altogether. The head and thorax of the White Ermine have a soft furry covering of fine white hairs, with the male moth featuring magnificent comb-like antennae. The bright yellow poisonous abdomen, which can exude a colourful and distasteful secretion if threatened by predators, stands out against the white wings. If the moth is disturbed it may fall to the ground and feign death.

White Ermine Moth

Spilosoma lubricipeda   Order: *Lepidoptera*   Family: *Arctiidae*

DIAGRAMS ACTUAL SIZE

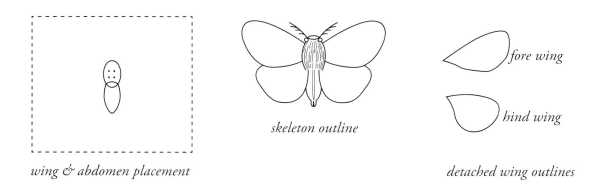

wing & abdomen placement

skeleton outline

fore wing

hind wing

detached wing outlines

REQUIREMENTS

quilter's muslin: 20 cm (8 in) square

10 cm (4 in) embroidery hoop

needles

crewel/embroidery size 10

sharps size 12

milliners/straw size 9

chenille size 18

sharp yarn darner sizes 14–18

beads & wire

Mill Hill petite beads 42014 *(black)*

33 gauge white covered wire:

four 12 cm (4½ in) lengths

*Note: I worked the spots in the wings
with tiny, purplish black, antique
glass seed beads (these beads were the
inspiration to embroider this moth).
As the beads are less than 1 mm in
diameter (size 22–24), I needed to use
a size 16 beading needle and fine cotton
lace thread (size 150/2). If you do not
have access to similar beads, French
knots, worked with black stranded
thread, are a good substitute.*

thread

white stranded thread:
Soie d'Alger 4098 (Blanc Optique) or DMC Blanc

black stranded thread:
Soie d'Alger Noir or DMC 310

dark gold stranded thread: S
oie d'Alger 2536 or DMC 976

pearl metallic thread:
Kreinik Cord 032c

copper/black metallic thread:
Kreinik Cord 215c

nylon clear thread:
Madeira Monofil 60 col. 1001

METHOD

. . . .

Trace the thorax and abdomen outline and wing placement dots to the background fabric.

WINGS

1. Mount the muslin into a small hoop and trace four wing outlines—a right and a left fore wing and a right and a left hind wing. As the wings will be embroidered with white thread, press masking tape over the traced lines to remove excess graphite, thus reducing the risk of 'grey' stitches.

forewing

2. Using tweezers, shape a length of wire around a wing outline diagram, leaving two tails of wire at the base of the wing. Shape a right and a left fore wing and a right and a left hind wing.

hind wing

3. With one strand of white thread in a crewel needle, couch then buttonhole stitch the shaped wire to the muslin, over the traced wing outline.

fore wing

4. Work the outer edge of the wing (inside the wire) with a row of long and short buttonhole stitch, then embroider the remainder of the wing surface in long and short stitch. Make sure all stitches are worked in a direction towards the inner corner of the wing.

hind wing

5. With pearl metallic thread in a milliners needle, work the veins with fly and single feather stitches, using the diagrams as a guide.

6. The wings of the White Ermine Moth are scattered with tiny black spots, varying greatly in pattern and number and with very few spots in the hind wings. The spots may be worked with small French knots, using one strand of black thread, or with tiny beads (see note in Requirements), using the diagrams as a guide to placement.

completed wings

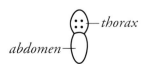

abdomen—⟍   ⟋—thorax

abdomen placement

completed thorax & abdomen

ABDOMEN

1. Outline the thorax and the abdomen with small back stitches, using white thread for the thorax and gold thread for the abdomen.

2. Using 6 strands of gold thread in a chenille needle, pad the abdomen, inside the outline, with four long straight stitches. With one strand of thread, work five evenly spaced couching stitches over the padding (the abdomen will be worked in raised stem stitch over these bars).

3. With one strand of black thread in a tapestry needle, work a row of raised chain stitch down the centre of the abdomen (to form a slightly textured centre line), working the stitches over the couched bars towards the tail.

4. Using one strand of gold thread, work five rows of raised stem stitch on either side of the centre line, to cover the abdomen. Work each row alternately, towards the tail.

5. With 2 strands of white thread, work a few Turkey knots at the end of the abdomen to form a tufted tail, working the securing stitches at the back of the work (behind the abdomen).

To Complete the Moth

1. Carefully cut out the wings. Use a large yarn darner to insert the wire tails of the wings through the two pairs of dots inside the thorax outline. Apply the hind wings first, inserting the wire tails separately through the two lower dots, then the fore wings through the two upper dots (the wings will slightly overlap). Bend the wire tails under the wings and secure to the backing fabric with tiny stitches using white thread, making sure that the stitches do not protrude beyond the wingspan. Trim the wire tails when the moth is finished.

wing placement

2. Using 2 strands of white thread, and starting at the abdomen end of the thorax, work 'rows' of Turkey knots to fill the abdomen, working all stitches between the wings and inside the upper outline (I worked seven 'rows' with 2 to 4 stitches in each row—4, 3, 2, 2, 3, 4, 3). Using small sharp scissors and an eyebrow comb, cut and comb the Turkey knots to form the fluffy thorax characteristic of this moth.

thorax

3. With 2 strands of thread, work two small satin stitches at the top of the thorax to form the head. Using nylon thread in a sharps needle, stitch a black petite bead on either side of the head for the eyes.

4. With one strand of copper/black metallic thread in a milliners needle, work each antenna with three single feather stitches. Work two tiny straight stitches in front of the head for the mouth parts.

completed antennae

finished moth actual size

Order: Lepidoptera Family Geometridae

Geometers

The Geometridae are a large, worldwide family of moths whose
caterpillars have characteristic looping movements. Unlike most
caterpillars, those of the geometers have legs at each end but none
in the middle, hence their method of crawling entails the arching
of the body into a loop then extending forward as if measuring
the distance spanned. From this action has been derived the term
'geometer' and the family name Geometridae, which means 'earth-
measuring'. The caterpillars are also known as loopers or inch-worms.

The adult moths are rather frail insects and very weak fliers.
They have a slender abdomen, broad, thin wings, often marked with
incredibly fine and intricate patterns, and long, slender legs. When
resting, the moth holds its wings flush with the surface and the
antennae close to the body. The often mottled colours of their wings,
combined with this flat, shadowless posture, provides very effective
camouflage for these moths.

Large Emerald Moth, *Geometra papilionaria*

Among lepidopterans green wings are
something of an exception, but among
the geometrids there are many green
species. The largest of these, the **Large
Emerald Moth**, Geometra papilionaria,
has delicate blue-green wings crossed
with faint wavy lines. As distinct from
the female, the male has pectinate
(comb-like) antennae. The species
inhabits birch, hazel and beech woods
from lowlands to mountains.

Large Emerald Moth

Geometra papilionaria   Order: *Lepidoptera*   Family: *Geometridae*

DIAGRAMS ACTUAL SIZE

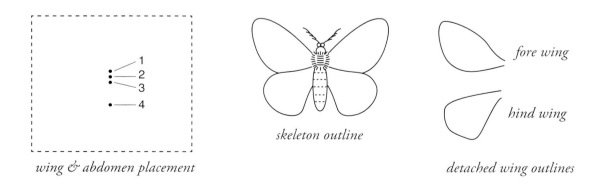

wing & abdomen placement   *skeleton outline*   *detached wing outlines*

REQUIREMENTS

quilter's muslin: 20 cm (8 in) square

10 cm (4 in) embroidery hoop

needles

crewel/embroidery size 10

sharps size 12

milliners/straw size 9

chenille size 18

sharp yarn darner sizes 14–18

beads & wire

3 mm blue/purple bead

Mill Hill petite beads 42028 *(ginger)*

33 gauge white covered wire:
  four 10 cm (4 in) lengths

thread

white stranded thread:
Cifonda Art Silk White or DMC Blanc

very pale green stranded thread:
Cifonda Art Silk 491 or DMC 3813

light green stranded thread:
Cifonda Art Silk 492 or DMC 503

medium green stranded thread:
Cifonda Art Silk 493 or DMC 502

dark green stranded thread:
Cifonda Art Silk 494 or DMC 501

light gold stranded thread:
Cifonda Art Silk 48 or DMC 729

medium gold stranded thread:
Soie d'Alger 3815 or DMC 167

ecru stranded thread:
DMC Ecru

variegated dark green/gold chenille thread:
col. Fire

METHOD

. . . .

Transfer the wing and abdomen placement dots to the background fabric.

WINGS

1. Mount the muslin into a small hoop and trace four wing outlines—a right and left fore wing and a right and left hind wing. Both the fore and hind wings are worked as follows.

2. Using very pale green thread in a sharps needle, couch wire around the wing outline leaving two tails of wire at the base of the wing. Buttonhole stitch the wire to the muslin.

forewing wire

3. The wings are embroidered, inside the wire outline, with rows of buttonhole stitch and encroaching satin stitch. To provide guidelines for these rows, lightly pencil in seven lines as shown. With dark green thread, work the row at the wing edge first with close, long buttonhole stitches (the ridge of the buttonhole is next to the wire).

4. Work the remainder of the wing with seven rows of straight stitches blending into each other (encroaching satin stitch), blending the first row into the long buttonhole stitches (leaving a narrow strip of dark green inside the wire). Refer to the diagram for row colours:

Buttonhole row: dark green —
Row 1: light green —
Row 2: white —
Row 3: very pale green —
Row 4: light green —
Row 5: very pale green —
Row 6: light green —
Row 7: light green —

fore wing

hind wing

completed wings

5. With medium green thread, work the veins with fly and buttonhole stitches, using the diagram as a guide. To make the green thread as fine as possible, dampen and twist just before stitching.

6. Embroider a row of seven spots on the edge of the wing, between the veins. Each spot is worked with two satin stitches in white thread.

padding

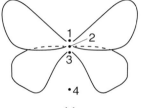

coaching stitch abdomen

To Complete the Moth

1. Both the abdomen and the thorax are padded with 14 strands of medium gold thread in a chenille needle (7 strands doubled). To pad the abdomen, make one stitch from 3 to 4. Cross the tails of padding thread behind the stitch (at the back), and hold each end with masking tape (retain the thread in the needle at the back until required to pad the thorax).

2. With one strand of medium gold thread in a crewel needle, work four couching stitches over the padding (catching in the tails of thread behind the abdomen), then, changing to a fine tapestry needle, cover the abdomen with six rows of raised stem stitch, working over these couching stitches towards the tail.

3. Carefully cut out the wings and apply by inserting the wire tails through the upper three dots as shown, using large yarn darners. Apply the hind wings first, inserting the wire tails separately through 2 and 3, then the fore wings through 1 and 2 (the wings share hole 2). Bend the wire tails under the wings and secure to the backing fabric with tiny stitches using ecru thread, making

padding

sure that the stitches do not protrude beyond the wingspan. Trim the wire tails when the moth is finished.

4. Using the retained medium gold thread, make a padding stitch from 1 to 3—this will be wrapped with chenille thread to form the thorax. With chenille thread in the largest yarn darner, come out near 1, make three wraps around the padding stitch then insert the needle near 3. Make sure the chenille does not twist and adjust the tension of the wraps (thus the fluffiness of the thorax) as desired. To facilitate the wrapping, do not tighten or secure the padding thread until the stitch has been wrapped with chenille. Use stranded thread to secure all threads at the back.

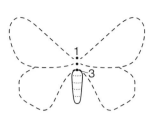

5. With one strand of dark green thread, apply a 3 mm bead for the head, working the stitches towards the thorax. To form the eyes, apply two petite beads, one stitch through both beads, above the head bead. Work a couching stitch between the beads, then another stitch between the petite beads then through the 3 mm bead.

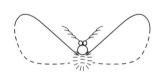

6. Using light gold thread, dampened if necessary to make it smooth, work each antenna with four stem stitches, spacing the stitches to produce a comb-like effect.

finished moth actual size

*completed thorax
& abdomen*

Order: Lepidoptera Family Hepialidae

Ghost Moths, Swift Moths

Some of the handsomest moths, easily rivalling the butterflies, belong to the family Hepialidae. The ghost moths of the genus Aenetus, found in Indonesia, New Guinea, New Caledonia, Australia and New Zealand, have many large species (wingspan up to 150 mm), with colours ranging from pinks, greens and blues to deep golds and pearly whites. The larvae (caterpillars) are mainly tunnellers in the stems or roots of living trees and sometimes in the ground.

The Splendid Ghost Moth, Aenetus mirabilis, has pastel aqua-green fore wings and shiny white hind wings which attract females as he flies at dusk. Aenetus mirabilis is one of several species of Australian ghost moths whose large wood-boring caterpillars, known as witchetty grubs, were collected and consumed by some Aboriginal peoples in arid regions to supplement their protein supply.

Splendid Ghost Moth, *Aenetus mirabilis*

Splendid Ghost Moth

Aenetus mirabilis Order: *Lepidoptera* Family: *Hepialidae*

DIAGRAMS ACTUAL SIZE

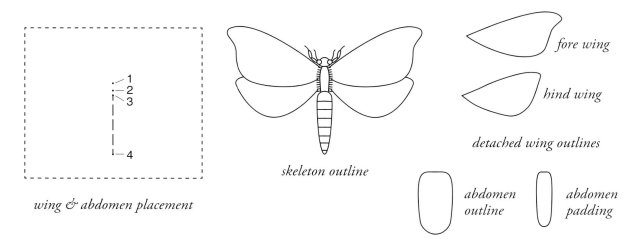

wing & abdomen placement

skeleton outline

fore wing

hind wing

detached wing outlines

abdomen outline

abdomen padding

REQUIREMENTS

hand-painted silk satin:
30 cm (12 in) square (either purchase
hand-painted fabric from one of the
many available suppliers or paint
your own)

quilter's muslin: 30 cm (12 in) square
ivory kid: 5 cm (2 in) square
 (I used an old kid glove)
white felt: 2.5 cm (1 in) square
25 cm (10 in) embroidery hoop

needles
sharps sizes 10 and 12
crewel/embroidery size 10
sharp yarn darner sizes 14–18

beads & wire
3 mm bronze bead
Mill Hill petite beads 40374
 (blue/purple)
33 gauge white covered wire:
 four 12 cm (4½ in) lengths

thread
pale green stranded thread:
Cifonda Art Silk 491 or DMC 3813

off-white stranded thread:
Cifonda Art Silk Off-white or DMC 3865

ecru stranded thread:
DMC Ecru

gold rayon machine embroidery thread:
Madeira Rayon No. 40 col.1070

copper/black metallic thread:
Kreinik Cord 215c

variegated gold and beige chenille threads:
cols. Paprika and Neutral

clear nylon thread:
Madeira Monofil No. 60: col.1001

dark nylon thread:
Madeira Monofil No. 60: col.1000

METHOD

Transfer the wing and abdomen placement dots to the background fabric.

As my aim was use as many different techniques as possible to create these moths and butterflies, I chose to interpret the wings of the Splendid Ghost Moth with hand-painted silk satin that I painted with metallic acrylic fabric paint (Lumiere by Jaquard). I have included a brief description of the process; however, if painting your own fabric, follow the instructions provided for the materials you are using.

1. Mount a piece of ivory silk satin into a large plastic embroidery hoop. Mix Pearl White, Metallic Olive and a touch of Pearl Blue fabric paint to produce a pale green. Mix several shades of the colour then paint a selection onto half of the fabric in the hoop. Mix Pearl White and a touch of Metallic Gold to produce a creamy white. Mix several shades of the colour then paint a selection onto the remaining half of the fabric in the hoop. Allow to dry for 24 hours.

2. Remove the fabric from the hoop and fix the paint by ironing on the reverse side for a few minutes.

WINGS

1. Mount the dyed satin and muslin backing fabric into the hoop (if the painted satin is stiff there is no need for the backing fabric). A larger hoop has been recommended to allow more choice when selecting the sections of painted fabric to be used for the wings.

2. Using tweezers, shape lengths of wire around the wing outline diagrams, leaving two tails of wire at the base of the wing. Shape a right and a left fore wing, and a right and a left hind wing. Transfer the shaped wires to the

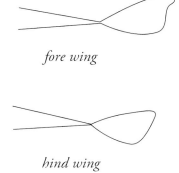

fore wing

hind wing

fore wing

hind wing

completed wings

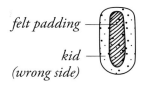

felt padding

kid
(wrong side)

completed abdomen

fabric surface, selecting an area of pale green for the fore wings and an area of creamy white for the hind wings. Hold the wire tails in place with masking tape and check that the shapes have not been distorted.

3. Using a size 10 sharps needle, couch then buttonhole stitch the shaped wire to the background fabric, using pale green thread for the fore wings and off-white thread for the hind wings.

4. With the gold rayon thread in a size 12 sharps needle, work the veins with a combination of fly and buttonhole stitches, using the diagrams as a guide.

ABDOMEN

The leather abdomen is shaped in the hand before being couched to the background fabric with dark nylon thread.

1. Paint a small strip of the ivory kid with pale green fabric paint. Cut an abdomen shape from the ivory kid, using the abdomen outline as a guide and placing the tail end over a painted section of the kid. To pad the abdomen, cut a padding shape from felt. Fold the sides of the kid towards each other, enclosing the felt padding, and catch the edges together with overcast stitches, using clear nylon thread in a size 12 sharps needle. Do not stitch right to the tip of the abdomen. Mould the leather into the abdomen shape with your fingers.

2. Using dark nylon thread, apply the abdomen shape to the background fabric (over a line between 3 and 4) with seven couching stitches (segment lines), angling the needle under the abdomen shape. Work the centre couching stitch first, then three stitches on either side, squeezing the tail of the abdomen into a point with tweezers as you work the lower stitches. Pull the stitches slightly to form slight indentations at the segment lines.

To Complete the Moth

1. Carefully cut out the wings and apply by inserting the wire tails through the two upper dots, using a large yarn darner. First apply the hind wings, inserting the wire tails through 2, then the fore wings at 1 (the wings will slightly overlap). Bend the wire tails under the wings and secure to the backing fabric with tiny stitches using ecru thread, making sure that the stitches do not protrude beyond the wingspan. Trim the wire tails when the butterfly is finished.

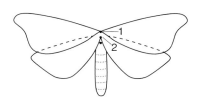

wing placement

2. The thorax is worked with three straight stitches across the centre of the wings (from 1 to 3), using chenille thread in the largest yarn darner. Using variegated chenille, select a dark gold section of thread and work two stitches, side by side. Select a beige section of chenille and work a stitch on top/between the gold to form a centre stripe (for maximum control of the chenille, all stitches can be made with separate lengths of thread, inserted from the front). Make sure the chenille does not twist and adjust the tension of the stitches (thus the fluffiness of the thorax), as desired. Secure the tails of chenille with clear nylon thread (retain thread to apply the beads).

leg stitch diagram

3. Using clear nylon thread, stitch a 3 mm bead close to the top of the thorax for the head (keep the hole in the bead parallel to the top of the thorax). Bring the needle through to the front and stitch a bronze/purple petite bead on either side of the head bead for the eyes, taking the needle through the hole of the bead several times so that the eyes are suspended on either side of the head.

leg placement

4. Using two strand of pale green thread, work a leg on either side of the head—two chain stitches and a long tie-down stitch for each leg.

5. With one strand of copper/black metallic thread, make a stitch on either side of the head bead for the antennae (taking the needle through the head bead if desired).

finished moth actual size

Order: Lepidoptera Family: Incurvariidae

Longhorns

Longhorn Moths are day-flying micro-moths, commonly seen in early summer. The males are active in sunshine, swarming around the tops of bushes and trees, while the females inhabit the undergrowth. The young larvae build flat cases out of pieces of leaf and feed in the leaf litter throughout autumn, pupating within the cases.

Longhorn Moth, *Adela reaumurella*

The glittering **Longhorn Moth**, Adela reaumurella, can frequently be seen clustering over bushes of yellow gorse flowers in summer. Often referred to as Fairy Moths, and sometimes mistaken for flies, these small insects look dark at first, but when their wings catch the light they flash bright gold against the black fluffy body. The wings have a feathered edge - the fore wings being metallic greenish gold in colour, the hind wings metallic bronze-plum. The distinguishing feature of these moths is the extraordinarily long antennae of the males -- up to six times the length of the body. Female moths have shorter antennae and a less hairy head. The wingspan of these tiny moths ranges from 14-18 millimetres.

Longhorn Moth

Adela reaumurella Order: *Lepidoptera* Family: *Incurvariidae*

DIAGRAMS ACTUAL SIZE

1
2

3

wing & abdomen placement

skeleton outline

fore wing

hind wing

detached wing outlines

REQUIREMENTS

light gold shot crystal organza:
   15 x 7.5 cm (6 x 3 in)
wine/black shot organza:
   15 x 7.5 cm (6 x 3 in)
gold metal organdie:
   15 cm (6 in) square
paper-backed fusible web:
   15 cm (6 in) square
10 cm (4 in) embroidery hoop

needles
sharps size 11 or 12
milliners/straw size 9
chenille size 18
sharp yarn darner sizes 14–18

beads & wire
Mill Hill antique glass bead 3036
   (wine/bronze)
Mill Hill petite beads 442014 *(black)*
33 gauge white covered wire (moth
   wings): four 9 cm (3½ in) lengths
   *(colour wire pale gold if desired: Copic
   YR24 Pale Sepia)*
28 gauge brass wire (moth antennae):
   one 15 cm (6 in) length

thread
pale gold rayon machine thread:
Madeira Rayon No. 40 col.1338

pale plum rayon machine thread:
Madeira Rayon No. 40 col.1358

dark brown stranded thread:
Soie d'Alger 4146 or DMC 838

ecru stranded thread:
DMC Ecru

pale gold metallic thread:
Madeira Metallic No. 30 col. 6032

wine/black metallic thread:
Kreinik Cord 208c

black chenille thread:
Au Ver à Soie Chenille à Broder: col. Noir

nylon clear thread:
Madeira Monofil No.60 col. 1001

METHOD

Transfer the wing and abdomen placement dots to the background fabric.

WINGS

1. Lay the rectangles of organza side by side, overlapping the long sides 1 cm (⅜ in). Apply fusible web to the resulting 'square' of organzas (use baking parchment to protect the iron and the ironing board). Fuse gold metal organdie to the 'square' of organzas, one layer of fabric rotated 45 degrees to be on the bias grain. Mount the fabrics into the hoop, organza side uppermost.

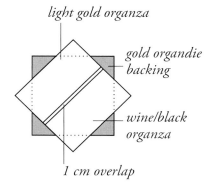

light gold organza

gold organdie backing

wine/black organza

1 cm overlap

2. Using tweezers, shape a length of wire around the wing outline diagram, leaving two tails of wire at the base of the wing. Shape a right and a left fore wing and a right and a left hind wing. Transfer the shaped wires to the fabric surface, positioning the fore wings over the light gold fabric and the hind wings over the wine/black fabric, holding the wire tails in place with masking tape. Check that the shapes have not been distorted.

3. Using pale gold rayon machine thread in a sharps needle, couch then buttonhole stitch the shaped wire to the background fabrics.

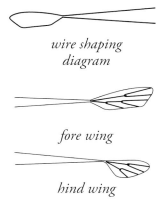

wire shaping diagram

fore wing

hind wing

4. With pale gold metallic thread in a milliners needle, work the veins in the fore wings with fly and buttonhole stitches, using the diagram as a guide.

5. With pale plum rayon thread in a sharps needle, work the veins in the hind wings with fly stitches, using the diagram as a guide.

completed wings

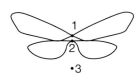

To Complete the Moth

1. Carefully cut out the wings and apply by inserting the wire tails through the upper two dots, using a large yarn darner. Apply the hind wings first, inserting the wire tails through 2, then the fore wings at 1. Bend the wire tails under the wings and secure to the backing fabric with tiny stitches using ecru thread, making sure that the stitches do not protrude beyond the wingspan. Trim the wire tails when the moth is finished.

2. The thorax is worked with black chenille thread in the largest yarn darner (to prevent the chenille from shredding). Work one straight stitch across the centre of the wings (from 1 to 2) adjusting the tension of the stitch, thus the fluffiness of the thorax, as desired (it is easier to insert each tail of chenille from the front). Secure the tails of chenille at the back with a few stitches worked in stranded thread.

3. The abdomen is worked with a wrapped stitch using 7 strands of dark brown thread in a chenille needle. Bring the needle out at 3 and insert at the base of the thorax. Repeat to make a double stitch. Bring the needle out again at 3 and wrap the double stitch back to the thorax (sliding the needle under and around the stitch), adjusting the tension of the wrapping to form the abdomen (this resembles a bullion knot).

4. Using nylon thread in a sharps needle, apply a wine/bronze antique bead at the top of the thorax for the head, working the stitches from side to side through the bead. Stitch a petite black bead on either side of the head for eyes then take the needle through all three beads and couch between each bead.

5. With one strand of wine/black metallic thread in a milliners needle, work the legs with straight stitches using the diagram as a guide. Work two straight stitches for each of the two inner segments and one straight stitch for the outer segment of each leg.

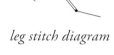

leg stitch diagram

6. To form the antennae, fold the length of brass wire in half and insert the folded end through to the back, under the head bead, using a fine yarn darner. Secure the wire end behind the thorax. Shape the wire into smooth, curved antennae by pulling it between your fingers. Trim to the desired length, 4–5 cm (2 in) for a male, 2.5 cm (1 in) for a female.

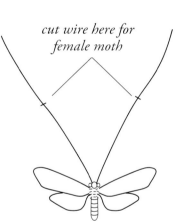

cut wire here for female moth

finished moth actual size

Blues, Coppers and Hairstreaks

The Lycaenidae family, comprising several thousand small to medium-sized butterflies, may be found in all regions of the world, usually inhabiting their preferred environment of grasslands and meadows rich in wild flowers. This family of swift flying, jewel-like butterflies includes the Blues, the Coppers and the Hairstreaks. Most species have brilliant metallic colours on the upper surface of the wings, usually shades of blue (the Blues), but sometimes coppery orange-red (the Coppers), while the more modestly coloured Hairstreaks feature fine white lines on the underside of the wings. While subject to enormous variation, the under sides of the wings of most lycaenids are a different and paler colour than the upper surface and are often spotted and streaked in intricate patterns, thus rendering the butterfly almost invisible when at rest. Males and females of the same species may be different in colour, with the females often being dull brown and inconspicuous. There are two members of Family Lycaenidae in the specimen box, the Chalkhill Blue Butterfly, Lysandra coridon, and the Purple-shot Copper Butterfly, Lycaena alciphron.

Chalkhill Blue Butterfly, *Lysandra coridon*

The **Chalkhill Blue**, Lysandra coridon, like many Blues, has males that are brightly coloured to attract females, and females that are an inconspicuous dark brown. The pale silvery-blue male has white-edged wings, with dark markings around the fore wings and a row of spots on the hind wings. The butterflies feed on nectar from many wildflowers, and are also attracted to dung, which provides them with essential salts. The Chalkhill Blue used to be seen in great numbers on chalk and limestone downlands in England, France and central Europe, but their numbers are now in decline due to the depletion of their food supply.

Chalkhill Blue Butterfly

Lysandra coridon Order: *Lepidoptera* Family: *Lycaenidae*

DIAGRAMS ACTUAL SIZE

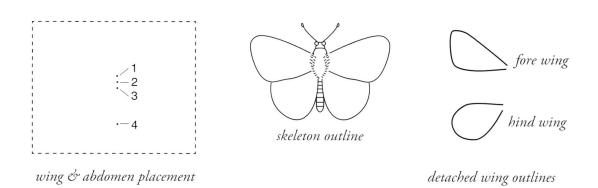

wing & abdomen placement

skeleton outline

fore wing

hind wing

detached wing outlines

REQUIREMENTS

quilter's muslin: 20 cm (8 in) square

10 cm (4 in) embroidery hoop

needles

sharps size 11 or 12

milliners/straw size 9

chenille size 18

sharp yarn darner sizes 14–18

beads & wire

3 mm blue/purple bead

Mill Hill petite beads 40374

  (blue/purple)

33 gauge white covered wire:

  four 10 cm (4 in) lengths

thread

dark grey stranded thread:

Cifonda Art Silk 215 or DMC 317

medium grey stranded thread:

Cifonda Art Silk 213 or DMC 318

light grey stranded thread:

Cifonda Art Silk 211 or DMC 762

medium blue stranded thread:

Cifonda Art Silk 987 or DMC 334

light blue stranded thread:

Cifonda Art Silk 986 or DMC 3325

steel-grey stranded thread:

Soie d'Alger 3443 or DMC 414

ecru stranded thread:

DMC Ecru

silver metallic thread:

Madeira Metallic No. 30 col. 6031

silver/black metallic thread:

Madeira Metallic No. 40 col. 442

variegated grey/brown chenille thread:

col. Pecan

METHOD

. . . .

Transfer the wing and abdomen placement dots to the background fabric.

WINGS

Mount the muslin into a small hoop and trace four wing outlines—a right and left fore wing and a right and left hind wing.

Fore Wings

1. Using light blue thread in the sharps needle, couch wire around the wing outline leaving two tails of wire at the base of the wing. Buttonhole stitch the wire to the muslin, working the sides of the wing in light blue and the corners and outer edge in light grey.

2. To form the markings on the outer edge of the wing, work 7 evenly spaced straight stitches over the wire (inside the buttonhole ridge) with medium grey thread.

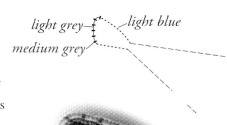

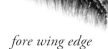

fore wing edge markings

3. The wings are embroidered, inside the wire outline, with rows of buttonhole stitch and encroaching satin stitch. To provide guidelines for these rows, lightly pencil in seven lines as shown. With medium grey thread, work the row at the wing edge first with close, long buttonhole stitches (the ridge of the buttonhole is next to the wire).

Buttonhole row: medium grey
Row 1: light grey
Row 2: light grey
Row 3: light blue
Row 4: light blue
Row 5: medium blue
Row 6: medium blue
Row 7: medium blue

4. Work the remainder of the wing with seven rows of straight stitches blending into each other (encroaching satin stitch), blending the first row into the long buttonhole stitches (leaving a narrow strip of medium grey inside the wire). Refer to the diagram for row colours:

5. With silver metallic thread in the milliners needle, work the veins with fly, single feather and straight stitches, using the diagram and the wing edge markings as a guide to placement.

completed fore wing

light blue
light grey
medium grey

Hind Wings

1. Using light blue thread, couch wire around the wing outline, leaving two tails of wire at the base of the wing. Buttonhole stitch the wire to the muslin, working the sides of the wing in light blue and the corners and outer edge in light grey.

2. To form the markings on the outer edge of the wing, work 8 evenly spaced straight stitches over the wire (inside the buttonhole ridge) with medium grey thread.

hind wing edge markings

3. The wings are embroidered, inside the wire outline, with rows of buttonhole stitch and encroaching satin stitch. To provide guidelines for these rows, lightly pencil in five lines as shown. With medium grey thread, work the row at the wing edge first with close, long buttonhole stitches (the ridge of the buttonhole is next to the wire).

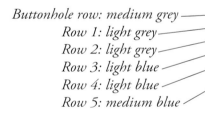

Buttonhole row: medium grey
Row 1: light grey
Row 2: light grey
Row 3: light blue
Row 4: light blue
Row 5: medium blue

4. Work the remainder of the wing with five rows of straight stitches blending into each other (encroaching satin stitch), blending the first row into the long buttonhole stitches (leaving a narrow strip of medium grey inside the wire). Refer to the diagram for row colours:

5. Work the veins in silver metallic thread with fly, single feather and straight stitches, using the diagram and the wing edge markings as a guide to placement.

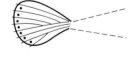

6. Using one strand of dark grey thread in the milliners needle, work seven French knots, between the veins, to form a row of spots on the edge of the wing.

completed hind wing

To Complete the Butterfly

1. Carefully cut out the wings and apply by inserting the wire tails through the three upper dots as shown, using large yarn darners. Apply the hind wings first, inserting the wire tails through 2 and 3, then the fore wings through 1 and 2 (the wings share hole 2). Bend the wire tails under the wings and secure to the muslin backing with tiny stitches using ecru thread, making sure that the stitches do not protrude beyond the wingspan. Trim the wire tails when the butterfly is finished.

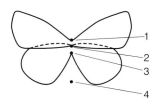

2. The thorax is worked with three straight stitches across the centre of the wings (from 1 to 3), using chenille thread in the largest yarn darner. Make sure the chenille does not twist and adjust the tension of the stitches, thus the fluffiness of the thorax, as desired. Use stranded thread to stitch the chenille tails to the backing fabric.

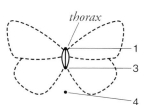

3. The abdomen is worked with a wrapped stitch, using 7 strands of steel-grey thread in the chenille needle. Bring the needle out at 4 and insert at 3 (the base of the thorax). Repeat to make a double stitch. Bring the needle out again at 4 and wrap the double stitch back to the thorax (sliding the needle under and around the stitch), adjusting the tension of the wrapping to form the abdomen (this resembles a bullion knot).

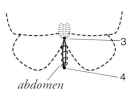

4. With one strand of steel-grey thread, apply a 3 mm bead for the head, working the stitches towards the thorax. To form the eyes, apply two petite beads, one stitch through both beads, above the head bead. Work a couching stitch between the beads.

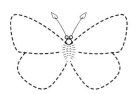

5. To work the antennae, make a small chain stitch (for the clubbed end) with a long tie-down stitch to the head, using silver/black metallic thread in the milliners needle. Refer to the diagram for placement—do not mark the antennae dots on the background fabric as they may show

finished butterfly actual size

Order: Lepidoptera Family: Lycaenidae

Blues, Coppers & Hairstreaks

The Lycaenidae family, comprising several thousand small to medium-sized butterflies, may be found in grasslands and meadows rich in wild flowers. This family of swift flying, jewel-like butterflies includes the Blues, the Coppers and the Hairstreaks. Most species have brilliant metallic colours on the upper surface of the wings, usually shades of blue (the Blues), but sometimes coppery orange-red (the Coppers).

Purple-shot Copper Butterfly, *Lycaena alciphron*

The **Purple-shot Copper Butterfly**, Lycaena alciphron, is one of the brilliant coppery-gold lycaenids. The male of this delightful species carries every colour of the rainbow on his wings -- shades of coppery-purple adorn the fore wings, blending to yellowish mauve hind wings, all sprinkled with purple-black spots. The dark-rimmed wings have an iridescent purple sheen which looks spectacular in sunlight.

Purple-shot Copper Butterfly

Lycaena alciphron (syn. Heodes alciphron)
Order: *Lepidoptera* Family: *Lycaenidae*

DIAGRAMS ACTUAL SIZE

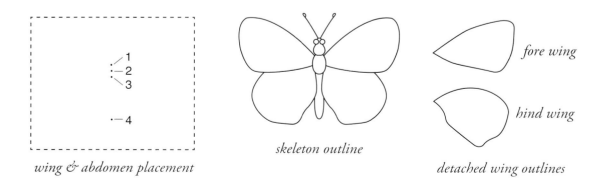

wing & abdomen placement

skeleton outline

fore wing

hind wing

detached wing outlines

REQUIREMENTS

....

vintage silk taffeta ribbon in shades of
  mauve and yellow: 20 cm (8 in)
  length *(hand-dyed silk ribbon or
  fabric may be substituted)*
silk organza: 20 cm (8 in) square
paper-backed fusible web:
  20 cm (8 in) square
15 cm (6 in) embroidery hoop

needles
sharps sizes 10 and 12
milliners/straw size 9
chenille size 18
sharp yarn darner sizes 14–18

beads & wire
3 mm blue/purple bead
Mill Hill petite beads 40374
  (blue/purple)
33 gauge white covered wire:
  four 12 cm (4½ in) lengths
  *(colour wire burgundy and copper if
  desired: Copic R59 Copic Cardinal,
  Copic YR14 Caramel)*

thread
burgundy stranded thread:
Cifonda Art Silk 145 or DMC 902

medium copper stranded thread:
Cifonda Art Silk 103 or DMC 301

medium purple stranded thread:
Cifonda Art Silk 125 or DMC 550

*Note: The above are the colours that I used for the
wings. Select threads to match your fabric.*

dark purple stranded thread:
Soie d'Alger 3316 or DMC 939

ecru stranded thread:
DMC Ecru

copper metallic thread:
Madeira Metallic Art 9803 col. 3027

silver/black metallic thread:
Madeira Metallic No. 40 col. 442

nylon clear thread:
Madeira Monofil No. 60 col. 1001

variegated purple chenille thread:
col. Copper mauve

METHOD

....

Transfer the wing and abdomen placement dots to the background fabric.

As my aim was use as many different techniques and materials as possible to create these butterflies, I chose to interpret the Purple-shot Copper Butterfly with a piece of old mauve-yellow, silk moiré taffeta ribbon. Hand-dyed silk ribbon or fabric may be substituted.

To facilitate the mounting of the ribbon into a hoop, fuse a 20 cm (8 in) length of ribbon to a square of silk organza using paper-backed fusible web cut to the same size as the ribbon (protect the iron and ironing board with baking parchment).

WINGS

1. Mount the fused ribbon-organza fabric into the hoop. A larger hoop is recommended to allow more choice when selecting the sections of ribbon to be used for the wings. My ribbon was shaded from mauve to yellow—I used mauve for the fore wings, and yellow for the hind wings.

2. Using tweezers, shape lengths of wire around the wing outline diagrams, leaving two tails of wire at the base of the wing. Shape a right and a left fore wing and a right and a left hind wing. If desired, colour sections of the fore wing wires burgundy and copper using the diagram as a guide (the hind wing wires are all coloured copper). Transfer the shaped wires to the fabric surface, selecting an area of mauve for the fore wings and an area of yellow for the hind wings. Hold the wire tails in place with masking tape and check that the shapes have not been distorted.

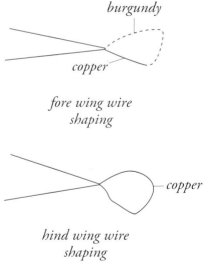

burgundy

copper

fore wing wire shaping

copper

hind wing wire shaping

Fore Wings

1. Using one strand of either burgundy or medium copper thread in size 10 sharps needles, couch the shaped wire to the ribbon fabric, working the stitches in burgundy along the upper and outer edges of the wing and medium copper along the lower edge, parking the colour not in use to the side.

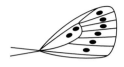

fore wing

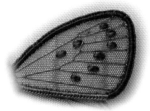

completed fore wing

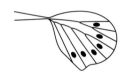

hind wing

*completed hind
wing*

abdomen

2. Buttonhole stitch the wire to the ribbon fabric, working the upper and outer edges of the wing in burgundy, and the lower edge in medium copper.

3. With the copper metallic thread in a size 12 sharps needle, work the veins with fly and buttonhole stitches, using the diagram as a guide.

4. Using medium purple thread in a size 12 sharps needle, embroider eight spots in each fore wing, working each spot with five satin stitches. Refer to the diagram for placement.

Hind Wings

1. Using medium copper thread, couch wire around the wing outline leaving two tails of wire at the base of the wing. Buttonhole stitch the wire to the ribbon.

2. With the copper metallic thread in a size 12 sharps needle, work the veins with fly and buttonhole stitches, using the diagram as a guide.

3. Using medium purple thread in a size 12 sharps needle, embroider six spots in each hind wing, working each spot with five satin stitches. Refer to the diagram for placement.

To Complete the Butterfly

1. To pad the abdomen, make one stitch from 3 to 4, with 14 strands of dark purple thread in a chenille needle (7 strands doubled). Cross the tails of padding thread behind the stitch (at the back), and hold both ends with masking tape.

2. With one strand of dark purple thread in a crewel needle, work five couching stitches over the padding (catching in the tails of thread behind the abdomen), then, changing to a fine tapestry needle, cover the abdomen with six rows of raised stem stitch, working over these couching stitches towards the tail.

3. Carefully cut out the wings and apply by inserting the wire tails through the upper two dots, using a large yarn darner. Apply the hind wings first, inserting the wire tails through 2, then the fore wings at 1 (the wings will overlap slightly). Bend the wire tails under the wings and secure to the backing fabric with tiny stitches using ecru thread, making sure that the stitches do not protrude beyond the wingspan. Trim the wire tails when the butterfly is finished.

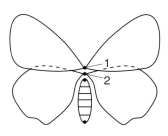

wing placement

4. The thorax is worked with two straight stitches across the centre of the wings (from 1 to 3), using a purple section of the variegated chenille thread in the largest yarn darner (for maximum control of the chenille, the stitches can be made with separate lengths of thread, inserted from the front). Make sure the chenille does not twist and adjust the tension of the stitches (thus the fluffiness of the thorax), as desired. Use nylon thread to secure all threads at the back.

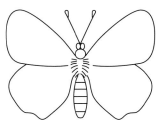

thorax, head & antennae placement

5. With one strand of nylon thread, apply a 3 mm bead for the head, working the stitches towards the thorax. To form the eyes, apply two petite beads, one stitch through both beads, above the head bead. Work a couching stitch between the beads, then another stitch between the petite beads then through the 3 mm bead.

6. To work the antennae, make a long fly stitch with a tiny chain stitch at each end (to form the clubbed tip), using silver/black metallic thread in the milliners needle. Refer to the diagram for placement.

finished butterfly actual size

Order: Lepidoptera Family: Morphidae

Morphos

One of the world's most beautiful butterflies, the male Morpho rhetenor, gets its sapphire sheen not from pigment but from a layer of scales that reflects only blue light. This butterfly is a member of the small family Morphidae (morpho meaning 'beautiful'), which occurs only in the tropical rainforests of South and Central America.

Blue Morpho Butterfly, *Morpho rhetenor*

Many male Morpho butterflies, usually more colourful than the females, have upper wings of shimmering metallic shades of blue, green or white, sharply contrasting with the drab brown spotted underside, common to all species. The sudden opening of the wings, whose span can range from 7.5 cm (3 inches) to an imposing 20 cm (8 inches), may serve to dazzle predators, while the ultra-violet light reflected from the wing surface informs other males of their presence, males of the species being very territorial. Morpho butterflies feed on the juices of fermenting fruit and fungi on the forest floor.

The iridescent blue colours of the morpho wing result from the way light is reflected or broken up by specially structured scales on the wing. These scales, which are arranged in layers, reflect up to 70 per cent of the light falling on them, including ultra-violet, producing different shades of blue. Having wing colours that are structural, thus fade-proof, not only makes these butterflies highly attractive to collectors, but led to the wings of the **Blue Morpho** butterflies being used widely for butterfly wing 'pictures' and jewellery, such as brooches and pendants, mainly between the 1920s and 1950s. Many early butterfly wing jewellery items made in England were set in sterling silver and feature fine filigree work at the edges. In the past, the butterflies were collected in the wild, but today, blue Morphos are bred commercially for sale.

Blue Morpho Butterfly

Morpho rhetenor (male)
Order: *Lepidoptera* Family: *Morphidae*

DIAGRAMS ACTUAL SIZE

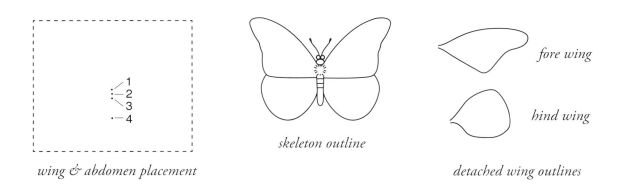

1
2
3
4

wing & abdomen placement

skeleton outline

fore wing

hind wing

detached wing outlines

REQUIREMENTS

metallic-blue elastane fabric:
  15 cm (6 in) square
teal organza: 15 cm (6 in) square
paper-backed fusible web:
  15 cm (6 in) square
10 cm (4 in) embroidery hoop

needles
sharps size 10
chenille size 18
sharp yarn darner sizes 14–18

beads & wire
Mill Hill seed bead 374
Mill Hill petite beads 42014 *(black)*
33 gauge white covered wire:
  four 12 cm (4½ in) lengths
  (colour wire blue and brown if
  desired: Copic B18 Copic Lapis
  Lazuli, Copic E57 Light Walnut)

thread
blue stranded thread;
Cifonda Art Silk 685 or DMC 3842

medium brown stranded thread:
Cifonda Art Silk 50 or DMC 801

light grey stranded thread:
Cifonda Art Silk 212 or DMC 415

dark rust stranded thread:
Soie d'Alger 4143 or DMC 300

ecru stranded thread:
DMC Ecru

blue/black metallic thread:
Kreinik Cord 202c

brown/black metallic thread:
Kreinik Cord 201c

variegated blue/brown chenille thread:
col. Amber Marine

METHOD

. . . .

Transfer the wing and abdomen placement dots to the background fabric.

WINGS

1. Fuse paper-backed fusible web to organza, then fuse the organza to the back of the metallic-blue fabric (fuse fabrics between sheets of baking parchment for protection). Mount the fabric sandwich into a small hoop.

2. Using tweezers, shape a length of wire around the wing outline diagram, leaving two tails of wire at the base of the wing. Shape a right and a left fore wing and a right and a left hind wing. If desired, colour the wires brown and blue using the diagram as a guide. Transfer the shaped wires to the fabric surface, holding the wire tails in place with masking tape. Check that the shapes have not been distorted.

3. The wire is stitched to the background fabric with either blue or medium brown thread (each in a sharps needle), as indicated by the diagram. Couch the wire to the fabric with blue or medium brown thread, parking the colour not in use to the side. Then buttonhole stitch the wire to the fabric, with either blue or medium brown thread as required.

medium brown

blue

wire shaping

blue

medium brown

wire shaping

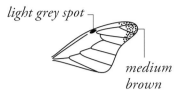

light grey spot

medium brown

fore wing

medium brown

hind wing

completed wings

3

4

abdomen placement

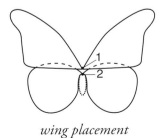

1
2

wing placement

4. Embroider the wing markings, inside the wire edge, with medium brown thread. Work the brown edge on the tip of fore wing in satin stitch and the border on the lower hind wing with stem stitch. Using light grey thread, embroider a spot inside the front edge of each fore wing, with three satin stitches.

5. With blue/black metallic thread in a sharps needle, work the veins with fly and buttonhole stitches, using the diagram as a guide.

To Complete the Butterfly

1. The abdomen is worked with a wrapped stitch, using 7 strands of dark rust thread in the chenille needle. Bring the needle out at 4 and insert at 3. Repeat to make a double stitch. Bring the needle out again at 4 and wrap the double stitch back to 3 (sliding the needle under and around the stitch), adjusting the tension of the wrapping to form the abdomen (this resembles a bullion knot).

2. Carefully cut out the wings and apply by inserting the wire tails through the two upper dots as shown, using large yarn darners. Apply the hind wings first, inserting both the wire tails through 2, then the fore wings through 1 (the wings will slightly overlap). Bend the wire tails under the wings and secure to the muslin backing with tiny stitches using ecru thread, making sure that the stitches do not protrude beyond the wingspan. Trim the wire tails when the butterfly is finished.

3. The thorax is worked with one straight stitch across the centre of the wings (from 1 to 3), using a doubled length of chenille thread in the largest yarn darner. Make sure the chenille does not twist and adjust the tension of the stitch, thus the fluffiness of the thorax, as desired. Use stranded thread to stitch the chenille tails to the backing fabric.

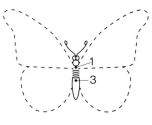

thorax placement

4. With one strand of dark rust thread, apply a seed bead for the head, working the stitches towards the thorax. To form the eyes, apply two petite beads, one stitch through both beads, above the head bead. Work several couching stitches between the beads.

5. To work the antennae, make a long fly stitch with a tiny straight stitch at each end (to form the clubbed tip), using brown/black metallic thread in the sharps needle. Refer to the diagram for placement—do not mark the antennae dots on the background fabric as they may show.

finished butterfly actual size

Owlet Moths

Owlet Moths are members of the family Noctuidae, the largest family of Lepidoptera with over 20000 known species. They are mostly night-flying, as the name noctua would indicate (Latin for 'owl'), but are attracted to lights at night. Ranging in size from small to very large, many species have intricate and very fine markings on their greyish brown fore wings, which not only are a guide to their identification, but also ensure superb camouflage.

The hind wings of many owlet moths are also grey or brown, but in some species the hind wings are yellow, red or blue, usually with dark markings. A beautiful example is the **Large Yellow Underwing Moth**, Noctua pronuba, which has bright yellow hind wings with a dark brownish black band around the outer edge. This large, day-flying moth, conspicuous in flight because of its brightly coloured hind wings, can be seen throughout summer in a variety of locations. This moth's colour scheme is very effective. Its drab, mottled, brownish grey fore wings, folded over its hind wings when at rest, renders it almost undetectable from the surrounding tree bark and foliage. If threatened, it can produce a startling display of bright yellow, thus aiding its escape. The caterpillars are considered a pest. Known as cutworms, they feed at night on a wide variety of low-growing plants such as turnips and strawberries, cutting the plant off near the ground.

Large Yellow Underwing Moth, *Noctua pronuba*

Large Yellow Underwing

Noctua pronuba Order: *Lepidoptera* Family: *Noctuidae*

DIAGRAMS ACTUAL SIZE

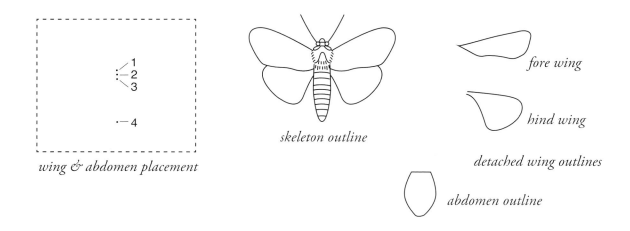

1
2
3

4

wing & abdomen placement

skeleton outline

fore wing

hind wing

detached wing outlines

abdomen outline

REQUIREMENTS

brownish grey smooth cotton fabric:
  20 cm (8 in) square

quilter's muslin: 20 cm (8 in) square

dark gold suede leather:
  2.5 cm (1 in) square

paper-backed fusible web:
  at least 20 cm (8 in) square

paints: watercolour or acrylic in shades
  of brown, grey and rust

small brush or sponge

two 10 cm (4 in) embroidery hoops

needles

crewel/embroidery size 10

sharps size 11 or 12

milliners/straw size 9

sharp yarn darner sizes 14–18

beads & wire

3 mm bronze bead

Mill Hill petite beads 42014 *(black)*

33 gauge white covered wire:
  four 12 cm (4½ in) lengths
  (colour wires grey and yellow if desired:
  Copic W7 Warm Grey, Copic Y15
  Cadmium Yellow)

thread

brown/grey stranded thread:
Soie d'Alger 3344 or DMC 3790

yellow stranded thread:
Cifonda Art Silk 174 or DMC 742

dark brown stranded thread:
Cifonda Art Silk 225A or DMC 3371

ecru stranded thread:
DMC Ecru

dark gold rayon machine thread:
Madeira Rayon No. 40 col. 1173

rust/gold metallic thread:
Madeira Metallic No. 40 col. 482

brown/black metallic thread:
Kreinik Cord 201c

variegated rust/brown chenille thread:
col. Amber Marine

dark nylon clear thread:
Madeira Monofil No. 60 col. 1000

Method

. . . .

Transfer the wing and abdomen placement dots to the background fabric.

Wings
Fore Wings

The fore wings of most noctid moths are drab brownish grey with fine markings that resemble bark. To achieve this mottled effect, I applied painted paper-backed fusible web to a brownish grey smooth cotton background fabric as follows:

1. Mix the paint with water then, using a brush or a sponge, apply to the web side of the paper-backed fusible web in a pattern of irregular narrow lines in browns, greys and rusts.

Hints:
- *Do not use too much water.*
- *Make sure the paint is not too thick.*
- *Paint a larger piece of web than required, then select a square that looks suitably 'mottled'.*

completed fore wing

2. Allow the paint to dry thoroughly (wrinkles will occur in the paper), place the square over the background fabric (paper side uppermost), then iron carefully to transfer the painted web to the fabric. Allow to cool then remove the paper backing and mount the fabric into a hoop, painted side uppermost (the fabric will feel a little tacky to start with but this effect soon disappears).

3. Using tweezers, shape a length of wire around the fore wing outline diagram, leaving two tails of wire at the base of the wing. Shape a right and a left fore wing. Transfer the shaped wires to the fabric surface, selecting a suitable 'mottled' section of the painted fabric, and hold the wire tails in place with masking tape. Check that the shapes have not been distorted.

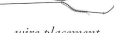

wire placement

4. With one strand of brown/grey thread in a crewel needle, couch then buttonhole stitch the wires to the fabric.

vein sitches

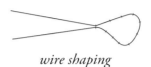

wire shaping

vein sitches

completed hind wing

5. Using dark nylon thread in a sharps needle, work the veins with fly, buttonhole and straight stitches, using the diagram as a guide (the veins in this moth are barely discernible).

Hind Wings

1. Mount the muslin into a small hoop and trace a right and left hind wing outline.

2. Using yellow thread in a sharps needle, couch wire around the wing outline leaving two tails of wire at the base of the wing. Buttonhole stitch the wire to the muslin.

3. With dark brown thread, work a row of close, long buttonhole stitches inside the wire at the wing edge.

4. Work the remainder of the wing in long and short stitch with yellow thread, blending the stitches into the brown border.

5. Using dark gold rayon thread, work the veins with fly and straight stitches, using the diagram as a guide.

ABDOMEN

The leather abdomen is shaped in the hand before being couched to the background fabric.

abdomen placement

1. Cut an abdomen shape from dark gold suede, using the abdomen outline as a guide. Fold the sides of the leather towards each other and catch together with overcast stitches, using nylon thread in a sharps needle (do not stitch right to the tip of the abdomen). Mould the leather into the abdomen shape with your fingers.

2. Using brown/black metallic thread in a straw needle, apply the abdomen shape to the background fabric (over the abdomen placement line between 3 and 4) with seven couching stitches, angling the needle under the abdomen shape. Work the centre couching stitch first then the couching stitches on either side, squeezing the tail of the abdomen into a point with tweezers as you work the lower stitch.

completed abdomen

To Complete the Moth

1. Carefully cut out the wings and apply by inserting the wire tails through the three upper dots as shown, using large yarn darners. Apply the hind wings first, inserting the wire tails through 2 and 3, then the fore wings through 1 and 2 (the wings share hole 2). Bend the wire tails under the wings and secure to the muslin backing with tiny stitches using ecru thread, making sure that the stitches do not protrude beyond the wingspan. Trim the wire tails when the moth is finished.

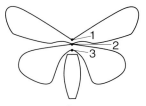

wing placement

2. The thorax is worked with three straight stitches across the centre of the wings (from 1 to 3), using chenille thread in the largest yarn darner. Using variegated chenille, select a rust section and work two stitches side by side. Select a section of brown chenille and work a stitch on top/between to form a centre stripe (for maximum control of the chenille, all stitches can be made with separate lengths of thread, all inserted from the front). Make sure the chenille does not twist and adjust the tension of the stitches (thus the fluffiness of the thorax), as desired. Secure the tails of chenille with nylon thread.

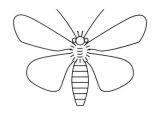

3. Using nylon thread in a sharps needle, stitch a 3 mm bead close to the top of the thorax, for the head (keeping the hole in the bead parallel to the top of the thorax). Bring the needle through to the front and stitch a black petite bead on either side of the head bead for the eyes, taking the needle through the hole of the bead several times so that the eyes are suspended on either side.

completed head & thorax

4. With one strand of rust/gold metallic thread in a sharps needle, make a stitch on either side of the head bead for the antennae. Work a small fly stitch at the top of the head for the mouthparts.

finished moth actual size

Order: Lepidoptera Family: Nymphalidae

Fritillaries, Admirals, Emperors and Aristocrats

The family Nymphalidae is one of the largest and best-known families of butterflies, with more than four thousand species represented in all world regions. With wingspans varying from 25 mm to 130 mm, these butterflies feature an extensive array of colouring, pattern and wing shapes. Some have very beautifully coloured wings, leading to exotic common names such as Purple Emperor, Red Admiral, Peacock and Painted Lady. Also known as Brush-footed Butterflies, the nymphalids hold their short, hairy, non-functional front legs forward, close to the head. Consequently, they all appear to have only four legs instead of six. There are two members of the family Nymphalidae in the specimen box, the Camberwell Beauty, Nymphalis antiopa, and the Purple Fuchsia Butterfly, Anaea tyrianthina.

Camberwell Beauty Butterfly, *Nymphalis antiopa*

Nymphalis antiopa, known as the **Camberwell Beauty** in the British Isles, and the Mourning Cloak in Europe and North America, is a nymphalid native to Eurasia and North America. It migrates to Britain from Scandinavia each year. This large, exquisite butterfly, with wings like maroon velvet, was first discovered in Britain in 1748, at the village of Camberwell, two miles south of London Bridge. The light-coloured border of both pairs of wings clearly distinguishes the Camberwell Beauty from all other members of this family. It was given various names by early entomologists, including White Petticoat, due to the pale hem-like wing edges. The wings feature a row of bright blue spots on a dark grey band between the creamy yellow border and dark red wing surface. The Camberwell Beauty has a strong fluttering and gliding flight, often soaring over the tops of the willows and birches that it favours. It is not attracted to flowers, but feeds on oozing tree sap and ripe fruit, particularly blackberries.

Camberwell Beauty

Nymphalis antiopa Order: *Lepidoptera* Family: *Nymphalidae*

DIAGRAMS ACTUAL SIZE

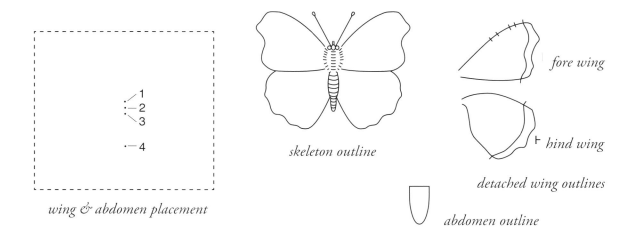

wing & abdomen placement

skeleton outline

fore wing

hind wing

detached wing outlines

abdomen outline

REQUIREMENTS

quilter's muslin: 20 cm (8 in) square

maroon kid leather:

  2.5 cm (1 in) square

12.5 cm (5 in) embroidery hoop

needles

sharps size 10 and 12

sharp yarn darner sizes 14–18

beads & wire

Mill Hill seed bead 3033 *(maroon)*

Mill Hill petite beads 42028 *(ginger)*

33 gauge white covered wire:

  four 15 cm (6 in) lengths *(colour
  wire maroon if desired: Copic R59
  Cardinal)*

thread

maroon stranded thread:
Cifonda Art Silk 533 or DMC 814

dark red stranded thread:
Cifonda Art Silk 530 or DMC 815

dark grey stranded thread:
Rajmahal Art Silk 25 or DMC 3799

blue stranded thread:
Cifonda Art Silk 182 or DMC 3838

light yellow stranded thread:
Cifonda Art Silk 1112 or DMC 3078

ecru stranded thread:
DMC Ecru

wine/black metallic thread:
Kreinik Cord 208c

gold/bronze metallic thread:
Madeira Metallic No.40 col.482

variegated maroon/brown chenille thread:
col. Amber Marine

nylon clear thread:
Madeira Monofil No. 60 col. 1001

Method

....

Transfer the wing and abdomen placement dots to the background fabric.

Wings

1. Mount the muslin into the hoop and trace four wing outlines—a right and left fore wing and a right and left hind wing—include the internal line indicating the yellow edge of the wing and the markings on the upper fore wing.

2. Using tweezers, shape a length of wire around the wing outline diagram, leaving two tails of wire at the base of the wing. Shape a right and a left fore wing and a right and a left hind wing. If desired, colour the sides of the wires maroon using the diagram as a guide.

3. The wire is stitched to the background fabric with either maroon or light yellow thread using the diagram as a guide (thread one strand of each into size 10 sharps needles). Couch the wire around the wing outline with either maroon or light yellow thread, parking the colour not in use to the side. Buttonhole stitch the wire to the muslin, working the sides of the wing in maroon and the outer edge in light yellow (also the top edge markings on the fore wings).

4. The wings are embroidered, inside the wire outline, with eight rows of satin stitch or encroaching satin stitch. To provide guidelines for these rows, lightly pencil in seven lines as shown (the traced line inside the edge is one of the seven lines).

5. Using light yellow thread, work a row of padded satin stitch at the outer edge of the wing. First, work a row of split back stitch inside the edge of the wire then a few padding stitches. Work the satin stitches towards the wire, enclosing the row of split stitch and the traced line. Embroider the wing markings, inside the top edge of the fore wings, in satin stitch.

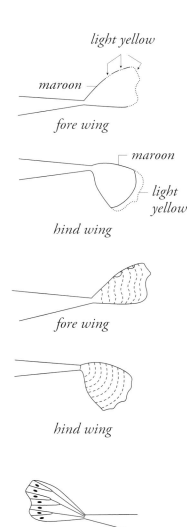

6. With dark grey thread, work the second row in satin stitch, inserting the needle just into the edge of the yellow satin stitches.

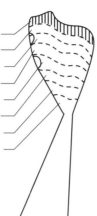

Row 1: light yellow satin stitch
Row 2: dark grey satin stitch
Row 3: maroon encroaching satin stitch
Row 4: dark red encroaching satin stitch
Row 5: maroon encroaching satin stitch
Row 6: dark red encroaching satin stitch
Row 7: maroon encroaching satin stitch
Row 8: maroon encroaching satin stitch

7. Using maroon and dark red thread, work the remainder of the wing with six rows of encroaching satin stitch (rows of straight stitches merging into each other), blending row 3 into the band of dark grey satin stitches. Refer to the diagram for row colours:

completed fore wing

completed hind wing

8. With wine/black metallic thread in a size 10 sharps needle, work the veins with fly, and single feather stitches, using the diagrams as a guide.

9. This butterfly has a row of blue spots at the edge of each wing (seven in the fore wing and eight in the hind wing). Using one strand of blue thread, work each spot with six satin stitches, embroidering the spots on top of the row of dark grey satin stitch, between each vein.

Abdomen

The leather abdomen is shaped in the hand before being couched to the background fabric.

abdomen placement

1. Cut an abdomen shape from maroon leather, using the outline as a guide. Fold the sides of the leather towards each other and catch together with overcast stitches, using nylon thread in a size 12 sharps needle (do not stitch right to the tip of the abdomen). Mould the leather into the abdomen shape with your fingers.

couching stitches

2. Using wine/black metallic thread in a size 10 sharps needle, apply the abdomen shape to the background fabric (over the abdomen placement line between 3 and 4) with five or six couching stitches, angling the needle under the abdomen shape. Work one of the centre couching stitches first, then the couching stitches on either side, squeezing the tail of the abdomen into a point with tweezers as you work the lower stitches.

To Complete the Butterfly

1. Carefully cut out the wings and apply by inserting the wire tails through the three upper dots as shown, using large yarn darners. Apply the hind wings first, inserting the wire tails through 2 and 3, then the fore wings through 1 and 2 (the wings share hole 2). Bend the wire tails under the wings and secure to the muslin backing with tiny stitches using ecru thread, making sure that the stitches do not protrude beyond the wingspan. Trim the wire tails when the butterfly is finished.

2. The thorax is worked with three straight stitches across the centre of the wings (from 1 to 3), using chenille thread in the largest yarn darner. Using variegated chenille, select a maroon section and make two stitches side by side. Select a section of brown chenille and work a stitch on top/between the maroon chenille to form a centre stripe (for maximum control of the chenille, all stitches can be made with separate lengths of thread, all inserted from the front). Make sure the chenille does not twist and adjust the tension of the stitches (thus the fluffiness of the thorax), as desired. Secure the tails of chenille with nylon thread after the head is applied (to allow for final adjustments).

3. Using nylon thread in a sharps needle, stitch a maroon seed bead close to the top of the thorax, for the head (keep the hole in the bead parallel to the top of the thorax). Stitch a ginger petite bead on either side of the head bead for the eyes (take the needle through all three beads, then couch between them, to keep them close together).

4. To work the antennae, make a small chain stitch (for the clubbed end) with a long, loose tie-down stitch on either side of the head bead, using gold/bronze metallic thread in a size 10 sharps needle. Refer to the diagram for placement—do not mark the antennae dots on the background fabric as they may show. Work a small fly stitch, above the head bead, for the front legs.

completed abdomen

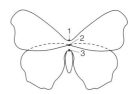

wing placement

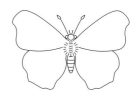

*completed thorax,
head & antennae*

*finished butterfly
actual size*

Order: Lepidoptera Family: Nymphalidae

Fritillaries, Admirals, Emperors and Aristocrats

The family Nymphalidae is one of the largest and best-known families of butterflies, with species represented in all regions of the world. With wingspans varying from 25 mm to 130 mm, these butterflies feature an extensive array of colouring, pattern and wing shapes. Some have very beautifully coloured wings, leading to exotic common names such as Purple Emperor, Red Admiral, Peacock and Painted Lady. Also known as Brush-footed Butterflies, the nymphalids hold their short, hairy, non-functional front legs forward, close to the head. Consequently, they all appear to have only four legs instead of six.

The rare **Purple Fuchsia Butterfly**, Anaea tyrianthina, is an example of one of the brilliantly coloured butterflies belonging to this family. Discovered in Bolivia in the nineteenth century, the exotic Anaea tyrianthina is one of the few high-altitude butterflies.

Purple Fuchsia Butterfly, *Anaea tyrianthina*

Purple Fuchsia Butterfly

Anaea tyrianthina Order: *Lepidoptera* Family: *Nymphalidae*

DIAGRAMS ACTUAL SIZE

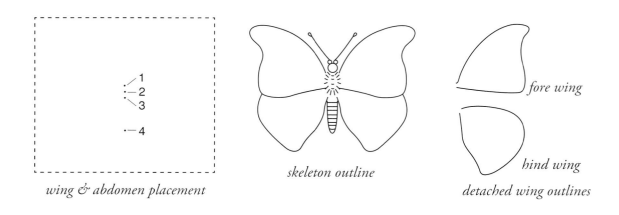

1
2
3
4

wing & abdomen placement

skeleton outline

fore wing

hind wing

detached wing outlines

The Butterfly & Moth Specimen Box

REQUIREMENTS

hand-dyed or painted silk fabric:
20 cm (8 in) square *(in shades of copper and gold; either purchase hand-dyed fabric or create your own)*
quilter's muslin: 20 cm (8 in) square
15 cm (6 in) embroidery hoop

needles
sharps size 10
crewel/embroidery size 10
chenille size 18
tapestry size 28
sharp yarn darner sizes 14–18

beads & wire
3 mm bronze bead
Mill Hill petite beads 40374
(blue/purple)
33 gauge white covered wire:
four 10 cm (4 in) lengths *(colour two wires copper and two gold if desired: Copic E07 Light Mahogany and Copic YR24 Pale Sepia)*

thread
copper stranded thread:
Cifonda Art Silk 104 or DMC 920

gold stranded thread:
Cifonda Art Silk 62 or DMC 435

Note: The above are the colours that I used for the wings. Select threads to match your fabric.

brown stranded thread:
Soie d'Alger 3435 or DMC 838

ecru stranded thread:
DMC Ecru

copper/black metallic thread:
Kreinik Cord 215c

rust/gold metallic thread:
Madeira Metallic No. 40 col. 482

variegated brown/mahogany chenille thread:
col. Cinnamon

METHOD

. . . .

Transfer the wing and abdomen placement dots to the background fabric.

As my aim was use as many different techniques and materials as possible to create these butterflies, I chose to interpret the Purple Fuchsia Butterfly with hand-dyed silk fabric that I painted myself, using Silk Designer dyes and gold Serti Gutta. I have included a brief overview of the process; however, if dyeing your own fabric, follow the instructions provided for the materials you are using.

1. Mount a piece of light weight ivory silk into a large plastic embroidery hoop. Using gutta in a bottle with a fine nozzle, draw the desired design outlines onto the silk fabric. Allow to dry. (The use of gutta is optional.)

2. Apply the fabric dye to the silk in the hoop with a paint brush or sponge. Allow to dry then remove from the hoop.

3. Wrap the silk loosely in clean calico or paper towel, then place the rolled fabric in a steamer over boiling water (I used a bamboo steaming basket over a wok). Steam for 1–2 hours to fix the gutta and the dye. Allow to cool then rinse several times with cold water to remove excess dye. Allow to almost dry before ironing on the back of the fabric.

WINGS

1. Mount the dyed silk and muslin backing fabric into the hoop (a coloured backing fabric may be substituted if desired). A larger hoop has been recommended to allow more choice when selecting the sections of dyed fabric to be used for the wings. My fabric had a section of coppery colours, which I used for the fore wings, and an area of golds which I used for the hind wings.

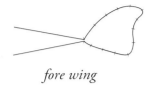

fore wing

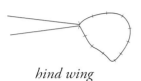

hind wing

fore wing

hind wing

2. Using tweezers, shape lengths of wire around the wing outline diagrams, leaving two tails of wire at the base of the wing. Shape a right and a left fore wing (using copper-coloured wire if desired), and a right and a left hind wing (with gold-coloured wire). Transfer the shaped wires to the fabric surface, selecting an area of copper for the fore wings and an area of gold for the hind wings. Hold the wire tails in place with masking tape and check that the shapes have not been distorted.

3. Using a sharps needle, couch then buttonhole stitch the shaped wire to the background fabric, using copper thread for the fore wings and gold thread for the hind wings.

4. With the copper/black metallic thread in a sharps needle, work the veins with fly and buttonhole stitches, using the diagrams as a guide.

completed wings

To Complete the Butterfly

1. To pad the abdomen, make one stitch from 3 to 4, with 14 strands of brown thread in a chenille needle (7 strands doubled). Cross the tails of padding thread behind the stitch (at the back), and hold both ends with masking tape.

2. With one strand of brown thread in a crewel needle, work three couching stitches over the padding (catching in the tails of thread behind the abdomen), then, changing to a fine tapestry needle, cover the abdomen with six rows of raised stem stitch, working over these couching stitches towards the tail.

abdomen placement

3. Carefully cut out the wings and apply by inserting the wire tails through the upper two dots, using a large yarn darner. Apply the hind wings first, inserting the wire tails through 2, then the fore wings at 1 (the wings will slightly overlap). Bend the wire tails under the wings and secure to the backing fabric with tiny stitches using ecru thread, making sure that the stitches do not protrude beyond the wingspan. Trim the wire tails when the butterfly is finished.

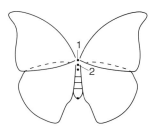

wing placement

4. The thorax is worked with two straight stitches across the centre of the wings (from 1 to 3), using a dark brown section of the variegated chenille thread in the largest yarn darner (for maximum control of the chenille, both stitches can be made with separate lengths of thread, inserted from the front). Make sure the chenille does not twist and adjust the tension of the stitches (thus the fluffiness of the thorax) as desired. Use stranded thread to secure all threads at the back.

5. With one strand of brown thread, apply a 3 mm bead for the head, working the stitches towards the thorax. To form the eyes, apply two petite beads, one stitch through both beads, above the head bead. Work a couching stitch between the beads, then another stitch between the petite beads then through the 3 mm bead.

head & eyes placement

6. To work the antennae, make a long fly stitch with a tiny chain stitch at each end (to form the clubbed tip), using rust/gold metallic thread in the crewel needle. Refer to the diagram for placement.

finished butterfly actual size

Order: Lepidoptera Family: Papilionidae

Apollos, Swallowtails & Birdwings

The family Papilionidae, which includes the Apollos, Birdwings and Swallowtails, contains the largest and some of the most splendid of all butterflies. Distributed throughout the world, they are generally powerful fliers and are among the most conspicuous butterflies in the countries where they are found. The attractive colours and wing shapes of many species of this family, and their relatively large size, has ensured that they have received a great deal of attention and study from lepidopterists throughout the world. Particularly fascinating are the enormous Birdwing Butterflies, mainly found in the Australian region, with a wingspan of up to 25 cm (10 inches) or more, while the smaller Apollos are quite different, with their rounded semi-transparent wings and bodies densely covered with hair.

Swallowtail Butterfly, *Papilio machaon*

Caterpillar of the Swallowtail Butterfly

The **Swallowtail Butterflies**, so-called as most have extensions on the hind wings which give the appearance of a swallow's tail, may be found in temperate or tropical zones of most countries. The Swallowtail Papilio machaon is one of the most handsome of the species. Also known as the Common Yellow Swallowtail and the Old World Swallowtail, this striking butterfly is yellow with black wing and vein markings and a wingspan of 8-10 cm (3-4 inches). The hind wings have a prominent tail which features a distinctive red and blue 'eye-spot'. The butterfly has a strong and fast flight, but frequently pauses to hover over flowering umbelliferous plants (such as fennel, parsley and dill) and sip nectar.

Swallowtail Butterfly

X *Papilio machaon* Order: *Lepidoptera* Family: *Papilionidae*

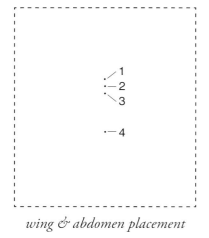

wing & abdomen placement

DIAGRAMS ACTUAL SIZE

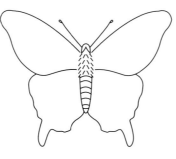

skeleton outline

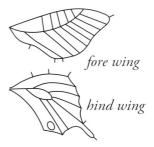

fore wing

hind wing

detached wing outlines

REQUIREMENTS

quilter's muslin: 20 cm (8 in) square

12.5 cm (5 in) embroidery hoop

needles

crewel/embroidery size 10

sharps size 12

milliners/straw size 9

chenille size 18

sharp yarn darner sizes 14–18

beads & wire

3 mm bronze/purple bead

Mill Hill petite beads 40374

  (bronze/purple)

33 gauge white covered wire:

  four 15 cm (6 in) lengths *(colour*

  sections of wire dark grey if desired:

  Copic W7 Warm Grey)

thread

black stranded thread:

Cifonda Art Silk Black or DMC 310

dark grey stranded thread:

Cifonda Art Silk 215 or DMC 317

light yellow stranded thread:

Cifonda Art Silk 1114 or DMC 744

medium yellow stranded thread:

Cifonda Art Silk 1116 or DMC 743

blue stranded thread:

Cifonda Art Silk 989B or DMC 796

red stranded thread:

Cifonda Art Silk 254A or DMC 817

medium brown stranded thread:

Soie d'Alger 4534 or DMC 610

dark grey stranded thread:

Soie d'Alger 3446 or DMC 3799

ecru stranded thread:

DMC Ecru

slate/gold metallic thread:

Madeira Metallic No. 40 col. 484

variegated brown/grey chenille thread:

col. Hunter Olive

METHOD

Transfer the wing and abdomen placement dots to the background fabric.

WINGS

1. Mount the muslin into a small hoop and trace four wing outlines—a right and a left fore wing and a right and a left hind wing. Include the vein lines and wing edge markings.

2. Using tweezers, shape a length of wire around the wing outline diagram, leaving two tails of wire at the base of the wing. Shape a right and a left fore wing and a right and a left hind wing. If desired, colour the black and grey sections of the wires dark grey using the diagram as a guide (leave the yellow sections uncoloured).

Fore Wings

1. Using one strand of black thread in a sharps needle, couch the shaped wire around the traced fore wing outline on the muslin, working a couching stitch at each colour change mark. Buttonhole stitch the wire to the muslin, working the top edge of the wing in black, the outer edge in light yellow and the lower edge in black, light yellow and grey as shown in the diagram.

2. With light yellow thread, work a row of stem stitch along the inside upper edge of the wing, close to the buttonhole stitches. Using black thread, work a row of stem stitch next to the yellow row.

3. Using black thread, work a row of outline stitch along the curved centre vein line. Starting at this centre line, embroider the veins in the lower section of the wing in split back stitch, working towards the wire edge. At the end of each vein line, work two overcast stitches over the wire, inside the ridge of the buttonholed edge (these form the black markings at the edge of the wing).

4. With black, work a row of buttonhole stitch inside the outer edge of the wing aligning the stitches with the vein lines. Make the stitches 2.5–3 mm (⅛ in) in length.

Note: A row of yellow spots will be worked over these stitches at a later stage.

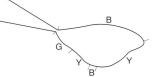

G *grey*
Y *light yellow*
B *black*

vein stitches

black buttonhole stitch

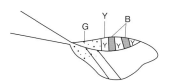

G *grey*
Y *light yellow*
B *black*

completed fore wing

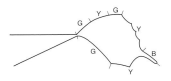

G *grey*
Y *light yellow*
B *black*

5. Using grey thread, work a row of encroaching satin stitch into the row of black buttonhole stitch, keeping the stitches within the vein lines. Make the stitches about 3 mm in length, bringing the needle out about 1 mm beyond the edge of the buttonhole stitches.

Hint: To ensure the desired blend of colours, slide the point of the needle between the stitches in the previous row (encroaching satin stitch).

6. With black thread, work a row of encroaching satin stitch into the row of grey, keeping the stitches within the vein lines. Again, make the stitches about 3 mm in length, bringing the needle out about 1 mm beyond the edge of the previous row of stitches.

7. Embroider the remaining section of the wing, up to the curved centre vein line, in long and short stitch, blending from light to medium yellow except for the inner section of the wing which blends to grey.

8. Work the upper segment of the wing in blocks of satin stitch in black, medium yellow and grey as shown.

9. Using light yellow thread, work a row of eight spots at the outer edge of the wing, three satin stitches for each spot, working the stitches between the vein lines.

Hind Wings

1. Using one strand of light yellow thread, couch the shaped wire around the traced hind wing outline on the muslin, working a couching stitch at each colour change mark. Buttonhole stitch the wire to the muslin, working in grey, light yellow or black according to the edge markings shown in the diagram.

2. Work a row of outline stitch around the curved centre vein line. Starting at this centre line, embroider the veins in the lower section of the wing in split back stitch, working towards the wire edge. At the end of each vein, work two overcast stitches over the wire, inside the ridge of the buttonholed edge (these form the black markings at the edge of the wing).

3. With black, work a row of buttonhole stitch inside the outer edge of the wing, leaving the inner segment of the wing unstitched. Make the stitches 2.5–3 mm (1/8 in) in length and align them with the vein lines.
Note: A row of yellow spots will be worked over these stitches at a later stage.

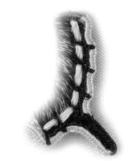

4. With blue thread, work a row of encroaching satin stitch into the row of black buttonhole stitch, keeping the stitches within the vein lines. Make the stitches about 3 mm in length, bringing the needle out about 1 mm beyond the edge of the buttonhole stitches.
Hint: To ensure the desired blend of colours, slide the point of the needle between the stitches in the previous row (encroaching satin stitch).

5. With black thread, work a row of encroaching satin stitch into the row of blue, keeping the stitches within the vein lines. Again, make the stitches about 3 mm in length, bringing the needle out about 1 mm beyond the edge of the previous row of stitches.

6. Embroider the remaining section of the wing, up to the curved central lobe, in long and short stitch, blending from light yellow to medium yellow. Work the central lobe in medium yellow.

7. Work a row of buttonhole stitch in light yellow at the outer edge of the inner segment. Embroider the segment in long and short stitch, blending from light to medium yellow, then to grey at the inner corner.

8. Using red thread, embroider a satin stitch spot at the outer edge of the inner segment (nine satin stitches). Work two fly stitches in blue above the

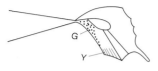

G *grey*
Y *light yellow*

B *black*
Bl *blue*
R *red*

spot, then two fly stiches in black above the blue stitches.

9. Using light yellow thread, work a row of six spots at the outer edge of the wing, three satin stitches for each spot, working the stitches between the vein lines.

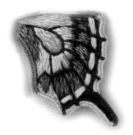

*completed
hind wing*

To Complete the Butterfly

1. To pad the abdomen, make one stitch from 3 to 4, with 14 strands of brown thread in a chenille needle (7 strands doubled). Cross the tails of padding thread behind the stitch (at the back), and hold both ends with masking tape.

*abdomen
placement*

2. With one strand of brown thread in a size 10 crewel needle, work five evenly spaced couching stitches over the padding, catching in the tails of padding thread behind the abdomen (the tails will be trimmed later). The abdomen will be embroidered in raised stem stitch over these couching stitches so they need to be snug but not too tight.

3. With one strand of thread in a tapestry needle, work seven rows of raised stem stitch—two rows in brown, the centre three rows in dark grey, then two more rows in medium brown, working each row towards the tail.

4. Carefully cut out the wings and apply by inserting the wire tails through the two upper two dots as shown, using large yarn darners. Apply the hind wings first, inserting both wire tails through 2, then the fore wings through 1 (the wings will overlap slightly). Bend the wire tails under the wings and secure to the backing fabric with tiny stitches using ecru thread, making sure that the stitches do not protrude beyond the wingspan. Trim the wire tails when the butterfly is finished.

wing placement

5. The thorax is worked with three straight stitches across the centre of the wings (from 1 to 3), using chenille thread in the largest yarn darner. Using variegated chenille, select a medium brown section of thread and work two stitches side by side. Select a section of dark grey chenille and work a stitch on top/between the brown to form a centre stripe (for maximum control of the chenille, all stitches can be made with separate lengths of thread, all inserted from the front). Make sure the chenille does not twist and adjust the tension of the stitches (thus the fluffiness of the thorax), as desired.
Secure the tails of chenille with nylon thread after the head is applied (to allow for final adjustments).

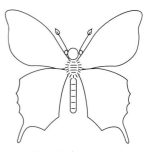

head & thorax placement

6. Using nylon thread in a sharps needle, stitch a 3 mm bead close to the top of the thorax, for the head (keep the hole in the bead parallel to the top of the thorax). Bring the needle through to the front and stitch a bronze/purple petite bead on either side of the head bead for the eyes, taking the needle through the hole of the bead several times so that the eyes are suspended on either side.

7. With one strand of gold/bronze metallic thread in a sharps needle, make a stitch on either side of the head bead for the antennae (taking the needle through the head bead if desired). Work a tiny chain stitch at the end of the antennae if desired.

finished butterfly actual size

Order: Lepidoptera Family: Pieridae

Whites, Brimstones and Sulphurs

The Pieridae is a large family of mainly white or yellow butterflies—the Whites, Jezebels, Orange-tips, Brimstones and Sulphurs. Widely distributed through the world, many species are migratory, while several of the Whites, such as the familiar Cabbage Butterfly, are pests of economic importance.

The word 'butterfly' was probably first used to describe the common butter-coloured insect, *Gonepteryx rhamni*, the **Brimstone Butterfly**. Often the first and last butterfly to be seen each year in Europe, the Brimstone emerges from its overwintering sites of ivy bushes and hollow logs in early spring, often while there are still remnants of snow to be seen, and enters hibernation again in late autumn. Eventually, butterfly became the general term for all species while the Brimstone acquired its present name, which relates to the colour of sulphur. Only the male has the sulphur-yellow coloured upper wings after which the species has been named; the female is paler. Both sexes have a reddish orange spot on each of their wings and a pale yellowish green underside. When at rest, the colour, shape and unusually pronounced veins of the closed wings, gives the butterfly a very leaf-like appearance, allowing it to blend in with the vegetation in which it hibernates. A powerful flier, the Brimstone frequents the edges of woodland and hedgerows, seeking out nectar from wild flowers such as primroses, knapweed and thistles, being strongly attracted to yellow and purple blossoms.

Brimstone Butterfly, *Gonepteryx rhamni*

Brimstone Butterfly

Gonepteryx rhamni Order: *Lepidoptera* Family: *Pieridae*

DIAGRAMS ACTUAL SIZE

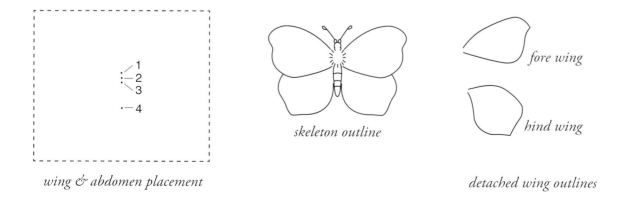

skeleton outline

fore wing

hind wing

wing & abdomen placement

detached wing outlines

REQUIREMENTS

yellow/orange organza: 15 cm (6 in)
square or shaded organza ribbon
bright yellow satin:
 15 cm (6 in) square
10 cm (4 in) embroidery hoop

needles
sharps size 11 or 12
crewel/embroidery size 10
chenille size 18
tapestry size 28
sharp yarn darner sizes 14–18

beads & wire
3 mm blue/bronze bead
Mill Hill petite beads 40374
 (blue/purple)
33 gauge white covered wire:
 four 10 cm (4 in) lengths *(colour
wire yellow if desired: Copic Y15
Cadmium Yellow)*

thread
yellow stranded thread:
Cifonda Art Silk 1117 or DMC 725

copper stranded thread:
Cifonda Art Silk 63 or DMC 3776

orange stranded thread:
Cifonda Art Silk 135A or DMC 946

beige stranded thread:
Soie d'Alger 3834 or DMC 640

ecru stranded thread:
DMC Ecru

yellow rayon machine thread:
Madeira Rayon No. 40 col. 1024

rust/gold metallic thread:
Madeira Metallic No. 40 col. 482

variegated beige/grey chenille thread:
col. Neutral

METHOD

. . . .

Transfer the wing and abdomen placement dots to the background fabric.

WINGS

1. Mount organza and the satin backing fabric into the hoop. If using ribbon, cut several 18 cm (7 in) lengths and tack both long edges to the satin backing before mounting into the hoop. If using a variegated ribbon, select lengths of the desired colour.

fore wing

2. Using tweezers, shape a length of wire around the wing outline diagram, leaving two tails of wire at the base of the wing. Shape a right and a left fore wing and a right and a left hind wing. Transfer the shaped wires to the fabric surface, holding the wire tails in place with masking tape. Check that the shapes have not been distorted.

hind wing

3. Using yellow stranded thread in a sharps needle, couch then buttonhole stitch the shaped wire to the background fabric.

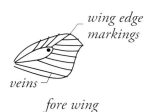

wing edge markings

veins

fore wing

4. To form the markings on the outer edge of the wing, work straight stitches over the wire (inside the buttonhole ridge) with copper thread, using the diagram as a guide to placement (eleven for the front wing and nine for the back wing).

5. Using orange thread, embroider the spot in each wing with six satin stitches.

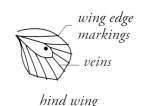

wing edge markings

veins

hind wing

6. With yellow machine thread in a sharps needle, work the veins with fly and buttonhole stitches, using the diagram and the wing edge markings as a guide.

Brimstone Butterfly **127**

abdomen placement

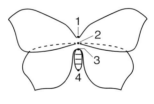

coaching the abdomen

wing placement

To Complete the Butterfly

1. Both the abdomen and the thorax are padded with 14 strands of beige thread in a chenille needle (7 strands doubled). To pad the abdomen, make one stitch from 3 to 4. Cross the tails of padding thread behind the stitch (at the back), and hold both ends with masking tape (retain the thread in the needle at the back until required to pad the thorax).

2. With one strand of beige thread in a crewel needle, work three couching stitches over the padding (catching in the tails of thread behind the abdomen), then, changing to a fine tapestry needle, cover the abdomen with six rows of raised stem stitch, working over these couching stitches towards the tail.

3. Carefully cut out the wings and apply by inserting the wire tails through the upper three dots as shown, using large yarn darners. Apply the hind wings first, inserting the wire tails through 2 and 3, then the fore wings through 1 and 2 (the wings share hole 2). Bend the wire tails under the wings and secure to the backing fabric with tiny stitches using ecru thread, making sure that the stitches do not protrude beyond the wingspan. Trim the wire tails when the butterfly is finished.

4. Using the retained beige thread, make a padding stitch from 1 to 3—this will be wrapped with chenille thread to form the thorax. With chenille thread in the largest yarn darner, come out near 1, make three wraps around the padding stitch then insert the needle near 3. Make sure the chenille does not twist and adjust the tension of the wraps (thus the fluffiness of the thorax), as desired. To facilitate the wrapping, do not tighten or secure the padding thread until the stitch has been wrapped with chenille. Use stranded thread to secure all threads at the back.

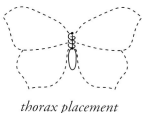

thorax placement

5. With one strand of beige thread, apply a 3 mm bead for the head, working the stitches towards the thorax. To form the eyes, apply two petite beads, one stitch through both beads, above the head bead. Work a couching stitch between the beads, then another stitch between the petite beads then through the 3 mm bead.

head & eyes placement

6. To work the antennae, make a long fly stitch with a tiny chain stitch at each end (to form the clubbed tip), using rust/gold metallic thread in the crewel needle. Refer to the diagram for placement.

finished butterfly actual size

Order: Lepidoptera Family:Saturniidae

Giant Silk Moths, Emperor Moths, Royal Moths

Among the largest of the Lepidoptera, the Saturniidae family includes giant Silk Moths, Royal Moths and Emperor Moths. They are found worldwide with the majority occurring in wooded tropical or subtropical regions. Adult saturniids are characterised by large, heavy bodies covered in hair-like scales, lobed wings, reduced mouthparts and small heads. These moths are sometimes brightly coloured, and often have translucent eye-spots on their wings. The name Saturniidae is derived from the concentric rings, reminiscent of the planet Saturn, that surround the eye-spots of some family members. Most adults have a wingspan ranging from 3 to 15 cm, but some tropical species, such as the Atlas Moth, may boast incredible wingspans of up to 30 cm.

The most spectacular of the giant silk moths are the Luna or Moon Moths, said to have been named for the moon-like spots on both the fore and hind wings. With a wingspan of 7 to 12 cm (2¾-5 in), the Indian Moon Moth, Actias selene, is one of the most exquisite of the species, with pale diaphanous green wings extending into long fluttering tails on the hind wings, prominent eye-spots, and golden feathery antennae. The legs are dark rose-pink, as is the band across the top edge of the fore wings. The head of the moth is small (it does not feed at all as an adult -- it lives off the energy stored in its body during the caterpillar stage). The large, startling eye-spots on the wings of a moon moth probably divert predators away from the delicate body. Similarly, the long trailing tails of the hind wings will break off if attacked.

Indian Moon Moth, *Actias selene*

Indian Moon Moth

Actias selene Order: *Lepidoptera* Family: *Saturniidae*

DIAGRAMS ACTUAL SIZE

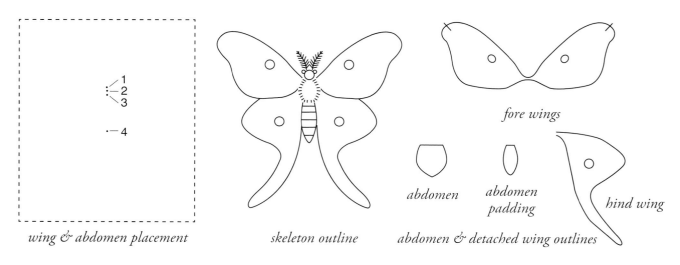

wing & abdomen placement

skeleton outline

fore wings

abdomen

abdomen padding

hind wing

abdomen & detached wing outlines

REQUIREMENTS

quilter's muslin: 20 cm (8 in) square

ivory kid: 2.5 cm (1 in) square
 (I used an old kid glove)

white felt: 2.5 cm (1 in) square

15 cm (6 in) embroidery hoop

needles

crewel/embroidery size 10

sharps size 12

milliners/straw size 9

sharp yarn darner sizes 14–18

beads & wire

3 mm gold sequins

Mill Hill petite beads 42014 *(black)*

33 gauge white covered wire:
 one 25 cm (10 in) length and two
 18 cm (7 in) lengths *(colour part of
 longer wire dark pink if desired: Copic
 R59 Cardinal)*

thread

dark pink stranded thread:
Soie d'Alger 4623 or DMC 3721

medium green stranded thread:
Soie d'Alger 2132 or DMC 3364

pale green stranded thread:
Soie d'Alger 242 or DMC 3348

lime green stranded thread:
Soie d'Alger 2221 or DMC 472

light gold stranded thread:
Soie d'Alger 2223 or DMC 734

medium pink stranded thread:
Cifonda Art Silk 114 or DMC 3712

ecru stranded thread:
DMC Ecru

gold metallic thread:
Madeira Metallic No. 30 col. 6034

green/black metallic thread:
Kreinik Very Fine (#4) Braid col. 850

cream chenille thread:
Au Ver à Soie Chenille à Broder: col. Creme

nylon clear thread:
Madeira Monofil No. 60 col. 1001

METHOD

Transfer the wing and abdomen placement dots to the background fabric.

WINGS

Mount the muslin into the hoop and trace the wing outlines—the joined right and left fore wings and a right and left hind wing. Include the marks indicating the dark pink edge on the upper fore wings.

Fore Wings

The distinctive dark pink upper edge of the Indian Moon Moth's fore wings appears to be an unbroken line. To achieve this effect, the wings are traced side by side (joined in the centre), allowing for a length of wire to be stitched across the entire top edge.

1. Using tweezers, shape the 25 cm (10 in) length of wire around the fore wings outline diagram, having a continuous length of wire across the top edges of the wings and two tails of wire in the centre of the lower edges of the wings. If desired, colour the top edge of the fore wings dark pink using the marks as a guide.

wire placement

2. The wire is stitched to the background fabric with either dark pink or light gold thread using the diagram as a guide (thread one strand of each into crewel needles). Couch the wire around the wing outline with either dark pink or light gold thread, parking the colour not in use to the side, then buttonhole stitch the wire to the muslin, working the lower and side edges of the wings in light gold and the upper edge in dark pink.

3. The wings are embroidered, inside the wire outline, with rows of buttonhole and long and short stitch, blending the three shades of green (thread painting). Take care to follow the direction guidelines when working all stitches. With lime green thread, work the row at the wing edge first with close, long and short buttonhole stitch (the ridge of the buttonhole is next to the wire).

4. Work the remainder of the wing with four rows of long and short stitch, blending the first row into the buttonhole stitches. Refer to the diagram for row colours:

Buttonhole row: lime green
Row 1: pale green long and short stitch
Row 2: medium green long and short stitch
Row 3: pale green long and short stitch
Row 4: medium green long and short stitch

guidelines for stitch direction

The wings have golden ocelli ('eyes'), each with a dark edge on one side and a pink spot in the centre.

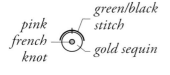

pink french knot
green/black stitch
gold sequin

5. Using the diagram to position, apply a gold sequin to each wing with three stitches in nylon thread. To work the dark edge, make a loose stitch across the sequin with green/black metallic thread then couch this stitch in place at the edge of the sequin with nylon thread. Secure the tails at the back.
Work a French knot in the centre of the sequin with one strand of medium pink thread.

6. With gold metallic thread in a milliners needle, work the veins with fly and single feather stitches, using the diagram as a guide.

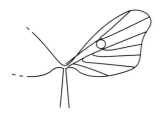

vein stitches

completed fore wing

Hind Wings

1. With one strand of light gold thread in a crewel needle, couch wire around the hind wing outline leaving two tails of wire at the base of the wing. Buttonhole stitch the wire to the muslin.

2. The wings are embroidered with rows of buttonhole and long and short stitch, blending the three shades of green. Take care to follow the direction guidelines when working all stitches (including the tail). With lime green thread, work the row at the wing edge first with close long and short buttonhole stitches, working the buttonhole stitches at an angle along the narrow tails of the wing (embroider any remaining space in the tails with straight stitches blended into the buttonhole).

3. Work the remainder of the wing with four rows of long and short stitch, blending the first row into the buttonhole stitches. Refer to the diagram for row colours:

wire placement

Buttonhole row: lime green
Row 1: pale green long and short stitch
Row 2: medium green long and short stitch
Row 3: pale green long and short stitch
Row 4: medium green long and short stitch

guidelines for stitch direction

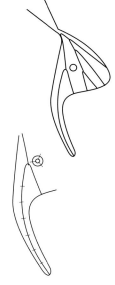

completed hind wing

abdomen placement

completed abdomen

5. Using the diagram to position, apply a gold sequin to each wing with three stitches in nylon thread. To work the dark edge, make a loose stitch across the sequin with green/black metallic thread, then couch this stitch in place at the edge of the sequin with nylon thread. Secure the tails at the back. Work a French knot in the centre of the sequin with one strand of medium pink thread.

6. With gold metallic thread in a milliners needle, work the veins with fly and single feather stitches, using the diagram as a guide. Work a fly stitch with a long 'leg' to form a vein along the centre of the narrow tail of the wing. Couch this long stitch in place with nylon thread.

ABDOMEN

The leather abdomen is shaped in the hand before being couched to the background fabric with nylon thread.

1. Cut an abdomen shape from ivory kid, using the outline as a guide. To pad the abdomen, cut a padding shape from felt and thin card. Fold the sides of the leather towards each other, enclosing the card and felt padding (place the felt next to the kid), and catch the edges together with overcast stitches, using nylon thread in a sharps needle. Do not stitch right to the tip of the abdomen. Mould the leather into the abdomen shape with your fingers.

2. Using nylon thread, apply the abdomen shape to the background fabric (over a line between 3 and 4) with five or six couching stitches, angling the needle under the abdomen shape. Work one of the centre couching stitches first, then the couching stitches on either side, squeezing the tail of the abdomen into a point with tweezers as you work the lower stitches.

TO COMPLETE THE MOTH

1. Carefully cut out the wings and apply by inserting the wire tails through the three upper dots, using large yarn darners. Apply the hind wings first, inserting the wire tails through 2 and 3. To apply the fore wings, insert the wire tails through 1 (the dark pink upper edge will be slightly raised). Bend the wire tails under the wings and secure to the muslin backing with tiny stitches using ecru thread, making sure that the stitches do not protrude beyond the wingspan. Do not trim any wire tails until the moth is finished.

2. The thorax and head are worked with ivory chenille thread. Cut a 12 cm (5 in) length of chenille and fold in half. Stitch the chenille to the centre of the fore wings (just below the ridge of dark pink buttonhole) by working a couching stitch across the fold of the chenille. Using a yarn darner, insert the tails of chenille through to the back, just above the top edge of the abdomen. Make sure the chenille does not twist and adjust the tension of the stitches (thus the fluffiness of the thorax), as desired. Secure the tails of chenille with nylon thread.

3. The head and eyes of the Indian Moon Moth are partially hidden by the top edge of the wings. To form the head, cut a 10 cm (4 in) length of chenille and work a short 'stitch' above the centre of the fore wings, inserting the needle under the top edge of the wings (it is easier to insert both tails of the 'stitch' from the front). Using nylon thread, stitch a petite black bead on either side of the head for eyes.

4. The Indian Moon Moth has large feathered antennae. With gold metallic thread in a milliners needle, work each antenna with a row of close fly stitches, using the diagram as a guide (the antennae are leaf shaped).

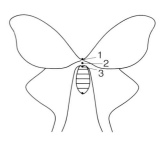

wing placement

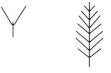

antenae stitch guide

finished moth actual size

Order: Lepidoptera Family: Satyridae

Browns, Satyrs & Glasswings

Members of the large family Satyridae may be found in all regions of the world. While the wings vary greatly in size, shape and pattern, the majority of the species is predominantly shades of brown, with the distinguishing feature being the characteristic ocelli (eye-spots), which may be found on either the upper or lower surface of the wings. These false eyes serve to confuse predators such as bird and lizards.

One of the most unusual and beautiful groups of satyrs, subfamily Haeterinae, may be found in tropical South America. Often called Glasswings, many of these butterflies have transparent wings with brilliant patches of colour. The Glasswing Butterfly, Cithaerias aurorina, lives in the tropical rainforests of Peru. Its transparent wings have a network of golden veins, with a dazzling patch of rose-pink and characteristic eye-spot on each hind wing. In this environment of dappled light and shade, the almost entirely transparent butterfly, flying close to the ground and settling frequently, is almost impossible to detect, making it a difficult target for predators.

The nineteenth-century English naturalist, Henry Walter Bates, wrote of a glasswing butterfly observed near the Amazon River: 'its wings transparent except for a spot of violet or rose, [it] looked like a wandering petal as it flew low over dead leaves in gloomy shade'.

Glasswing Butterfly, *Cithaerias aurorina*

Glasswing Butterfly

Cithaerias aurorina Order: *Lepidoptera* Family: *Satyridae*

DIAGRAMS ACTUAL SIZE

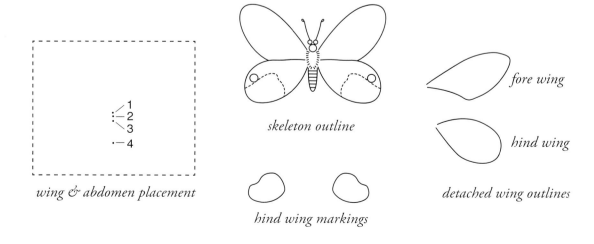

wing & abdomen placement

skeleton outline

hind wing markings

fore wing

hind wing

detached wing outlines

REQUIREMENTS

pearl metal organdie:
  15 cm (6 in) square
rose-pink silk: 2.5 cm (1 in) square
paper-backed fusible web:
  2.5 cm (1 in) square
clear 'crystal' plastic (medium weight):
  8 cm (4 in) circle
gilt Very Fine Pearl Purl: about 25 cm
Post-it note
  (or removable self-adhesive label)
10 cm (4 in) embroidery hoop
beeswax

needles
sharps size 12
milliners size 9
chenille size 18
sharp yarn darner sizes 14–18

beads & wire
3 mm blue/bronze bead
Mill Hill petite beads 40374
  (blue/bronze)
28 gauge uncovered wire:
  four 11 cm (4½ in) lengths
two 3 mm steel-blue sequins

thread
dark gold stranded thread:
DMC 782

gold fine silk thread:
YLI Silk Stitch 50 col. 79

ecru stranded thread:
DMC Ecru

gold fine metallic thread:
Madeira Metallic No. 30 col. 6032

gold/black metallic thread:
Madeira Metallic No. 40 col. 425

dark gold chenille thread:
col. Paprika

nylon clear thread:
Madeira Monofil No. 60 col. 1001

METHOD

Transfer the wing and abdomen placement dots to the background fabric.

WINGS

To replicate the transparent nature of the wings of the Glasswing Butterfly they are worked on a piece of clear plastic backed with a layer of pearl metal organdie. Small shapes of pink silk are sandwiched between these two layers to form the markings for the hind wings.

1. Mount a square of pearl metal organdie into a small hoop. Trace the hind wing markings onto paper-backed fusible web and fuse to the back of the pink silk. Cut out the shapes and fuse to the right side of the pearl organdie in the hoop (use a sheet of baking parchment between the iron and the fabrics and a small board underneath the hoop for support). The shapes need to be placed with care—position them so that they will be in the lower corner of the hind wings. The remaining fabric is for the fore wings.

2. Using the hind wing diagram as a guide, attach a sequin for an eye-spot to each wing (just above the pink marking) with a few stitches in nylon thread (or use a minute amount of glue applied with a pin).

3. Lay the circle of plastic over the organdie (and wing markings) and attach at the sides of the hoop with masking tape, keeping the plastic taut.

4. Trace templates for the right and left hind wings from the adhesive strip of a Post-it note. Cut out the right and left wing templates and stick them to the plastic circle, taking care to position them over the right and left wing markings. Carefully lay the pearl purl around the outside edge of a wing template and cut an accurate length. Thread a piece of uncovered wire through the purl, leaving tails of equal length at each end. Repeat for the other hind wing.

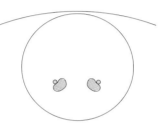

hind wing markings placement

wire placement

vein stitches

completed fore wing

vein stitches

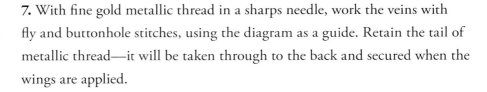

completed hind wing

5. Shape the wired pearl purl around the hind wing template, leaving two tails of wire at the base of the wing that touch but do not cross. Check that the purl is the correct length (stretch if too short, remove wire and trim if too long). Place the shaped wired purl around the template, holding the tails of wire in place with masking tape. Using waxed silk thread in a sharps needle, couch the wired purl around the edge of the wing template, working the couching stitches through the plastic/organdie sandwich. Angle the needle under the purl and pull the stitches firmly so that they lie between the coils of purl (work stitches 1–3 coils apart). Take care when you insert the needle— once holes are made in the plastic they do not close up, and thus remain visible. Repeat for the remaining hind wing.

6. Cut templates for a right and a left fore wing and apply wired purl as above (the fore wings do not have any wing markings).

7. With fine gold metallic thread in a sharps needle, work the veins with fly and buttonhole stitches, using the diagram as a guide. Retain the tail of metallic thread—it will be taken through to the back and secured when the wings are applied.

To Complete the Butterfly

1. Carefully cut out the wings and apply by inserting the wire (and thread) tails through the upper three dots, using yarn darners. Apply the hind wings first, inserting the wire tails through 2 and 3, then the fore wings through 1 and 2 (the wings share hole 2). Bend the wire tails under the wings and secure to the backing fabric with tiny stitches using ecru thread, making sure that the stitches do not protrude beyond the wingspan. Secure the metallic thread from the veins, checking that the stitches inside the wings are taut. Trim the wire tails when the butterfly is finished.

2. The thorax is worked with dark gold chenille thread in the largest yarn darner (to prevent the chenille from shredding). Work two straight stitches across the centre of the wings (from 1 to 3) adjusting the tension of the stitch, thus the fluffiness of the thorax, as desired (it is easier to insert each tail of chenille from the front). Secure the tails of chenille at the back with a few stitches worked in stranded thread.

3. The abdomen is worked with a wrapped stitch using 7 strands of dark gold thread in a chenille needle. Bring the needle out at 4 and insert at the base of the thorax (3). Repeat to make a double stitch. Bring the needle out again at 4 and wrap the double stitch back to the thorax (sliding the needle under and around the stitch), adjusting the tension of the wrapping to form the abdomen (this resembles a bullion knot).

4. Using nylon thread in a sharps needle, apply a 3 mm bronze bead at the top of the thorax for the head, working the stitches towards the thorax. To form the eyes, apply two petite beads, one stitch through both beads, above the head bead. Work a couching stitch between the beads.

5. With one strand of gold/black metallic thread in a milliners needle, work a fly stitch above the eyes for the antennae—keep the stitches quite loose so that they curve a little. Work a French knot at the end of each antenna.

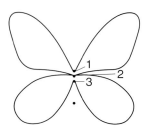

wing placement

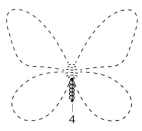

abdomen placement

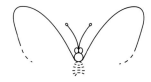

head & eyes placement

finished moth actual size

Order: Lepidoptera Family: Sesiidae

Clearwing Moths

Members of the family Sesiidae, of which there are more than 800 species, are remarkable both in appearance and behaviour. In body shape and colouration, most Clearwing Moths resemble various stinging insects such as bees, wasps and hornets, but unlike these they are defenceless. The narrow wings, which often have a metallic sheen, are often completely translucent with only the borders being covered in scales. The abdomen is usually conspicuously striped black and yellow or red with a characteristic tuft of long hairs at the tail.

The **Hornet Moth**, Sesia apiformis, with its black and yellow striped abdomen, yellow head and legs, and unusually small, transparent wings, is a most remarkable mimic of the common hornet. The moth is as large as a hornet and even has the hornet's rapid, rather jerky flight when disturbed, but it has more yellow and lacks the waist between the thorax and the abdomen. Protected from predators by its hornet-like appearance, it is quite harmless, and has no sting. A day-flying moth, Sesia apiformis can be seen throughout summer in parks, hedgerows and around pond edges. The moth lays its eggs in the bark at the base of poplar and willow trees, the caterpillars inhabiting the roots and lower parts of the trunk for two to three years before pupating in a cocoon of wood chippings.

Hornet Moth, *Sesia apiformis*

Hornet Moth

Sesia apiformis Order: *Lepidoptera* Family: *Sesiidae*

DIAGRAMS ACTUAL SIZE

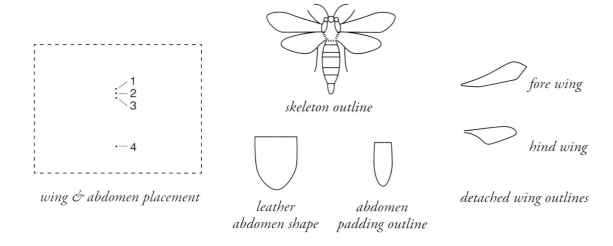

skeleton outline

fore wing

hind wing

1
2
3

4

wing & abdomen placement

leather
abdomen shape

abdomen
padding outline

detached wing outlines

REQUIREMENTS

clear 'crystal' plastic (medium weight):
    8 cm (3 in) circle

quilter's muslin: 20 cm (8 in) square

yellow kid leather:
    2.5 cm (1 in) square

yellow felt: 2.5 cm (1 in) square

thin card: 2.5 cm (1 in) square

10 cm (4 in) embroidery hoop

needles
sharps size 12

milliners size 8

sharp yarn darner sizes 14–18

beads & wire
yellow seed bead

Mill Hill petite beads 442014 *(black)*

33 gauge white covered wire:
    four 12 cm (4¾ in) lengths *(colour
    wire tan if desired: Copic E37 Sepia)*

thread
tan stranded thread:
DMC 780

ecru stranded thread:
DMC Ecru

copper/black fine metallic thread:
Kreinik Cord 215c

brown metallic thread:
Kreinik Very Fine (#4) Braid 022

curry metallic thread:
Kreinik Very Fine (#4) Braid 2122

variegated yellow/black chenille thread:
col. Fire

nylon clear thread:
Madeira Monofil No. 60 col. 1001

METHOD

Transfer the wing and abdomen placement dots to the background fabric.

WINGS

Both pairs of wings are stitched on clear plastic, mounted into a hoop as follows:

1. Mount muslin loosely into a small hoop. Stitch the circle of plastic on top of the muslin with long running stitches around the outside edge. Stretch the muslin (and plastic) until taut in the hoop, then cut a circle of muslin away from behind the plastic.

2. Using tweezers, shape a length of wire around the wing outline diagram, leaving two tails of wire at the base of the wing. Shape a right and a left fore wing and a right and a left hind wing. Transfer the shaped wires to the plastic surface, holding the wire tails in place with masking tape (temporarily hold the tip of the wing with a small piece of tape). Check that the shapes have not been distorted.

3. Using one strand of tan thread in a sharps needle, buttonhole stitch the shaped wire to the plastic, taking care to insert the needle close to the wire (once holes are made in the plastic they remain and are visible).

4. With copper/black metallic thread in a sharps needle, work the veins with fly, buttonhole and straight stitches, using the diagram as a guide. Retain the tail of metallic thread—it will be taken through to the back and secured when the wings are applied.

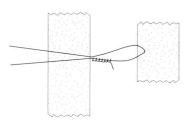

wire placement

fore wing

hind wing

completed wings

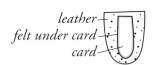

leather
felt under card
card

*abdomen
placement*

abdomen marking

completed abdomen

ABDOMEN

The padded yellow leather abdomen is shaped in the hand first before being couched to the background fabric.

1. Cut the larger abdomen shape from yellow leather, using the outline as a guide (the shape has side turnings added).

2. Trace the abdomen padding outline onto thin card. Cut out the shape. Cut a slightly smaller abdomen padding shape from yellow felt.

3. Sandwich the felt padding between the leather and the card. Fold the sides of the leather shape behind the card and catch the edges together with long overcast stitches, using nylon thread in a sharps needle (do not stitch right to the tip of the abdomen). Squeeze the lower edges of the leather together with tweezers to form a rounded point. Manipulate the padded leather into the abdomen shape with your fingers.

4. The Hornet Moth has a black segment in the centre of the abdomen (there are three visible segments on either side). I coloured the centre segment with a black marking pen (practise on a scrap of leather first).

5. Using brown metallic thread in a size 8 milliners needle, apply the abdomen shape to the background fabric (over the abdomen placement line 3–4) with six couching stitches, angling the needle under the abdomen shape. Work a couching stitch on each side of the black stripe in the centre of the abdomen, then two evenly spaced couching stitches on either side (squeeze the tail with tweezers to form a rounded point then couch around it to hold in place).

TO COMPLETE THE MOTH

1. Carefully cut out the wings and apply by inserting the wire (and thread) tails through the upper two dots, using a large yarn darner. Apply the hind wings first, inserting the wire tails through 2, then the fore wings at 1. Bend the wire tails under the wings and secure to the backing fabric with tiny stitches using ecru thread, making sure that the stitches do not protrude beyond the wingspan. Secure the metallic thread from the veins, checking

wing placement

that the stitches inside the wings are taut. Trim the wire tails when the moth is finished.

2. Using chenille thread in the largest yarn darner, work the thorax with three straight stitches across the centre of the wings (from 1 to 3). Using variegated chenille, select a dark yellow section and make two stitches side by side. Select a section of black chenille and work a stitch on top/between the yellow to form a centre stripe (for maximum control of the chenille, all stitches can be made with separate lengths of thread, all inserted from the front). Make sure the chenille does not twist and adjust the tension of the stitches (thus the fluffiness of the thorax), as desired. Secure the tails of chenille with nylon thread after the head is applied (to allow for final adjustments).

3. Using nylon thread in a sharps needle, apply a yellow seed bead at the top of the thorax for the head, working the stitches, from side to side through the bead. Stitch a petite black bead on each side of the head for the eyes, taking the needle through all three beads several times to draw the beads together. Work a couching stitch between each bead.

4. Carefully lift the wings and work the legs with one strand of curry metallic thread in a milliners needle, using the diagram as a guide. Work one chain stitch (from the edge of the thorax), then two straight stitches for each leg.

5. To work the antennae, make a loose, straight stitch on either side of the head with brown metallic thread in a milliners needle.

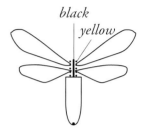

black
yellow

thorax placement

leg placement

completed thorax, head & antennae

finished moth actual size

Order: Lepidoptera Family: Zygaenidae

Burnets

The family Zygaenidae includes over a thousand species of day-flying moths found in practically all parts of the world, with the exception of North America. Many of these small to medium-sized moths, such as the Burnets, are brilliantly coloured and are often mistaken for butterflies. All the burnet moths are extremely poisonous, a fact advertised by their bright colouration, so although they fly slowly they are unpopular with predators. They have foul-tasting cyanide in their blood, which the caterpillars obtain from plants such as clover, and they can also squeeze drops of poison from their legs as a deterrent.

With their bright colouring, long narrow wings and slow flight, burnets are easily distinguishable from other lepidopterans, but it is not so easy to tell which species they belong to as their colours are very variable. Burnets usually have five or six spots on their greenish black fore wings -- these may be red, orange or white, or red spots with white borders. Some have translucent wings. The hind wings may be red, black or yellow, bordered with black, and mostly without spots.

The **Six-spot Burnet Moth**, Zygaena filipendulae, is the most common member of the genus. This day-flying moth is often to be seen in summer flying over sand dunes and cliff tops in seaside areas, and in meadows and cleared grassland from lowlands to quite high altitudes. Its greenish black fore wings have a metallic sheen and six red round spots. The hind wings are crimson, with narrow dark greenish black borders. Unusually for a moth, they have club-shaped antennae. All the burnets live in colonies, frequenting places where clover, trefoils and vetches grow.

Six-spot Burnet Moth, *Zygaena filipendulae*

Six-spot Burnet Moth

Zygaena filipendulae Order: *Lepidoptera* Family: *Zygaenidae*

DIAGRAMS ACTUAL SIZE

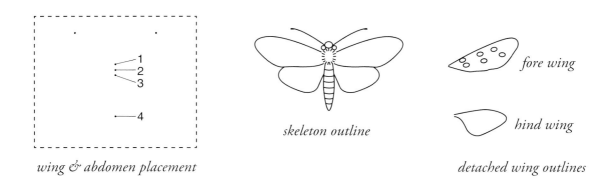

wing & abdomen placement

skeleton outline

fore wing

hind wing

detached wing outlines

REQUIREMENTS

black organza: 15 cm (6 in) square

grey/black metal organdie:
   15 cm (6 in) square

black cotton voile:
   two 15 cm (6 in) squares

red satin: 15 cm (6 in) square

paper-backed fusible web:
   15 cm (6 in) square

10 cm (4 in) embroidery hoop

needles

sharps size 11 or 12

milliners size 9

chenille size 18

sharp yarn darner sizes 14–18

beads & wire

3 mm black bead

Mill Hill petite beads 442014 *(black)*

33 gauge white covered wire:
   four 10 cm (4 in) lengths *(colour wire black if desired)*

thread

black rayon machine thread:
Madeira Rayon No. 40 col. 1000

red stranded thread:
Cifonda Art Silk 254A or DMC 817

black stranded thread:
Soie d'Alger col. Noir or DMC 310

ecru stranded thread:
DMC Ecru

green/black metallic thread:
Au Ver à Soie Metallics 209

red metallic thread:
Kreinik Cord 003c

black metallic thread:
Kreinik Very Fine (#4) Braid 005

black chenille thread:
Au Ver à Soie Chenille à Broder col. Noir

black patent leather 'thread': 2 mm wide (approximately 10 cm/4 in)

nylon clear thread:
Madeira Monofil No. 60 col. 1001

Method
....

Transfer the wing and abdomen placement dots to the background fabric.

Wings

Fore Wings

1. Fuse the black metal organdie to one of the pieces of black voile using the fusible web (this will stabilise the organdie). Place the black organza over the metal organdie then mount the fabrics into the hoop, organza side uppermost.

2. Using tweezers, shape a length of wire around the fore wing outline diagram, leaving two tails of wire at the base of the wing. Shape a right and a left fore wing. Transfer the shaped wires to the fabric surface, holding the wire tails in place with masking tape. Check that the shapes have not been distorted.

fore wing

3. Using black rayon machine thread in a sharps needle, couch then buttonhole stitch the shaped wire to the background fabric.

veins & wing markings.

4. Using red thread in a sharps needle, embroider six spots on each fore wing, working each spot with five or six satin stitches. Refer to the diagram for placement.

5. With green/black metallic thread in a milliners needle, work the veins with fly and buttonhole stitches, using the diagram as a guide.

completed fore wing

hind wing

vein stitches

completed hind wing

Hind Wings

1. Mount the red satin and a backing of black cotton voile, into the hoop.

2. Using tweezers, shape a length of wire around the hind wing outline diagram, leaving two tails of wire at the base of the wing. Shape a right and a left hind wing. Transfer the shaped wires to the fabric surface, holding the wire tails in place with masking tape. Check that the shapes have not been distorted.

3. Using black rayon machine thread in a sharps needle, couch then buttonhole stitch the shaped wire to the background fabric.

4. With red metallic thread in a milliners needle, work the veins with fly and buttonhole stitches, using the diagram as a guide.

abdomen placement

abdomen wrapping

completed abdomen

To Complete the Moth

1. The abdomen is padded with black stranded thread (7 strands), using the thread doubled in a chenille needle. Make a stitch from 3 to 4, then work a second stitch on top of the first. Hold the tails of thread behind the abdomen with masking tape.

2. The abdomen is formed by wrapping the padding stitches with the strip of patent leather, adjusting the tension to form a tapered tail. Using a chenille needle, bring the strip of leather to the front near 4, make approximately five wraps around the padding, taking care not to twist the leather, then sink through to the back near 3. Using one strand of black thread, secure the tails of leather and padding threads with a few stitches behind the abdomen then trim.

3. Carefully cut out the wings and apply by inserting the wire tails through the upper two dots, using a large yarn darner. Apply the hind wings first, inserting the wire tails through 2, then the fore wings at 1. Bend the wire tails under the wings and secure to the backing fabric with tiny stitches using ecru thread, making sure that the stitches do not protrude beyond the wingspan. Trim the wire tails when the moth is finished.

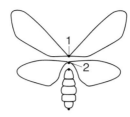

wing placement

4. The thorax is worked with black chenille thread in the largest yarn darner (to prevent the chenille from shredding). Work two straight stitches across the centre of the wings (from 1 to 3), adjusting the tension of the stitches, thus the fluffiness of the thorax, as desired. Secure the tails of chenille at the back with a few stitches worked in stranded thread.

completed thorax

5. Apply a 3 mm bead at the top of the thorax for the head, working the stitches, from side to side through the bead, with nylon thread. To apply the eyes, which are suspended on either side of the head bead, bring the needle up next to the head bead, thread on a petite bead and take the needle through the head bead; thread on another petite bead and take the needle back through the head bead. Repeat this 'figure of 8' movement several times then take the needle through to the back and secure.

eye placement

6. To work the antennae, make a loose, straight stitch on either side of the head with black metallic thread in a milliners needle. Refer to the diagram for placement.

*finished moth
actual size*

Order: Lepidoptera Family: Sphingidae

Hawkmoths & Sphinx Moths

Sphingidae is a family of moths commonly known as Hawkmoths and Sphinx Moths. Moderate to large in size, sphingids are distinguished by their rapid and sustained flying ability, which is facilitated by their narrow wings and streamlined abdomen. Some hawk moths, like the Hummingbird Hawkmoth, hover in mid-air while they feed on nectar from flowers and are sometimes mistaken for hummingbirds. The caterpillars are large, usually with a prominent horn at the rear. The family is well represented in the tropics but there are species in every region.

The **Elephant Hawkmoth**, Deilephila elpenor, is one the prettiest hawkmoths and is often mistaken for a 'pink butterfly'. A common species in most of Britain, this brightly coloured pink and green moth has a streamlined appearance and is found wherever willow herbs grow in profusion. They may be seen hovering in the evening, feeding on nectar from flowers such as honeysuckle, wild thyme, phlox and fuchsias. The female lays her eggs on the undersides of the leaves of these host plants. When the caterpillars hatch, they develop the prominent eye-spots and retractile front segments which suggest an elephant's trunk -- hence the common name for the species.

Elephant Hawkmoth, *Deilephila elpenor*

Elephant Hawkmoth

Deilephila elpenor Order: *Lepidoptera* Family: *Sphingidae*

DIAGRAMS ACTUAL SIZE

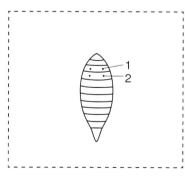

wing & abdomen placement

skeleton outline

fore wing

hind wing

detached wing outlines

REQUIREMENTS

quilter's muslin: 20 cm (8 in) square

12.5 cm (5 in) embroidery hoop

needles

crewel/embroidery size 10

sharps size 12

straw/milliners size 8

chenille size 20

tapestry size 28

sharp yarn darner sizes 14–18

beads & wire

Mill Hill petite beads 42014 *(black)*

33 gauge white covered wire:

  four 10 cm (4 in) lengths *(colour
  wire dark pink and green if desired:
  Copic RV09 Fuchsia, Copic YG63 Pea
  Green)*

thread

dark purple stranded thread:
Soie d'Alger 3326 or DMC 939

dark pink stranded thread:
Soie d'Alger 2945 or DMC 600

dark green stranded thread:
Soie d'Alger 2145 or DMC 580

medium green stranded thread:
Soie d'Alger 2144 or DMC 581

medium mauve stranded thread:
Soie d'Alger 4634 or DMC 3726

pale mauve stranded thread:
Soie d'Alger 4633 or DMC 316

ecru stranded thread:
DMC Ecru

copper metallic thread:
Madeira Metallic Art. 9803 col. 3027

burgundy/black metallic thread:
Kreinik Very Fine (#4) Braid col. 153V

METHOD

Transfer the thorax/abdomen outline (including internal segment lines) and wing placement dots to the background fabric.

WINGS

1. Mount the muslin into the hoop and trace the wing outlines—a right and left fore wing and a right and left hind wing. Include the marks indicating the colour changes on the edges of the wings.

2. Using tweezers, shape a length of wire around a wing outline diagram, leaving two tails of wire at the base of the wing. Shape a right and a left fore wing and a right and a left hind wing. If desired, colour sections of the wires dark pink and green using the diagram as a guide (leave the medium mauve section of the fore wing uncoloured).

Fore Wings

1. Using one strand of either dark pink or dark green thread in a crewel needle, couch the shaped wire around the traced fore wing outline, working the stitches in dark pink along the upper edge of the wing and dark green along the lower edge, parking the colour not in use to the side (do not stitch across the mauve outer edge).

2. Buttonhole stitch the wire to the muslin, working the upper edge of the wing in dark pink, the outer edge in medium mauve and the lower edge in dark green.

3. The wings are embroidered, inside the wire outline, with rows of buttonhole and long and short stitch, working all stitches in a direction towards the inner corner of the wing. With medium mauve thread, work the row at the wing edge first with close, long and short buttonhole stitch (the ridge of the buttonhole is next to the wire).

dark pink

medium mauve

dark green

fore wing

dark purple

dark pink

hind wing

4. Work the remainder of the wing with five rows of long and short stitch, blending the first row into the buttonhole stitches. Refer to the diagram for row colours:

vein stitches

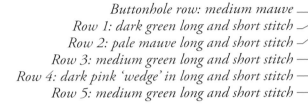

Buttonhole row: medium mauve
Row 1: dark green long and short stitch
Row 2: pale mauve long and short stitch
Row 3: medium green long and short stitch
Row 4: dark pink 'wedge' in long and short stitch
Row 5: medium green long and short stitch

completed forewing

5. With copper metallic thread in a sharps needle, work the veins with fly and single feather stitches, using the diagram as a guide.

Hind Wings

1. With one strand of dark pink thread, couch the shaped wire around the traced hind wing outline, working stitches at the inner corners, the colour change marks and around the outer edge of the wing.

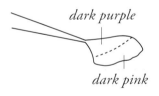

dark purple

dark pink

2. Buttonhole stitch the wire to the muslin, working the inner corners of the wing in dark purple and the outer edge in dark pink.

3. The wings are embroidered, inside the wire outline, with rows of buttonhole and long and short stitch, working all stitches in a direction towards the inner corner of the wing. With dark pink thread, work the row at the wing edge first with close, long and short buttonhole stitch (the ridge of the buttonhole is next to the wire).

veins

4. Work the remainder of the wing with long and short stitch, blending from dark pink to dark purple, using the inside line as a guide.

5. With copper metallic thread in a sharps needle, work the veins with fly and single feather stitches, using the diagram as a guide.

completed hindwing

To Complete the Moth

1. With one strand of dark pink thread, outline the thorax/abdomen in back stitch, working ten back stitches along each side, using the internal segment lines as a guide (one back stitch per segment line), and small back stitches at the tail and the head.

abdomen stitch diagram

2. Carefully cut out the wings. Use a large yarn darner to insert the wire tails of the wings through the two pairs of dots inside the thorax outline. Apply the hind wings first, inserting the wire tails separately through the two lower dots (2), then the fore wings through the two upper dots (1); the fore wings will overlap the hind wings. Bend the wire tails under the wings and secure to the backing fabric with tiny stitches using ecru thread, making sure that the stitches do not protrude beyond the wingspan. Do not trim any wire tails until the moth is finished. Keep the wings overlapped until the thorax and abdomen are worked.

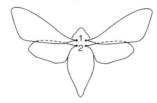

wing placement

3. Using 7 strands of medium green thread in a chenille needle, pad the thorax/abdomen, inside the outline, with five long straight stitches, using the diagram as a guide. To form a second layer of padding, work seven long straight stitches on top of the previous stitches.

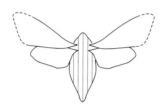

abdomen padding

4. Using one strand of medium green thread, work eleven couching stitches across the abdomen using the back stitches on each side as a guide. Carefully raise and move the wings, as required, to work the couching stitches on either side of the wing insertion points, and one between the wings. As the abdomen will be worked in raised stem stitch over these bars, the couching stitches need to be snug—not tight.

abdomen couching lines

Abdomen

Work the abdomen in raised stem stitch over the lower seven couched bars, bringing the needle out through the padding (above the seventh bar from the tail) and working all rows of stitches towards the tail.

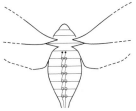

completed abdomen

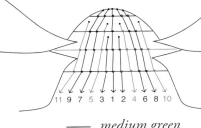

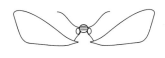
—— *medium green*
—— *dark pink*

head placement

*completed thorax,
head & antennae*

1. With one strand of dark pink thread in a tapestry needle, work two rows of raised stem stitch down the centre of the abdomen (over the lower seven bars), inserting the needle through a point at the end of the tail.

2. Using medium green thread, work five or six rows of raised stem stitch, alternately, on either side of the centre rows, inserting the needle above the lowest bar (the tail of the moth is pink).

3. With dark pink thread, work three rows of raised stem stitch on either side of the abdomen (alternately), working over the lowest bar and inserting the needle to form the pointed tail of the moth.

Thorax

The thorax is also worked in raised stem stitch, starting at the top edge and working the rows towards the abdomen, inserting the needle into the worked abdomen. To obtain the distinctive striped pattern of the thorax, work the rows of stem stitch in either dark pink or medium green over the top four bars, as shown on the diagram. Work the centre row first, over all four bars, then rows alternately on each side of this line.

Head & Antennae

1. With one strand of dark green thread, work five satin stitches across the top of the thorax for the head. Stitch a petite black bead on either side of the head for the eyes.

2. With one strand of burgundy metallic thread in a milliners needle, work a loose straight stitch on either side of the head for the antennae.

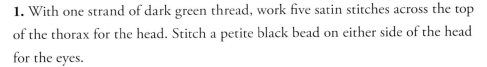

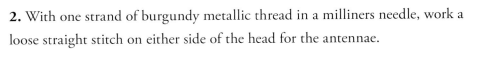

*finished moth
actual size*

Part 4

THE Projects

The four stumpwork projects in this section each include a moth or
butterfly among the flowers, with two of them featuring
the various stages of metamorphosis—the source of
much of the symbolism attached to these
creatures over the ages.

Dogwood & Green Lacewing

This embroidered panel was inspired by a striking dogwood shrub, *Cornus capitata*, encountered in Wanaka, New Zealand. Worked on ivory satin, in stumpwork and surface embroidery, this design features the bracts ('petals') in various phases of development—from the pale green buds and greenish pink young bracts, to the darker pinks of the more mature blossoms, all worked with detached 'petals' and raised beaded centres (the flower).

Several stages of the brilliant strawberry-like fruits are present—from pale orange-pink, through shades of rich red to dark purple. Nestled among the foliage are a Green Lacewing, *Chrysopa carnea*, with detached gauzy wings, beaded abdomen and long wire antennae, a Large Copper Butterfly, *Lycaena dispar*, with raised and surface embroidered wings, and a plump lime green caterpillar.

Dogwood shrub, Cornus capitata

'Dogwood' was present in the English vocabulary by the early seventeenth century. One theory suggests that the name was derived from the Old English word dagwood, from the use of its very hard wood for making dags -- daggers, arrows and skewers. This characteristic of the wood also explains an earlier English name for the Dogwood, 'Whipple-tree' (a whippletree is the part of a horse-drawn cart, linking the drawpole of the cart to the horses' harnesses.

The Dogwood, Cornus capitata (also known as the Himalayan Strawberry Tree), is a member of the family Cornaceae, a genus of mostly deciduous trees and shrubs best grown in cooler climates. (Cornus comes from the Latin word cornu, 'horn', referring to the hard wood.) The Dogwood is best known for its often large, petal-like bracts, in colours ranging from creamy whites, pale greens and yellows to a full array of pinks. The central 'button' (actually the flowerhead), is raised and looks like a cluster of beads. Cornus capitata has simple, smooth-edged leaves with the veins curving distinctively towards the leaf margins. The brilliant strawberry-like fruits appear in autumn and are very colourful -- at first green, they develop from pale orange-pink through shades of rich red to dark purple. Dogwoods are popular food plants for birds, flying-foxes and for the larvae of many species of butterflies and moths.

Dogwood shrub, *Cornus capitata*

DIAGRAMS ACTUAL SIZE

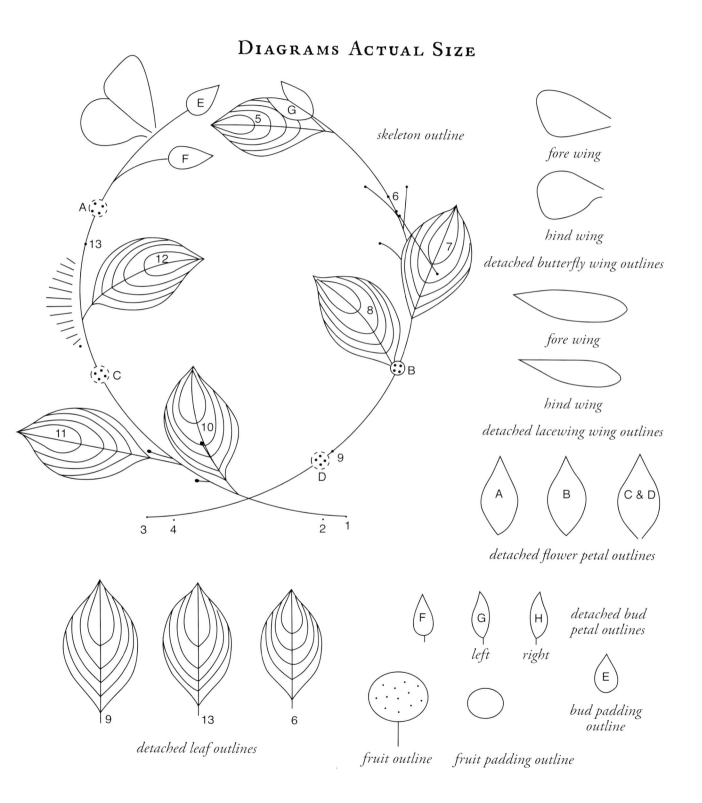

skeleton outline

fore wing

hind wing

detached butterfly wing outlines

fore wing

hind wing

detached lacewing wing outlines

A   B   C & D

detached flower petal outlines

F   G   H   detached bud petal outlines

left   right

E

bud padding outline

detached leaf outlines

fruit outline   fruit padding outline

Green Lacewing, Chrysopa carnea

Green Lacewing, *Chrysopa carnea*

The Green Lacewing, Chrysopa carnea, with its translucent lace-like wings, is most often seen in summer, perching on shrubs and low vegetation. These delicate insects have long thin antennae, a slender green abdomen and large wings covered by a lacework of veins. The wings are usually held over the body in a tent-like fashion when at rest. Green Lacewings are sometimes called Golden-eyes because their eyes are metallic orange-yellow in colour.

Chrysopa carnea is a useful insect, with both adults and larvae feeding on soft-bodied insects such as aphids. The female Lacewing deposits her eggs at the tips of very slender thread-like stalks (in places frequented by aphids) to help protect them from predators.

Large Copper Butterfly, Lycaena dispar

The **Large Copper Butterfly**, Lycaena dispar, is a European species with shiny metallic-looking wings. It inhabits moist areas, such as undeveloped riverbanks and wetlands, where it feed on various weedy plants. Sadly, this species of the Lycaenidae family became extinct in Britain in 1864 after its fenland home was reclaimed for agriculture. The upper wings are bright coppery orange with dark grey borders. The underside of the front wings is bright yellowy orange with black spots and grey edges; the hind wings are silvery bluish grey with small black spots and fiery orange borders.

Large Copper Butterfly, *Lycaena dispar*

OVERALL REQUIREMENTS

....

This is the complete list of requirements for this embroidery. For ease of use, the requirements of each individual element are repeated under its heading—for example, Dogwood requirements, Lacewing requirements.

ivory satin background fabric:
  35 cm (14 in) square
quilter's muslin (or calico) backing fabric:
  35 cm (14 in) square
  tracing paper
  (I use GLAD Bake/baking parchment)

quilter's muslin: *five 20 cm (8 in) squares*
red cotton fabric (homespun): *15 cm (6 in) square*
pale orange cotton fabric (homespun):
  15 cm (6 in) square
dark purple cotton fabric (homespun):
  15 cm (6 in) square
pale green organza: *15 cm (6 in) square*
pearl metal organdie: *15 cm (6 in) square*
white felt: *5 x 8 cm (2 x 3 in)*
paper-backed fusible web: *5 x 8 cm (2 x 3 in)*
  light coloured tracing/carbon paper
  (e.g. Clover Charcopy): 5 x 8 cm (2 x 3 in)

28 cm (11 in) embroidery hoop or stretcher bars
13 cm (5 in) embroidery hoops
10 cm (4 in) embroidery hoops

needles
crewel/embroidery sizes 3–10
milliners/straw sizes 1 and 9
sharps sizes 10 and 12
tapestry size 26 or 28
chenille size 18
sharp yarn darners sizes 14–18
embroidery equipment *(see page 264)*

3 mm purple/green glass beads
  (Hot Spotz SBXL-449)
Mill Hill seed bead 374 *(purple/green)*
Mill Hill antique beads 3059 *(green)*
Mill Hill petite beads 42037 *(green)*
Mill Hill petite beads 42028 *(ginger)*
Mill Hill petite beads 42033 *(orange)*

33 gauge white covered wire (flower petals):
  sixteen 15 cm (6 in) lengths
33 gauge white covered wire (bud petals):
  five 9 cm (3½ in) lengths
33 gauge white covered wire (leaves):
  three 15 cm (6 in) lengths
  (colour green if desired: Copic G99 Olive)
33 gauge white covered wire (butterfly):
  two 10 cm (4 in) lengths
28 gauge silver uncovered wire (wings):
  four 15 cm (6 in) lengths
32–34 gauge brass wire (antennae):
  10 cm (4 in) length

OVERALL REQUIREMENTS

THREAD   *Note: DMC colour equivalents are close but not always an exact match for the Soie d'Alger and Cifonda colours used.*

silver metallic thread (lacewing):
  Madeira Metallic Art. 03 col. 3010
slate/black metallic thread (lacewing):
  Kreinik Cord 225c
silver/black metallic thread (butterfly):
  Kreinik Cord 105c
thick silver/black metallic thread (butterfly):
  Madeira Metallic No. 40 col. 442
pale green rayon machine thread (lacewing):
  Madeira Rayon 40 col. 1047
variegated pale grey chenille thread (butterfly):
  col. Neutral
nylon clear thread:
  Madeira Monofil 60 col. 1001

dark olive stranded thread (stems):
  Soie d'Alger 3735 or DMC 934
dark green stranded thread
  (stems, leaves, lacewing):
  Soie d'Alger 2135 or DMC 3345
medium green stranded thread (leaves):
  Soie d'Alger 2134 or DMC 3346
light green stranded thread (leaves):
  Soie d'Alger 2124 or DMC 3347

dark lime stranded thread (flowers):
  Soie d'Alger 2123 or DMC 470
medium lime stranded thread (flowers):
  Soie d'Alger 242 or DMC 3348
light lime stranded thread (flowers):
  Soie d'Alger 241 or DMC 772
white stranded thread (flowers):
  Soie d'Alger Blanc or DMC Blanc
dark coral stranded thread (stems, fruit):
  Soie d'Alger 2916 or DMC 3328
medium coral stranded thread (leaves):
  Soie d'Alger 2915 or DMC 3712

very dark pink stranded thread (flowers):
  Soie d'Alger 1024 or DMC 335
dark pink stranded thread (flowers):
  Soie d'Alger 3012 or DMC 899
medium pink stranded thread (flowers):
  Soie d'Alger 3011 or DMC 3326
light pink stranded thread (flowers):
  Soie d'Alger 1021 or DMC 963
very pale pink stranded thread (flowers):
  Soie d'Alger 4147 or DMC 819
dark purple stranded thread (fruit):
  Soie d'Alger 3326 or DMC 939
light orange stranded thread (fruit):
  Soie d'Alger 641 or DMC 3825
steel-grey stranded thread (butterfly):
  Soie d'Alger 3443 or DMC 414

dark grey stranded thread (butterfly):
  Cifonda Art Silk 215 or DMC 317
medium grey stranded thread (butterfly):
  Cifonda Art Silk 212 or DMC 318
light grey stranded thread (butterfly):
  Cifonda Art Silk 211 or DMC 762
light blue stranded thread (butterfly):
  Cifonda Art Silk 181 or DMC 159
medium copper stranded thread (butterfly):
  Cifonda Art Silk 103 or DMC 3776
light copper stranded thread (butterfly):
  Cifonda Art Silk 102 or DMC 402

dark yellow stranded thread (butterfly):
  Cifonda Art Silk 175 or DMC 742
orange stranded thread (butterfly):
  Cifonda Art Silk 135A or DMC 947
black stranded thread (butterfly):
  Cifonda Art Silk Black or DMC 310

---

dark moss stranded thread (caterpillar):
  DMC 581
medium moss stranded thread (caterpillar):
  DMC 166

Or there, almost invisible against a leaf, is the lacewing, with green gauze wings and golden eyes, shy and secretive, descendant of an ancient race that lived in Permian times.
Rachel Carson, Silent Spring, *1962.*

PREPARATION

1. Mount the satin background fabric and the cotton backing into the 28 cm (11 in) embroidery hoop or frame. The fabrics need to be kept very taut.

2. Using a fine lead pencil, trace the skeleton outline onto tracing paper. Turn the tracing paper over and draw over the outline on the back (do not make the lines too dark).

3. Attach the tracing, right side up, to the satin in the hoop, using strips of masking tape on all sides. Check that the design is aligned with the straight grain of the fabric.

4. Place a tracing board (or small book) inside the back of the hoop for support, then transfer the design by tracing over the outline with a tracing pen or stylus.

Note: Take care to use the minimum amount of lead when tracing. If your outlines are too dark, gently press the traced outlines with pieces of masking tape or Magic Tape to remove any excess graphite.

ORDER OF WORK

1. STEMS
2. BACKGROUND LEAVES
3. BACKGROUND BUD PETALS
4. BACKGROUND BUTTERFLY WINGS
5. CATERPILLAR
6. FRUIT
7. BUDS
8. BUTTERFLY
9. GREEN LACEWING
10. FLOWERS
11. DETACHED LEAVES

METHOD: DOGWOOD

Dogwood 'flowers' *are actually the button-like head in the centre of a whorl of large white or pink bracts. For convenience, the bracts are referred to as petals in these instructions.*

REQUIREMENTS

quilter's muslin: *four 20 cm (8 in) squares*

red cotton fabric (homespun): *15 cm (6 in) square*

pale orange cotton fabric (homespun): *15 cm (6 in) square*

dark purple cotton fabric (homespun): *15 cm (6 in) square*

white felt: *5 x 8 cm (2 x 3 in)*

paper-backed fusible web: *5 x 8 cm (2 x 3 in)*

light coloured tracing/carbon paper
(e.g. Clover Charcopy): 5 x 8 cm (2 x 3 in)

Mill Hill antique beads 3059 *(green)*

Mill Hill petite beads 42037 *(green)*

Mill Hill petite beads 42028 *(ginger)*

Mill Hill petite beads 42033 *(orange)*

THREAD REQUIREMENTS

dark olive stranded thread:
  Soie d'Alger 3735 or DMC 934
dark green stranded thread:
  Soie d'Alger 2135 or DMC 3345
medium green stranded thread:
  Soie d'Alger 2134 or DMC 3346
light green stranded thread:
  Soie d'Alger 2124 or DMC 3347
dark lime stranded thread:
  Soie d'Alger 2123 or DMC 470
medium lime stranded thread:
  Soie d'Alger 242 or DMC 3348
light lime stranded thread:
  Soie d'Alger 241 or DMC 772
white stranded thread:
  Soie d'Alger Blanc or DMC Blanc
dark coral stranded thread:
  Soie d'Alger 2916 or DMC 3328

medium coral stranded thread:
  Soie d'Alger 2915 or DMC 3712
very dark pink stranded thread:
  Soie d'Alger 1024 or DMC 335
dark pink stranded thread:
  Soie d'Alger 3012 or DMC 899
medium pink stranded thread:
  Soie d'Alger 3011 or DMC 3326
light pink stranded thread:
  Soie d'Alger 1021 or DMC 963
very pale pink stranded thread:
  Soie d'Alger 4147 or DMC 819
dark purple stranded thread:
  Soie d'Alger 3326 or DMC 939
light orange stranded thread:
  Soie d'Alger 641 or DMC 3825
nylon clear thread:
  Madeira Monofil 60 col. 1001

STEMS

The flower stems are worked in raised stem stitch over a padding of stranded thread. See diagram opposite.

Left Flower Stem

1. Using 7 strands of dark olive thread in a chenille needle, insert the needle at 1 (from the front) and bring out at 2. Adjust the tails of padding thread to be of equal length (14 strands altogether).

2. With one strand of dark olive thread in a size 10 crewel needle, couch the padding threads along the left stem line to A, working the stitches 3 mm apart. Insert both tails of padding through to the back at the edge of circle A. Hold these tails of thread out of the way with masking tape—they will be trimmed later. As the stems will be worked in raised stem stitch, do not make the couching stitches too tight—just snug.

3. Using a single strand of thread in a tapestry needle, work the stem with rows of stem stitch as follows:

- Starting at C with dark coral thread, work a row of raised stem stitch to 2.
- The next four rows finish at staggered points (like satin stitch) between 2 and 1.
- Starting at A with dark olive thread, work raised stem stitch to the end of the stem.
- Starting at A with dark coral thread, work raised stem stitch to the end of the stem.
- Starting at A with dark olive thread, work raised stem stitch to the end of the stem.
- Starting at A with dark coral thread, work raised stem stitch to the end of the stem.
- Starting at A with dark green thread, work raised stem stitch to 1.
- Starting at A with dark olive thread, work raised stem stitch to 1.

To neaten the end of the stem, work a detached chain stitch from 1 to 2 with one strand of dark olive thread. Trim the padding threads.

Right Flower Stem

1. Using 7 strands of dark olive thread in a chenille needle, insert the needle at 3 and bring out at 4. Adjust the tails of padding thread to be of equal length.

2. With one strand of dark olive thread, couch the padding threads along the right stem line (over the worked stem) to the base of leaf 7. Insert both tails of padding through to the back at the base of leaf 7. Hold these tails of thread out of the way with masking tape.

3. Using a single strand of thread in a tapestry needle, work the stem with rows of stem stitch as follows:

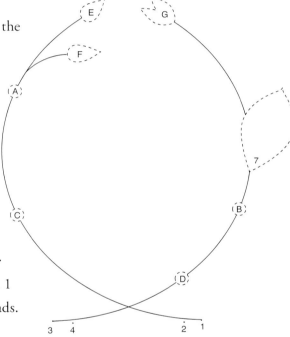

working the stems

- Starting at 4 with dark olive thread, work a row of raised stem stitch to B.
- Starting at 4 with dark olive thread, work a row of raised stem stitch to 7.
- The next four rows commence at staggered points (like satin stitch) between 4 and 3.
- Starting between 4 and 3 with dark olive thread, work raised stem stitch to 7.
- Starting between 4 and 3 with dark green thread, work raised stem stitch to 7.
- Starting between 4 and 3 with dark olive thread, work raised stem stitch to 7.
- Starting between 4 and 3 with dark green thread, work raised stem stitch to 7.
- Starting at 3 (note change from 4) with dark olive thread, work raised stem stitch to 7.

To neaten the end of the stem, work a detached chain stitch from 3 to 4 with one strand of dark olive thread. Trim the padding threads.

Left Bud Stem

1. Using seven strands of medium lime thread in a chenille needle, bring the needle out at the base of bud E.

2. With one strand of medium lime thread in a size 10 crewel needle, couch the padding thread along the stem line to the upper edge of circle A, working the stitches 2.5 mm apart. Hold the tails of the padding thread with masking tape.

3. Using a single strand of thread in a tapestry needle, work the stem with rows of stem stitch as follows:

- Starting at E with light orange thread, work a row of raised stem stitch to A.
- Starting at E with very pale pink thread, work a row of raised stem stitch to A.
- Starting at E with light lime thread, work a row of raised stem stitch to A.
- Starting at E with medium lime thread, work a row of raised stem stitch to A.

4. Using 7 strands of medium lime thread, bring the needle out at the base of bud F.

5. With one strand of medium lime thread, couch the padding thread along the stem line to join the upper bud stem at A.

6. Using a single strand of thread in a tapestry needle, work the stem with rows of stem stitch as for the previous bud stem. Trim the padding threads.

Right Bud Stem

1. Using 7 strands of medium lime thread in a chenille needle, bring the needle at the base of bud G.

2. With one strand of medium lime thread, couch the padding thread along the stem line to the upper edge of leaf 7. Hold the tails of padding thread with masking tape.

3. Using a single strand of thread in a tapestry needle, work the stem with rows of stem stitch as for the left bud stems. Trim the padding threads.

Note: The fruit stems are not worked at this stage.

BACKGROUND LEAVES

The leaves of the dogwood have very distinct veins which vary in colour from coral to light green. All the background leaves (see diagram page 167) are embroidered in the same manner—rows of stem stitch worked side by side, from one leaf edge to the other, taking the thread under the central vein. Each leaf varies a little with the shades of thread used.

Leaf 11 (dark)

1. Using one strand of dark green thread, work the leaf outline in stem stitch.

2. With 3 strands of dark coral thread, work the lower half of the central vein in stem stitch, changing to one strand of medium coral for the upper half.

3. Work a row of split stitch on either side of the central vein with one strand of dark green thread (this prevents a white gap showing on either side of the vein).

4. Work the lower side veins in stem stitch with one strand of dark coral thread, changing to medium coral or dark lime for the remaining side veins.

vein stitches

5. Using dark green thread, embroider the leaf surface (between the veins) with rows of stem stitch, working from one leaf edge to the other, taking the thread under the central vein.

Note: You may find it easier to work steps 4 and 5 concurrently, starting from the base of the leaf.

Leaves 7 & 12 (dark-medium)

1. Using one strand of dark green thread, work the leaf outline in stem stitch.

2. With 2 strands of medium coral thread, work the lower half of the central vein in stem stitch, changing to one strand for the upper half.

3. Work a row of split stitch on either side of the central vein with medium green thread.

4. Work the lower side veins in stem stitch with medium coral thread, changing to dark lime for the remaining side veins.

5. Embroider the lower leaf segments (between the veins) with rows of stem stitch using dark green thread, changing to medium green for the upper segments.

Leaf 10 (medium)

1. Using one strand of medium green thread, work the leaf outline in stem stitch.

2. With 2 strands of medium coral thread, work the lower half of the central vein in stem stitch, changing to one strand of dark lime for the upper half.

3. Work a row of split stitch on either side of the central vein with medium green thread.

4. Work the lower side veins in stem stitch with one strand of medium coral thread, changing to dark lime or medium lime for the remaining side veins.

completed leaf 12

5. Using medium green thread, embroider the leaf surface with rows of stem stitch, working from one leaf edge to the other, taking the thread under the central vein.

Leaves 5 & 8 (medium-light)

1. Using one strand of medium green thread, work the leaf outline in stem stitch.

2. With 2 strands of dark lime thread, work the lower half of the central vein in stem stitch, changing to one strand for the upper half.

3. Work a row of split stitch on either side of the central vein with medium green thread.

4. Work the lower side veins in stem stitch with dark lime thread, changing to medium lime for the remaining side veins.

5. Embroider the lower leaf segments with rows of stem stitch using medium green thread, changing to light green for the upper segments.

DETACHED LEAVES

Mount a square of muslin into a small hoop and trace the three detached leaves from the diagram on page 167 (check that they are the right way up). It is a good idea to number them—6, 9 and 13. Use 15 cm (6 in) lengths of wire, coloured green if desired.

Leaf 9 (dark)

1. Using one strand of dark coral thread, couch wire along the central vein, one end of the wire at the tip of the leaf. Overcast stitch the wire to the muslin along the central vein, working the lower half of the vein in dark coral thread and changing to medium coral for the upper half.

2. Using dark green thread, couch the remaining wire around the leaf outline, bending into a point at the tip and ending with a tail of wire at the base of the leaf (do not trim the wire tail—it will be wrapped later to form a stem).

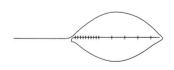

wire placement

Buttonhole stitch the wire to the muslin around the outside edge of the leaf.

3. With dark green thread, work a row of split stitch on either side of the central vein.

4. Work the lower side veins in stem stitch with one strand of dark coral thread, changing to medium coral or dark lime for the remaining side veins.

5. Using dark green thread, embroider the leaf surface (between the veins) with rows of stem stitch, working from one wired leaf edge to the other, taking the thread under the central vein.

Note: I found it easier to work steps 4 and 5 concurrently, starting from the base of the leaf.

Leaf 6 (medium)

1. Using one strand of dark lime thread, couch wire along the central vein, one end of the wire at the tip of the leaf. Overcast stitch the wire to the muslin along the central vein, working the lower half of the vein in medium coral thread and changing to dark lime for the upper half.

2. Using medium green thread, couch the remaining wire around the leaf outline, bending into a point at the tip and ending with a tail of wire at the base of the leaf (do not trim the wire tail). Buttonhole stitch the wire to the muslin around the outside edge of the leaf.

3. With medium green thread, work a row of split stitch on either side of the central vein.

4. Work the lower side veins in stem stitch with one strand of medium coral thread, changing to dark lime or medium lime for the remaining side veins.

5. Using medium green thread, embroider the leaf surface with rows of stem stitch, working from one wired leaf edge to the other, taking the thread under the central vein.

completed leaf 6

Leaf 13 (medium-light)

1. Using one strand of dark lime thread, couch wire along the central vein, one end of the wire at the tip of the leaf. Overcast stitch the wire to the muslin along the central vein.

2. Using medium green thread, couch the remaining wire around the leaf outline, bending into a point at the tip and ending with a tail of wire at the base of the leaf (do not trim the wire tail). Buttonhole stitch the wire to the muslin around the outside edge of the leaf.

3. With medium green thread, work a row of split stitch on either side of the central vein.

4. Work the lower side veins in stem stitch with dark lime thread, changing to medium lime for the remaining side veins.

5. Using medium green thread, embroider the lower leaf segments with rows of stem stitch, changing to light green for the upper segments.

To Complete the Leaves

Do not apply the detached leaves until all other work on the piece is finished.

1. Carefully cut out the leaves. To form a wrapped stalk at the base of each leaf, attach one strand of dark green thread to the back of the leaf, then closely wrap at least 1 cm (3/8 in) of the wire tail. Secure the thread with a knot, retaining the thread tail.

2. Shape each leaf slightly before applying to the finished work. Using a yarn darner, insert the wrapped wire and thread tails through to the back, at the numbered points on the stem as shown on page 167, leaving a short wrapped stalk between the leaf and the main stem. Secure the tail of wire with a few small stitches at the back of the stem. Shape the leaves with tweezers and trim the wire tails.

FLOWERS

The dogwood flowers require sixteen detached petals which, while varying a little in size and colour, are all worked the same way. To avoid soiling the pale edges of the petals with a traced lead pencil outline, the wires are bent into a petal shape first, before applying to the muslin. Use tweezers, and the appropriate detached petal outline as a template, to bend the wires into the required petal shapes. Work all the petals on two hoops of muslin and keep aside until required.

1. Mount a square of muslin into a 13 cm (5 in) hoop and apply the wires for the detached petals for flowers A and B. Label each petal to avoid confusion.

2. Mount a square of muslin into a 13 cm (5 in) hoop and apply the wires for the detached petals for flowers C and D.

Flower A

Using petal outline A as a template, work four detached petals as follows:

1. Bend a 12 cm (4½ in) length of wire in half, then shape around the petal outline, having a point at the tip and leaving two tails of wire at the base that touch but do not cross.

2. With one strand of light pink thread in a size 10 crewel needle, couch the shaped wire to the muslin in the order as shown, starting with a waste knot and tail of thread beyond the tip of the petal. As the tip of the petal will eventually be worked in very dark pink thread, this first couching stitch needs to be able to be removed. Park the light pink thread to the side.

3. Buttonhole stitch the wire to the muslin, working the lower edges 5 mm (¼ in) with medium lime thread and changing to light pink for the upper edges, leaving the tip of the wire (2 mm from the tip) unstitched at this stage.

4. Embroider the petal in long and short stitch, starting at the base with dark lime thread, blending into medium lime then light pink. Just before the tip is

completed flower A

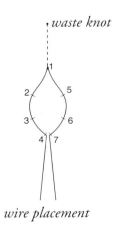

wire placement

reached, park the light pink thread to the side.

5. To work the tip of the petal, attach one strand of very dark pink (in a size 12 sharps needle) to the back of the petal, then buttonhole stitch the tip of the wire to the muslin, removing the light pink couching stitch as you go. Make sure that you bring the needle up inside the last light pink buttonhole stitch and insert into the first buttonhole stitch on the other side to avoid a gap between the light pink and very dark pink buttonhole stitches (a size 12 needle helps with this). Secure the thread at the back of the petal.

6. Retrieve the light pink thread and embroider up to the tip of the petal.

Flower B

Using petal outline B as a template, work four detached petals as follows:

completed flower B

1. Bend a 12 cm (4½ in) length of wire in half then shape around the petal outline, having a point at the tip and leaving two tails of wire at the base that touch but do not cross.

2. With one strand of very pale pink thread, couch the shaped wire to the muslin in the order as shown, starting with a waste knot and tail of thread beyond the tip of the petal, as for Flower A. Park the thread to the side.

3. Buttonhole stitch the wire to the muslin, working the lower edges 5 mm (¼ in) with light lime thread and changing to very pale pink for the upper edges, leaving the tip of the wire (2 mm from the tip) unstitched at this stage.

4. Embroider the petal in long and short stitch, starting at the base with light lime thread, blending into white then very pale pink. Just before the tip is reached, park the very pale pink thread to the side.

5. To work the tip of the petal, attach one strand of very dark pink (in a size 12 sharps needle) to the back of the petal, then buttonhole stitch the tip of the wire to the muslin, removing the very pale pink couching stitch as you go. Make sure that you bring the needle up inside the last very pale pink buttonhole stitch and insert into the first buttonhole stitch on the other side to avoid a gap between the very pale pink and very dark pink buttonhole stitches (a size 12 needle helps with this). Secure the thread at the back of the petal.

6. Retrieve the very pale pink thread and embroider up to the tip of the petal.

Flower C

Using petal outline C as a template, work four detached petals as follows:

1. Bend a 12 cm (4½ in) length of wire in half then shape around the petal outline, having a point at the tip and leaving two tails of wire at the base that touch but do not cross.

2. With one strand of light pink thread, couch the shaped wire to the muslin in the order as shown, starting with a waste knot and tail of thread beyond the tip of the petal, as for Flower A. Park the thread to the side.

3. Buttonhole stitch the wire to the muslin, working the lower edges 5 mm (¼ in) with medium pink thread and changing to light pink for the upper edges, leaving the tip of the wire unstitched.

4. Embroider the petal in long and short stitch, starting at the base with dark pink thread, blending into medium pink then light pink thread. Just before the tip is reached, park the light pink thread to the side.

5. To work the tip of the petal, attach one strand of very dark pink to the back of the petal, then buttonhole stitch the tip of the wire to the muslin, as for flower B, removing the couching stitch as you go. Secure the thread at the back of the petal.

completed flower C

6. Retrieve the light pink thread and embroider up to the tip of the petal.

Flower D

Using petal outline D as a template, work four detached petals as follows:

1. Bend a 12 cm (4½ in) length of wire in half, then shape around the petal outline, having a point at the tip and leaving two tails of wire at the base that touch but do not cross.

2. With one strand of light pink thread, couch the shaped wire to the muslin in the order as shown, starting with a waste knot and tail of thread beyond the tip of the petal, as for Flower A. Park the thread to the side.

3. Buttonhole stitch the wire to the muslin, working the lower edges 5 mm (¼ in) with medium pink thread and changing to light pink for the upper edges, leaving the tip of the wire unstitched.

4. Embroider the petal in long and short stitch, starting at the base with medium pink thread, blending into light pink, very pale pink then light lime thread. Just before the tip is reached, park the light lime thread to the side.

5. To work the tip of the petal, attach one strand of very dark pink (in a size 12 sharps needle) to the back of the petal, then buttonhole stitch the tip of the wire to the muslin, as for flower B, removing the couching stitch as you go. Secure the thread at the back of the petal.

6. Retrieve the light lime thread and embroider up to the tip of the petal.

completed flower D

To Complete the Flower

Each flower is completed in the same way.

1. Carefully cut out the petals and squeeze the tips with tweezers to make a sharper point (the tips of dogwood petals also curl over slightly).

2. Using a yarn darner, insert the wire tails of the four detached petals through the four dots inside the circle outline on the stem (four individual holes as close to each other as possible). Bend the wires behind the petals and secure to the backing fabric with small stitches using white thread. Do not cut the wires until the flower is finished.

petal placement

To work the beaded centre of the flower you will need sixteen green petite beads (42037), two green antique beads (3059) and nylon thread in a size 12 sharps

bead placement

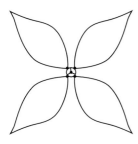

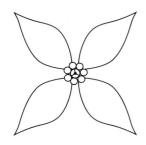

circular bead placement

completed beaded centre of flower

needle. Do not shape the petals until the beaded centre has been worked.

The beads are applied in layers as follows:

1. Stitch one antique bead in the centre of the petals to fill the gap. Stitch the bead in place with three or four stitches (the hole in the bead facing upwards like a doughnut), pulling the bead down to fill the space between the petal insertion points.

2. Bring the needle out through the centre bead and thread on an antique bead. Stitch on top of the first bead (the hole in the bead facing upwards) with three or four stitches. This now becomes the centre bead.

3. Using backstitch, apply eight petite beads evenly around the centre bead (carefully taking the needle through the petals and the background fabric), then pass the thread three times through these beads (like threading a necklace) to draw them into a tight circle. Take the needle through to the back.

4. Bring the needle through the centre bead, thread on a petite bead then take the needle back down through the centre, leaving the petite bead on its side to form a raised centre.

5. Using backstitch, apply seven petite beads evenly around the raised centre bead, taking the needle down through the space between the centre bead and the petite beads of the previous layer (this is easier than it sounds), then pass the thread three times through these beads (like threading a necklace) to draw them into a tight circle. Take the needle through to the back and secure.

Shape the petals then trim the wires.

FLOWER BUDS
Bud E

1. Trace base shape E on to paper-backed fusible web then fuse to white felt. Carefully cut out the shape.

2. Using medium lime thread in a size 10 crewel needle, apply the felt bud padding (web side up) to the background fabric with a few stab stitches, then outline the shape in buttonhole stitch (stitches about 1.5 mm apart).

3. Embroider the padded bud in satin stitch, enclosing the outline.

4. With one strand of dark pink thread in a size 12 sharps needle, work three satin stitches to form a point at the tip of the bud.

completed bud E

Bud F
Background Petal

1. Using one strand of light lime thread, outline the background petal in chain stitch, working each row from the base towards the tip.

2. Embroider the petal, inside the chain stitched outline, in long and short stitch, starting at the base with medium lime thread, blending into light lime then very pale pink.

3. With one strand of dark pink thread in a size 12 sharps needle, work three satin stitches to form a point at the tip of the bud petal.

Detached Petals

Mount a square of muslin into a 10 cm (4 in) hoop and apply the wires for the detached petals for buds F and G. Label each petal to avoid confusion.

Using petal outline F as a template, work three detached petals as follows:

1. Bend a 9 cm (3½ in) length of wire in half then shape around the petal outline, having a point at the tip and leaving two tails of wire at the base that touch but do not cross.

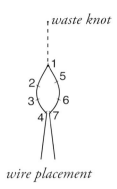

waste knot

wire placement

2. With one strand of light lime thread in a size 10 crewel needle, couch the shaped wire to the muslin in the order shown, starting with a waste knot and tail of thread beyond the tip of the petal. As the tip of the petal will eventually be worked in dark pink thread, this first couching stitch needs to be able to be removed.

3. Buttonhole stitch the wire to the muslin, leaving the tip of the wire (1.5 mm from the tip) unstitched at this stage.

4. Embroider the petal in long and short stitch, starting at the base with medium lime thread, blending into light lime then very pale pink. Just before the tip is reached, park the very pale pink thread to the side.

5. To work the tip of the petal, attach one strand of dark pink (in a size 12 sharps needle) to the back of the petal, then buttonhole stitch the tip of the wire to the muslin, removing the light lime couching stitch as you go. Make sure that you bring the needle up inside the last light lime buttonhole stitch and insert into the first buttonhole stitch on the other side to avoid a gap between the light lime and dark pink buttonhole stitches (a size 12 needle helps with this). Secure the thread at the back of the petal.

6. Retrieve the very pale pink thread and embroider up to the tip of the petal.

To Complete Bud F
1. Cut out the bud petals. Shape the petals slightly and squeeze the tip with tweezers to make a sharper point. Carefully cut off the right tail of wire from one petal and the left tail of wire from a second petal (these will become the side petals with one wire tail each).The remaining petal will be the middle petal with two wire tails.

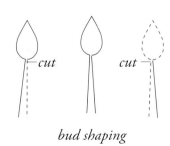

cut   *cut*

bud shaping

2. Using a yarn darner, insert the wire tails of the side petals through one hole at the base of the background petal (one petal will overlap the other). Bend the wire tails behind the background petal and secure with a few small stitches. Insert the middle petal wires through the same hole (this petal will be on top of the side petals) and secure the wire tails to the back of the stem. Shape the petals then trim the wires.

Bud G

Background Petals

1. Using one strand of light lime thread, outline the background petals in chain stitch, working each row from the base towards the tip (I embroidered over the leaf).

2. Embroider the petal, inside the chain stitched outline, in long and short stitch, starting at the base with light lime thread, blending into white then very pale pink.

3. With one strand of dark pink thread in a size 12 sharps needle, work three satin stitches to form a point at the tip of both bud petals.

Detached Petals

Using petal outline G as a template, work two detached petals as follows:

1. Bend a 9 cm (3½ in) length of wire in half, then shape around the petal outline, having a point at the tip and leaving two tails of wire at the base that touch but do not cross.

2. With one strand of light lime thread in a size 10 crewel needle, couch the shaped wire to the muslin as for Bud F, starting with a waste knot and tail of thread beyond the tip of the petal.

3. Buttonhole stitch the wire to the muslin, leaving the tip of the wire (1.5 mm from the tip) unstitched at this stage.

4. Embroider the petal in long and short stitch, starting at the base with light lime thread, blending into white then very pale pink. Just before the tip is reached, park the very pale pink thread to the side.

5. To work the tip of the petal, attach one strand of dark pink (in a size 12 sharps needle) to the back of the petal, then buttonhole stitch the tip of the

completed bud F

wire to the muslin, removing the light lime couching stitch as you go. Secure the thread at the back of the petal.

6. Retrieve the very pale pink thread and embroider up to the tip of the petal.

To Complete Bud G
1. Cut out the bud petals. Shape the petals slightly and squeeze the tip with tweezers to make a sharper point.

2. Using a yarn darner, insert the wire tails of both petals through one hole at the base of the background petals. Secure the wire tails to the back of the stem. Do not trim the wires until the beads have been stitched into the centre of the bud.

3. To work the beaded centre of the bud you will need nine green petite beads (42037) and nylon thread in a size 12 sharps needle.

Carefully lift up the petals and apply the beads as follows:

bead placement

- Bring the needle out 3 mm above the petal insertion point and slide on one bead. Stitch in place with three stitches, the hole in the bead facing upwards (like a doughnut).
- Stitch seven beads around the centre bead with backstitch, then pass the thread three times through these beads (like threading a necklace) to draw them into a tight circle.
- Bring the needle through the centre bead, thread on another bead then take the needle back through the centre, leaving the bead on its side to form a raised centre. Secure the thread.

Shape the petals then trim the wires.

completed bud G

FRUIT
The fruit of this dogwood ranges in colour from pinkish yellow, to shades of red and dark purple.

1. Trace six fruit padding shapes on to paper-backed fusible web then fuse to white felt. Carefully cut out the shapes and put aside until required.

2. Embroider the upper fruit stem lines in stem stitch—two rows side by side, using 2 strands of thread—one strand of light orange and one strand of medium lime thread—in a size 9 crewel needle.

Note: The lower fruit stems are not worked until after the fruit has been applied.

Yellow Fruit

1. Mount a square of pale orange cotton fabric into a small hoop. Trace two fruit outlines, including the stem line and inner dots. Leave a space between the fruits as they will be cut out with a seam allowance.

2. Using nylon thread in a size 12 sharps needle, stitch a ginger petite bead on top of each dot with three stitches, the hole in the bead facing upwards (like a donut).

bead placement

3. With 3 strands of light orange thread in a size 6 milliners needle, fill the fruit shape with French knots (one wrap). First work about five French knots around each bead then fill the remaining spaces between the beads and out to the edge.

4. With one strand of light orange thread in a size 10 crewel needle, work a row of running stitch around the fruit, about 1 mm away from the edge of the knots. Start and end the running stitch at the stem line, leaving two tails of thread on the front.

stitch guide for filling

5. Cut out the shape, about 1.5 mm away from the running stitch, avoiding the tails of thread.

6. Place a layer of padding behind the shape then pull the tails of thread to draw up the edges, enclosing the padding. Pull the tails of thread until the fruit is the size required then tie off (the gathered edges are now beneath the shape). Shape the fruit with your fingers before applying (a slightly oval shape).

7. Thread the tails into a needle and insert about 2 mm above the end of the fruit stem line. Check the position and reinsert the needle if necessary. Pull the tails of thread firmly and hold behind the stem line with masking tape.

fruit placement

completed yellow fruit

(Secure the tails of thread with a few stitches into the backing fabric after the fruit is stitched in place).

8. With one strand of light orange thread, apply the fruit shape with small invisible stab stitches, bringing the needle out from under the fruit and taking a small stitch into the fabric between the French knots. First work four stitches (north, south, east and west), then continue around the edge. Shape the fruit with your fingers.

Red Fruit

1. Mount a square of red cotton fabric into a small hoop. Trace two fruit outlines, including the stem line and inner dots.

2. Using nylon thread, stitch an orange petite bead on top of each dot with three stitches.

3. Using 3 strands of dark coral thread, fill the fruit shape with French knots.

Apply as for the yellow fruit, substituting dark coral thread. Before applying the red fruit, work the stem with a bullion knot, using 3 strands of dark olive thread in a size 1 milliners needle.

Purple Fruit

1. Mount a square of dark purple cotton fabric into a small hoop. Using a coloured tracing (carbon) paper, trace two fruit outlines, including the stem line and inner dots.

2. Using nylon thread in a size 12 sharps needle, stitch a ginger petite bead on top of each dot with three stitches.

completed red & purple fruit

3. Using 3 strands of dark purple thread, fill the fruit shape with French knots.

Apply as for the yellow fruit, substituting dark purple thread. Work each stem with a bullion knot, using 3 strands of dark olive thread in a size 1 milliners needle.

METHOD: CATERPILLAR

This caterpillar is the larva of the Large Copper Butterfly.
Work the caterpillar before applying the detached flower petals.

REQUIREMENTS

dark moss stranded thread: *DMC 581*
medium moss stranded thread: *DMC 166*
3 mm purple glass bead *(Hot Spotz SBXL-449)*

1. A caterpillar has twelve discernible body segments behind the head. These segments are indicated by the eleven internal lines on the caterpillar outline. Using one strand of medium moss thread in a size 10 crewel needle, outline the caterpillar in back stitch, working one back stitch per segment and one stitch across the head end. Leave a small gap between the lower outline and the stem to allow for the legs.

caterpillar outline

2. Using 6 strands of medium moss thread in a chenille needle, pad the caterpillar body (inside the outline), with laid satin stitches worked the length of the body. First work a few shorter stitches to pad the middle section then cover with the longer stitches. With one strand of thread, work eleven couching stitches over the padding, using the back stitches as a guide to placement. The caterpillar will be embroidered in raised stem stitch over these couching stitches, so they need to be snug but not too tight.

caterpillar padding

attaching the head

3. Using one strand of thread, stitch a 3 mm bead at the end of the caterpillar for the head (keeping the hole in the bead at right angles to the end of the caterpillar).

4. With one strand of medium moss thread in a tapestry needle, work a row of raised stem stitch along the lower edge of the caterpillar, starting at the tail end and inserting the needle next to the head bead. Continue working rows of raised stem stitch to cover the body of the caterpillar, working some short rows to allow for the shape of the body, and taking some rows through the head bead.

5. Using 3 strands of dark moss thread in a size 7 milliners needle, work eight French knots (below the appropriate segments) to represent the eight pairs of legs:

leg placement

- Work a French knot below the first three segments behind the head
- Miss two segments, then work French knots below the next four segments
- Miss two segments, then work a knot below the tails segment.
- Using tweezers, gently squeeze the legs to define their shape.

completed caterpillar

6. With one strand of dark moss thread in a size 9 milliners needle, work French knots for the spiracles along the lower half of the body. Work a knot in every segment except the first three and the last (eight knots in all). Work the French knots across a row of raised stem stitch (so they don't fall into the padding). Don't pull the stitches too tight.

METHOD: BUTTERFLY

....

This Copper Butterfly has two wings embroidered on the background fabric and two detached wings which are applied over them. Embroider the background wings before applying the detached wings.

REQUIREMENTS

quilter's muslin:
20 cm (8 in) square

3 mm bronze/blue bead

33 gauge white covered wire (butterfly):
two 10 cm (4 in) lengths

dark grey stranded thread:
Cifonda Art Silk 215 or DMC 317

medium grey stranded thread:
Cifonda Art Silk 212 or DMC 318

light grey stranded thread:
Cifonda Art Silk 211 or DMC 762

light blue stranded thread:
Cifonda Art Silk 181 or DMC 159

medium copper stranded thread:
Cifonda Art Silk 103 or DMC 3776

light copper stranded thread:
Cifonda Art Silk 102 or DMC 402

dark yellow stranded thread:
Cifonda Art Silk 175 or DMC 742

orange stranded thread:
Cifonda Art Silk 135A or DMC 947

black stranded thread:
Cifonda Art Silk Black or DMC 310

steel-grey stranded thread:
Soie d'Alger 3443 or DMC 414

silver/black metallic thread:
Kreinik Cord 105c

thick silver/black metallic thread:
Madeira Metallic No. 40 col. 442

variegated pale grey chenille thread:
col. Neutral

DETACHED FORE WING

1. Using one strand of dark yellow thread in a sharps needle, couch wire around the wing outline, leaving two tails of wire at the base of the wing. Buttonhole stitch the wire to the muslin, working the sides of the wing in dark yellow and the corners and outer edge in light grey.

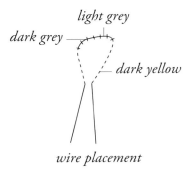

light grey

dark grey

dark yellow

wire placement

Buttonhole row: dark grey
Row 1: light grey
Row 2: light copper
Row 3: dark yellow
Row 4: medium copper
Row 5: dark yellow
Row 6: medium copper
Row 7: dark yellow

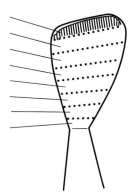

vein stitches

wire placement

2. To form the markings on the outer edge of the wing, work seven straight stitches over the wire (inside the buttonhole ridge) with dark grey thread

3. The wings are embroidered, inside the wire outline, with rows of buttonhole stitch and encroaching satin stitch. To provide guidelines for these rows, lightly pencil in seven lines as shown. With dark grey thread, work the row at the wing edge first with close, long buttonhole stitches (the ridge of the buttonhole is next to the wire).

4. Work the remainder of the wing with seven rows of straight stitches blending into each other (encroaching satin stitch), blending the first row into the long buttonhole stitches (leaving a narrow strip of dark grey inside the wire). Refer to the diagram for row colours:

5. With the fine silver/black metallic thread in a milliners needle, work the veins with fly and buttonhole stitches, using the diagram and the wing edge markings as a guide to placement.

6. With one strand of black thread, embroider six spots on the edge of the wings (inside the spaces between the veins), and three or four spots at random on the wing surface. Work each spot with three satin stitches.

DETACHED HIND WING

1. Using one strand of light grey thread, couch wire around the wing outline, leaving two tails of wire at the base of the wing, then buttonhole stitch the wire to the muslin.

2. To form the markings on the outer edge of the wing, work seven straight stitches over the wire (inside the buttonhole ridge) with dark grey thread.

3. The wings are embroidered, inside the wire outline, with rows of buttonhole stitch and encroaching satin stitch. To provide guidelines for these rows, lightly pencil in eight lines as shown. With dark grey thread, work the row at the wing edge first with close, long buttonhole stitches (the ridge of the buttonhole is next to the wire).

4. Work the remainder of the wing with eight rows of straight stitches blending into each other (encroaching satin stitch), blending the first row into the long buttonhole stitches (leaving a narrow strip of dark grey inside the wire). Refer to the diagram for row colours.

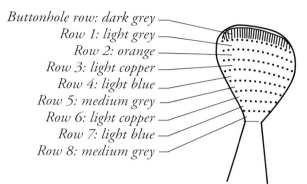

Buttonhole row: dark grey
Row 1: light grey
Row 2: orange
Row 3: light copper
Row 4: light blue
Row 5: medium grey
Row 6: light copper
Row 7: light blue
Row 8: medium grey

5. With the fine silver/black metallic thread in a milliners needle, work the veins with fly and buttonhole stitches, using the diagram and the wing edge markings as a guide to placement.

6. With black thread, embroider six spots on the edge of the wings (inside the spaces between the veins), then a row of four spots at the edge of the orange band. Work several more spots at random over the wing surface. Work each spot with three satin stitches.

vein stitches

BACKGROUND WINGS

1. The background wings, being the 'upper surface' of the butterfly, are both the same colour. Work the fore wing first, as it slightly overlaps the hind wing, then adjust the instructions as required to work the hind wing. Work the wing outline in chain stitch with one strand of thread, working the sides of the wing in dark yellow and the corners and outer edge in light grey.

2. To form the markings on the outer edge of the wing, work seven straight stitches over the chain stitch outline, with dark grey thread (six stitches for the hind wing). To replicate the edge of the detached wings, work a row of small stem stitches on the outer edge of the grey chain stitches with light grey thread (not next to the yellow chain stitches).

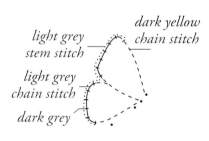

dark yellow chain stitch
light grey stem stitch
light grey chain stitch
dark grey

wing placement

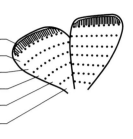

Buttonhole row: dark grey
Row 1: dark yellow
Row 2: medium copper
Row 3: dark yellow
Row 4: medium copper
Row 5: dark yellow

3. The wings are embroidered, inside the outline, with rows of buttonhole stitch and encroaching satin stitch as for the detached wings. To provide guidelines for these rows, lightly pencil in five lines as shown. With dark grey thread, work the row at the wing edge first with close, long buttonhole stitches (the ridge of the buttonhole is next to the row of chain stitch).

4. Work the remainder of the wing with five rows of straight stitches blending into each other (encroaching satin stitch), blending the first row into the long buttonhole stitches (leaving a narrow strip of dark grey inside the outline). Refer to the diagram for row colours:

vein stitches

5. With the fine silver/black metallic thread in the milliners needle, work the veins with fly and buttonhole stitches, using the diagram and the wing edge markings as a guide to placement.

TO COMPLETE THE BUTTERFLY

1. Both the abdomen and the thorax are padded with 14 strands of steel-grey thread (insert 7 strands of steel-grey thread into a chenille needle—make the tails the same length and use the thread double). To pad the abdomen, make one stitch from 3 to 4, holding the tails of thread behind the abdomen with masking tape and retaining the thread in the needle at the back until required to pad the thorax.

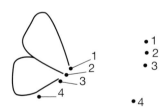

abdomen & thorax padding

2. With one strand of steel-grey thread in a size 10 crewel needle, work four couching stitches over the padding (catching in the tails of thread behind the abdomen), then, changing to a tapestry needle, cover the abdomen with six rows of raised stem stitch, working over these couching stitches towards the tail.

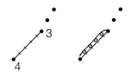

abdomen placement

3. Carefully cut out the detached wings and, using large yarn darners, insert the wire tails through the remaining dots, thus covering the background wings. Apply the fore wing first, inserting the wire tails through dots 1 and 2, then the hind wing through dots 2 and 3 (the wings share hole 2 and the back wing slightly overlaps the front wing). Bend the wire tails under the wings and secure to the back with tiny stitches. Trim the wire tails when the butterfly is finished.

background wing
fore wing
hind wing

wing placement

4. Using the retained steel-grey thread, make a padding stitch from 1 to 3—this will be wrapped with chenille thread to form the thorax. With chenille thread in the largest yarn darner, come out near 1, make two or three wraps around the padding stitch then insert the needle near 3. Make sure the chenille does not twist and adjust the tension of the wraps (thus the fluffiness of the thorax) as desired. To facilitate the wrapping, do not tighten or secure the padding thread until the stitch has been wrapped with chenille. Use stranded thread to secure all threads at the back.

thorax placement

5. With one strand of steel-grey thread, apply a 3 mm bead for the head, working the stitches towards the thorax.

6. Using the thicker silver/black metallic thread, work the antennae with two straight stitches, inserting the base of the stitches through the hole of the head bead. Work a French knot at the end of each straight stitch.

antennae, head & leg placement

7. With 2 strands of silver/black metallic thread in the milliners needle, work three straight stitches from the thorax, over the stem, to form the legs of the butterfly.

completed butterfly

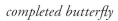

Method: Green Lacewing

The green lacewing has detached gauzy wings and a beaded abdomen.

Requirements

pale green organza:
15 cm (6 in) square

pearl metal organdie:
15 cm (6 in) square

3 mm purple/green glass beads
(Hot Spotz SBXL-449)

Mill Hill seed bead 374 *(purple/green)*

Mill Hill petite beads 42028 *(ginger)*

28 gauge silver uncovered wire (wings):
four 15 cm (6 in) lengths

32–34 gauge brass wire (antennae):
10 cm (4 in) length

pale green rayon machine thread:
Madeira Rayon 40 col. 1047

silver metallic thread:
Madeira Metallic Art. 03 col. 3010

slate/black metallic thread:
Kreinik Cord 225c

dark green stranded thread:
Soie d'Alger 2135 or DMC 3345

nylon clear thread:
Madeira Monofil 60 col. 1001

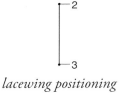

lacewing positioning

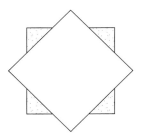

Preparation

Mark the position of the green lacewing on the background fabric, over the embroidered leaf, by making a stitch along the abdomen line (from 2 to 3) with a strand of scrap thread.

Detached Wings

1. Place the pale green organza over the pearl metal organdie, rotating one of the layers 45 degrees to be on the bias grain. Mount the fabrics into a small hoop, green organza side uppermost, making sure both layers are smooth and taut.

2. Using tweezers, bend the wire around the wing outline templates—two fore wings and two hind wings, leaving two tails of wire at the base of each wing that touch but do not cross. Place the wire shapes on the hoop of wing fabric, holding the wire tails in place with masking tape. Make sure that you have a right and a left fore wing and a right and a left hind wing.

3. Using one strand of pale green rayon machine thread in a size 10 sharps needle, stitch the wire to the wing fabric, with small, close, overcast stitches, working several stitches over both wires, at the base of the wing, to begin and end the stitching.

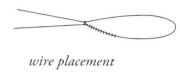

wire placement

4. Using silver metallic thread in the sharps needle, work the veins in each wing with three rows of single feather or feather stitch, using the diagram as a guide.

Note: It is safer to keep the tails of metallic thread at the front until the wings have been cut out, then insert them through the corner of the wing to the back. The tails of thread are secured after the wing has been applied to the main fabric.

vein stitches

5. Carefully cut out the wings (retaining the tails of metallic thread) and apply by inserting the wire and thread tails through the two upper dots, using a yarn darner. Apply the fore wings first, inserting the tails through 1, then the hind wings at 2. Make sure that the 'straighter' edge of each wing is the fore edge. Temporarily bend the wire tails under the wings, holding all tails in place with masking tape.

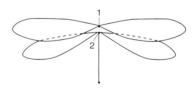

wing placement

THORAX

The thorax is worked with a bullion knot, using 7 strands of dark green thread in a small yarn darner. Bring the needle out below point 2 and insert above 1, working a curved bullion knot over the wing insertion points. Secure the thread at the back.

ABDOMEN

Select six 3 mm beads and one seed bead to form the abdomen of the lacewing. As the 3 mm beads may vary a little in size and colour, try to select beads of a similar shape that are greenish in colour. Using nylon thread in a sharps needle, apply the beads to the background fabric (along the abdomen line) as follows:

Bring the needle out 1.5 mm below 3, then remove the marking stitch.

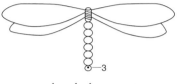

bead placement

Thread on the seed bead (the tail) and six 3 mm beads, then insert the needle next to the lower edge of the thorax. Repeat to make a second stitch through the beads.

Starting at the thorax end, work a couching stitch between each bead, keeping the beads as close together as possible. Take the needle back through all beads one more time then secure the thread at the back.

TO COMPLETE THE LACEWING

1. To secure the wire and thread tails of the wings, remove the masking tape and separate the thread tails from the wire tails. Bend the wire tails towards the abdomen line and hold on either side of the abdomen with tape, keeping the vein threads out of the way. Check the position of the wings on the front before securing the wires (the fore wings should overlap the hind wings in a tent-like fashion on either side of the abdomen). Stitch the wires to the backing (under the leaf) with green stranded thread, taking the stitches no further than the leaf edge. Do not trim the wires until the lacewing is finished.

2. Carefully pull each metallic thread tail (looking at the stitches in wings as you go) to make sure that the vein stitches are taut, then secure the metallic threads at the back.

3. Using nylon thread, stitch a 3 mm bead close to the top of the thorax, for the head—keeping the hole in the bead parallel to the top of the thorax. Bring the needle through to the front and stitch a ginger petite bead on either side of the head bead for the eyes, taking the needle through the hole of the head bead several times so that the eyes are suspended on either side. Secure the thread.

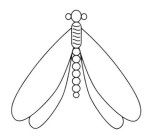

placing of head & eyes

4. Using a double strand of slate/black metallic thread in a size 9 milliners needle, work each leg with three straight stitches, using the diagram as a guide to length and position. As the legs are stitched towards the thorax, the wings will need to be gently lifted up when working the stitches.

5. To form the antennae, fold the length of brass wire in half and insert the folded end through to the back, under the head bead, using a fine yarn darner. Secure the wire end behind the thorax. Shape the wire into smooth, curved antennae by pulling between your fingers. Trim to the desired length.

Shape the wings, then trim the wire tails.

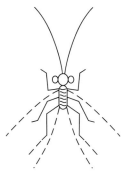

antennae placement

completed green lacewing

The Life Cycle of the *Swallowtail Butterfly*

Inspired by the wonder of metamorphosis, this embroidered panel features
the stages of the life cycle of the Swallowtail Butterfly, *Papilio machaon* —
ovum (egg), larva (caterpillar), chrysalis (pupa) and imago (butterfly):
nestled within the stems, buds and flowers of the preferred host plant,
Milk Parsley, *Peucedanum palustre* (also known as Marsh Hog's Fennel).

Worked on ivory satin, in stumpwork and surface embroidery,
this design contains beaded eggs, caterpillars in various stages of development,
a pupa worked in padded gold kid, and a butterfly with raised detached wings.
The Milk Parsley stems, leaves, buds and flowers are
embroidered with silks and beads.

Papilio machaon

Swallowtail Butterfly, Papilio machaon

The swallowtails, so-called as most have extensions on the hind wings which give the appearance of a swallow's tail, may be found in temperate or tropical zones of most countries. The Swallowtail, Papilio machaon, is one of the most handsome of the species. Also known as the Common Yellow Swallowtail and Old World Swallowtail, this striking butterfly is yellow with black wing and vein markings and a wingspan of 8-10 cm (3-4 in). The hind wings have a prominent tail which features a distinctive red and blue eye-spot. The butterfly has a strong and fast flight, but frequently pauses to hover over flowering umbelliferous plants such as fennel, parsley and dill and sip nectar.

Swallowtail Butterfly, *Papilio machaon*

Milk Parsley, *Peucedanum palustre*

Milk Parsley, Peucedanum palustre

Milk Parsley, Peucedanum palustre (also known as Marsh Hog's Fennel), is the preferred host plant for the British race of the Swallowtail Butterfly, found only in marshy areas such as the Norfolk Broads. The term 'milk' refers to the white sap found in the hollow, ridged stems of this plant, while 'parsley' references the deeply indented leaflets which are said to resemble parsley. As Milk Parsley is an umbelliferous plant, the bud and flower stalks all join in an umbrella-like fashion at the end of the stems.

DIAGRAMS ACTUAL SIZE

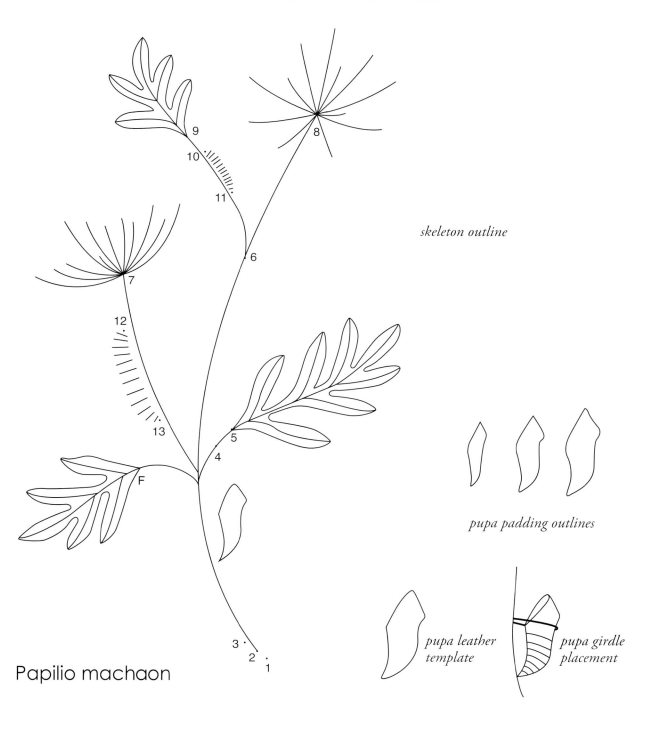

skeleton outline

pupa padding outlines

pupa leather template

pupa girdle placement

Papilio machaon

none

```

_The Swallowtail Butterfly_

# OVERALL REQUIREMENTS

.......................................................

_This is the complete list of requirements for this embroidery. For ease of use, the requirements of each individual element are repeated under its heading—for example, Milk Parsley requirements, Caterpillar requirements._

ivory satin background fabric: _35 cm (14 in) square_
quilter's muslin (or calico) backing fabric:
 _35 cm (14 in) square_
tracing paper _(I use GLAD Bake/baking parchment)_

quilter's muslin: _20 cm (8 in) square_
gold kid:
 _5 cm (2 in) square (colour kid green if desired: Copic G99 Olive)_
yellow felt: _5 x 8 cm (2 x 3 in)_
paper-backed fusible web: _5 x 8 cm (2 x 3 in)_

28 cm (11 in) embroidery hoop or stretcher bars
13 cm (5 in) embroidery hoop
_needles_
crewel/embroidery sizes 3–10
milliners/straw sizes 1 and 9
sharps sizes 10 and 12
tapestry size 26 or 28
chenille size 20
sharp yarn darners sizes 14–18
embroidery equipment _(see page 264)_

3 mm bronze/purple bead _(Hot Spotz SBXL-449)_
Mill Hill seed beads 0479 _(white)_
Mill Hill seed beads 3021 _(ivory)_
Mill Hill seed beads 0128 _(yellow)_
Mill Hill seed beads 0367 _(garnet)_
Mill Hill petite beads 40374 _(bronze/purple)_

33 gauge white covered wire:
 _four 15 cm (6 in) lengths (colour sections of wire dark grey if desired: Copic W7 Warm Grey)_

thin card (manila folder weight):
 _14 x 20 cm (5½ x 8 in)_
heavyweight (110 gsm) tracing paper
translucent removable tape
 _(e.g. Scotch Removable Magic Tape)_
```

THREAD

Note: DMC colour equivalents are close but not always an exact match for the Soie d'Alger and Cifonda colours used.

very dark green stranded thread (stems):
   Soie d'Alger 2126 or DMC 3345
dark green stranded thread (stems, leaves):
   Soie d'Alger 2125 or DMC 3346
   medium green stranded thread (stems, leaves, buds):
   Soie d'Alger 2124 or DMC 3347
light green stranded thread (stems, buds, flowers):
   Soie d'Alger 2123 or DMC 3348
very pale green stranded thread (flowers):
   Soie d'Alger 241 or DMC 772
cream stranded thread (flowers):
   Soie d'Alger Crème or DMC 3865
white stranded thread (flowers):
   Soie d'Alger Blanc or DMC Blanc

lime green stranded thread (caterpillar):
   DMC 907
black stranded thread (caterpillar): *DMC 310*
orange stranded thread (caterpillar): *DMC 946*
burnt orange stranded thread caterpillar):
   DMC 900
pale grey stranded thread (caterpillar):
   DMC 762 (pale grey)

black stranded thread (butterfly):
   Cifonda Art Silk Black or DMC 310
dark grey stranded thread (butterfly):
   Cifonda Art Silk 215 or DMC 317
light yellow stranded thread (butterfly):
   Cifonda Art Silk 1114 or DMC 744
medium yellow stranded thread:
   Cifonda Art Silk 1116 or DMC 743

blue stranded thread (butterfly):
   Cifonda Art Silk 989B or DMC 796
red stranded thread (butterfly):
   Cifonda Art Silk 254A or DMC 817
medium brown stranded thread (butterfly):
   Soie d'Alger 4534 or DMC 610
dark grey stranded thread (butterfly):
   Soie d'Alger 3446 or DMC 3799
ecru stranded thread (butterfly): *DMC Ecru*

slate/gold metallic thread (butterfly):
   Madeira Metallic No. 40 col. 484
dark grey metallic thread (caterpillar):
   Madeira Metallic No. 40 col. 360
gold/black metallic thread (pupa):
   Kreinik Cord 205c
iridescent white metallic thread (pupa):
   Couching thread 371 col. White Opal
gold sewing thread (pupa):
   Gutermann Polyester col. 488 sewing thread (Gold)
variegated brown/grey chenille thread (butterfly):
   col. Hunter Olive
medium green soft cotton padding thread (stems):
   DMC Soft Cotton 2470
lime green soft cotton padding thread (caterpillar):
   DMC Soft Cotton 2142
grey-green rayon machine thread (scientific name):
   Madeira Rayon No. 40 col. 1062
silk tacking thread
nylon clear thread:
   Madeira Monofil 60 col. 1001

PREPARATION

. . . .

1. Mount the satin background fabric and the cotton backing into the 28 cm (11 in) embroidery hoop or frame. The fabrics need to be kept very taut.

2. Cut a rectangle from thin card, 14 x 20 cm (5½ x 8 in). Place this rectangular template on the satin (checking that it is aligned with the straight grain of the fabric) and insert a fine needle at each corner point. Remove the template. Using fine silk or rayon machine thread in a sharps needle, make long stitches from each corner point, to form a stitched rectangle on the front fabric. This will be used as a reference grid when transferring the skeleton design outline and the line for the name of the butterfly (optional).

3. Using a fine lead pencil, trace the skeleton outline and rectangle outline of the design onto tracing paper. Do not trace the scientific name at this stage. Turn the tracing paper over and draw over the skeleton outline only—not the rectangle. With the tracing paper right side up, transfer the skeleton outline to the background fabric with a stylus, lining up the traced rectangle with the stitched rectangle (it helps to have a board underneath the frame of fabric to provide a firm surface).

Note: Take care to use the minimum amount of lead when tracing. If your outlines are too dark, gently press the traced outlines with pieces of masking tape or Magic Tape to remove any excess graphite.

METHOD: MILK PARSLEY

Milk Parsley, *one of the preferred host plants for the Swallowtail Butterfly, has hollow ridged stems and deeply indented leaves. As Milk Parsley is an umbelliferous plant, the bud and flower stalks all join in an umbrella-like fashion at the end of the stems.*

REQUIREMENTS

Mill Hill seed beads 0479 *(white)*

Mill Hill seed beads 3021 *(ivory)*

very dark green stranded thread:
Soie d'Alger 2126 or DMC 3345

dark green stranded thread:
Soie d'Alger 2125 or DMC 3346

medium green stranded thread:
Soie d'Alger 2124 or DMC 3347

light green stranded thread:
Soie d'Alger 2123 or DMC 3348

very pale green stranded thread:
Soie d'Alger 241 or DMC 772

cream stranded thread:
Soie d'Alger Crème or DMC 3865

white stranded thread:
Soie d'Alger Blanc or DMC Blanc

medium green soft cotton padding thread:
DMC Soft Cotton 2470

STEMS

The stems are worked in raised stem stitch, in shades of green, over a padding of soft cotton thread (one to three strands, depending on the thickness of the stem).

1. See diagram on next page. The lower section of the stem is padded with three lengths of soft cotton thread. With a 30 cm (12 in) length of soft cotton thread in a chenille needle, insert the needle at 1 (from the front) and bring out at 2. Adjust these tails of padding thread to be of equal length. Bring a 15 cm (6 in) length of soft cotton through from the back at 3, holding the tail of thread out of the way with masking tape (it will be trimmed later). Using one

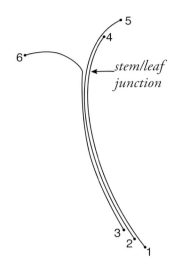

stem/leaf
junction

strand of dark green thread in a size 10 crewel needle, couch the three lengths of soft cotton thread along the lower stem line, working the couching stitches 3–4 mm apart. To produce a tapering stem, make the couching stitches 3 mm wide at the base, reducing to 2 mm halfway up the lower stem then tapering to 1 mm width just before the stem/leaf junction is reached. Make sure the couching stitches are just snug (not too tight), as nine rows of raised stem stitch will be worked over them.

2. Continue couching the two right side lengths of soft cotton thread along the right leaf stem, sinking one of the tails at 4 and the other at 5 (hold the tails out of the way with masking tape). Reduce the width of the couching stitches as the thickness of the padding reduces.

3. Couch the remaining length of soft cotton thread along the left leaf stem line, sinking the tail at 6.

4. With one strand of thread in a tapestry needle, work nine rows of raised stem stitch to cover the lower stems. The rows of stem stitch are worked in alternating shades of green to produce a striped effect, typical of the hollow stems of milk parsley. Start all rows, in a staggered fashion, along a line between 1 and 3 (i.e. row one starts at 1, row nine starts at 3), and finish each row at the point as listed.

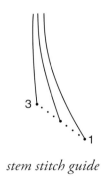

stem stitch guide

- Starting at 1 with dark green thread, work a row of raised stem stitch to 5.
- The next seven rows start at staggered points (like satin stitch) between 1 and 3.
- With very dark green thread, work a row of raised stem stitch to 5.
- With medium green thread, work a row of raised stem stitch to 5.
- With very dark green thread, work a row of raised stem stitch to 5.
- With medium green thread, work a row of raised stem stitch (the centre row), finishing at the junction of the leaf stems.
- With very dark green thread, work a row of raised stem stitch to 6.
- With medium green thread, work a row of raised stem stitch to 6.

- With very dark green thread, work a row of raised stem stitch to 6.
- Starting at 3 with dark green thread, work a row of raised stem stitch to 6.

To neaten the lower edge of the stem, work a long chain stitch from 1 to 3, with one strand of very dark green thread. Work a straight stitch inside the chain stitch if required. Trim all tails of soft cotton thread.

chain stitch placement

5. Refer to skeleton outline on page 207. Pad the left bud stem with one length of soft cotton, couched in place with one strand of medium green thread. Sink one tail of padding thread at the junction of the lower leaf stems and the other at 7. Work four rows of raised stem stitch to cover the left stem, starting the rows at the lower leaf junction and finishing at 7. Work the rows alternately in medium green and light green thread.

6. Pad the right flower stem with one length of soft cotton thread, couched in place with one strand of medium green thread. Sink one tail of padding thread at the junction of the lower leaf stems and the other at 8. Work four rows of raised stem stitch to cover the right stem, starting the rows at the lower leaf junction and finishing at 8. Work the rows alternately in medium green and light green thread.

7. Pad the upper leaf stem with one length of soft cotton thread, couched in place with one strand of medium green thread. Sink one tail of padding thread at the junction with the flower stem and the other at 9. Work four rows of raised stem stitch to cover the leaf stem, starting the rows at the junction with the flower stem (blending into the stem) and finishing at 9. Starting at the right side edge, work the rows in very dark green, medium green, very dark green and dark green.

LEAVES

The leaves are worked in padded satin stitch with one strand of thread in a size 10 crewel needle.

1. With medium green thread, work the veins in split stitch, connecting the centre vein to the row of medium green in the fleshy leaf stem.

2. Using dark green thread, outline the leaf in stem stitch then work padding stitches over the leaf surface. Embroider the leaf in satin stitch (enclosing the outline), working the stitches from the outside towards the vein (angle the needle under the vein). Start at the tip of each leaf margin and work one side at a time.

3. To make a smooth connection between the leaf and the stem, work a stitch from the lower edge of the leaf into the edge of the leaf stem.

completed milk parsley leaf

MILK PARSLEY BUDS

The bud stalks all join at the end of the stem. The bud stalks are worked in outline stitch (not stem stitch) as it produces a finer line.

1. With one strand of medium green thread, work the bud stalks in outline stitch, working from the end of each stalk towards the bud stem.

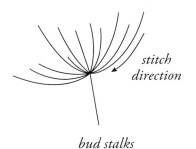

stitch direction

bud stalks

2. The buds are worked in satin stitch, 2–3 mm away from the top of the stalk, some with medium green thread and some with light green. Using one strand of either medium or light green thread in a crewel needle, work a bud with 9–10 satin stitches, all worked through the same two holes, 2–2.5 mm apart. With the same thread, work a straight stitch from the base of the bud to the top of the stalk. Embroider approximately five buds per stalk, less if the stalks are behind others. Work the front stalks first, then the back stalks.

3. Work sepals at the base of the stalks in outline stitch with medium green thread.

bud sepals

MILK PARSLEY FLOWERS

The flower stalks are worked in outline stitch (not stem stitch) as it produces a finer line.

1. With one strand of light green thread, work the flower stalks in outline stitch, working from the end of each stalk towards the flower stem.

2. Work the flower heads with a mixture of French knots (white, cream and very pale green) and beads (white and ivory):

Work the French knots with 6 strands of thread (one wrap), in a size 1 milliners needle.

Apply the beads with a double strand of matching thread in a size 10 crewel needle. Take one stitch through the bead, then another stitch 'around' the bead (through the same two holes but not through the bead—allowing the stitch to 'split' around the bead); this keeps the bead stable.

completed milk parsley buds

Start with a French knot at the end of a stalk, then work knots and apply beads to fill a rounded shape around the first knot. Take care not to make the blossoms too even or symmetrical. It is easier to have all threads and beads going at the same time.

completed milk parsley flower

METHOD: SWALLOWTAIL BUTTERFLY

This embroidered panel features the stages of the life cycle of the Swallowtail Butterfly—
ovum (egg), larva (caterpillar), chrysalis (pupa) and imago (butterfly).

REQUIREMENTS

quilter's muslin: *20 cm (8 in) square*

gold kid: 5 cm (2 in) square *(colour kid green if desired: Copic G99 Olive)*

yellow felt: *5 x 8 cm (2 x 3 in)*

paper-backed fusible web: *5 x 8 cm (2 x 3 in)*

3 mm bronze/purple bead *(Hot Spotz SBXL-449)*

Mill Hill seed beads 0128 *(yellow)*

Mill Hill seed beads 0367 *(garnet)*

Mill Hill petite beads 40374 *(bronze/purple)*

33 gauge white covered wire:

four 15 cm (6 in) lengths

(colour sections of wire dark grey if desired:

Copic W7 Warm Grey)

swallowtail butterfly,
larva & pupa

THREAD REQUIREMENTS

lime green stranded thread: *DMC 907*

black stranded thread: *DMC 310*

medium orange stranded thread: *DMC 946*

dark orange stranded thread: *DMC 900*

pale grey stranded thread: *DMC 762*

black stranded thread:
Cifonda Art Silk Black or DMC 310

dark grey stranded thread:
Cifonda Art Silk 215 or DMC 317

light yellow stranded thread:
Cifonda Art Silk 1114 or DMC 744

medium yellow stranded thread:
Cifonda Art Silk 1116 or DMC 743

blue stranded thread:
Cifonda Art Silk 989B or DMC 796

red stranded thread:
Cifonda Art Silk 254A or DMC 817

medium brown stranded thread:
Soie d'Alger 4534 or DMC 610

dark grey stranded thread:
Soie d'Alger 3446 or DMC 3799

ecru stranded thread: *DMC Ecru*

slate/gold metallic thread:
Madeira Metallic No. 40 col. 484

dark grey metallic thread:
Madeira Metallic No. 40 col. 360

gold/black metallic thread:
Kreinik Cord 205c

iridescent white metallic thread:
Couching thread 371 col. White Opal

gold sewing thread:
Gutermann Polyester col. 488 sewing thread

variegated brown/grey chenille thread:
col. Hunter Olive

lime green soft cotton padding thread:
DMC Soft Cotton 2142

grey/green rayon machine thread:
Madeira Rayon No. 40 col. 1062

silk tacking thread

nylon clear thread:
Madeira Monofil 60 col. 1001

Egg (ovum)

The female butterfly lays single yellow eggs on the leaves and stems of Milk Parsley.

With one strand of light yellow thread, stitch yellow beads at leaf or stem indentations for the eggs.

completed eggs

SMALL CATERPILLAR (LARVA)

After about ten to twelve days, the egg hatches to reveal a tiny black caterpillar with a white patch on its back (resembling a bird dropping), but as it grows it becomes more highly coloured and conspicuous.

Theoretically, this caterpillar should have thirteen segments plus a head. I soon gave up trying to replicate this—near enough was good enough! The caterpillar is worked in raised stem stitch over padding.

1. With 6 strands of black thread in a chenille needle, work four long stitches, between dots 10 and 11, to pad the caterpillar. With one strand of black thread, work 11–12 couching stitches over the padding, using the lines from the skeleton outline as a guide.

coaching stitch guide

2. Stitch a garnet seed bead at end of the padding (10) for the head, the hole in the bead parallel to the stem. Work approximately 6–8 rows of raised stem stitch, over the couching stitches, to fill the caterpillar, taking about four rows through the head bead.

3. The centre of the caterpillar has a whitish patch. Work satin stitches over two of the centre segments (3 satin stitches each) with one strand of pale grey thread. Leave a sliver of black showing between each band of grey.

caterpillar markings

4. Each segment has a black spike at the top. With one strand of black thread in a size 12 sharps needle, work a tiny straight stitch into each segment (aiming for 12), including one above the head.

5. Work two tiny French knots in each of eleven segments (I managed nine) using dark orange thread in a size 10 sharps needle. My notes had the word 'Crazy!' at the end—I can see why!

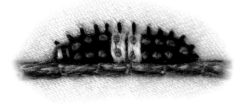

completed small caterpillar

Large Caterpillar (larva)

The caterpillar sheds its skin (moults) three times, becoming fully grown in six or seven weeks. By the third moulting the larva has developed the colours of a fully grown caterpillar—bands of black dotted with orange, alternating with pale green. In the last skin, the green caterpillar becomes much brighter. If disturbed, the caterpillar protrudes a forked, bright orange tubercle from just behind the head, the osmeterium, which emits a pungent odour.

1. The caterpillar has thirteen segments plus a head. On the skeleton outline, the caterpillar body is indicated by twelve straight lines and a dot at each end (12 and 13). With one strand of lime green thread, work a row of backstitch around the body as follows:

- Starting and ending at the dots and using the straight lines as a guide, work thirteen back stitches along the lower edge, leaving a small space for the legs (1 mm).
- Work a row of thirteen backstitches across the top edge, using the straight lines as a guide.

backstitch guide

2. With lime green soft cotton thread, doubled, in a chenille needle, make three long stitches inside the outline to pad the caterpillar (the first stitch in the centre, slightly shorter than the outline, a longer stitch at the lower edge, then slightly shorter at the top). Hold the tails out of the way at the back with masking tape—they will be trimmed when the caterpillar is finished. Using one strand of lime green thread, work twelve couching stitches over the padding, using the back stitches as a guide to placement. As the caterpillar will be worked in raised stem stitch, do not pull these stitches too tight.

3. Stitch a 3 mm bead at the end of the padding (12) for the head, the hole in the bead parallel to the stem.

4. With lime green thread in a tapestry needle, work rows of raised stem stitch over the couching stitches to cover the caterpillar, working short rows almost every alternate row (to allow for the tapering head and tail), and taking the needle through the head bead on each full row (approximately 16 rows).

5. With dark grey metallic thread in a size 9 milliners needle, work twelve couching stitches over the raised stem stitch to form the segment lines, pulling gently to form slight indentations (13 segments).

6. The pattern of bright stripes and spots on this caterpillar is worked with one strand of thread in a size 10 crewel needle:

- Using black thread, make two straight stitches, side by side, in the centre of each segment, working from the top edge of the caterpillar to almost two-thirds of the way down (the tail segment has only one black stitch).
- With medium orange thread, make three French knots (one wrap) in each segment except the last two. Make two knots in the second last segment and one knot in the tail segment. Take care to bring the needle up in one of the black stitches and down in the other so as not to split the 'stripe'.

leg placement

7. Work two bullion knots in medium orange thread, just above the head, to form the osmeterium. Using a size 9 milliners needle, work the 'upper' bullion with twelve wraps and the 'lower' bullion with ten wraps.

8. Using 4 strands of lime green thread, work the legs in French knots (one wrap) in the positions marked on the diagram (eight legs).

completed caterpillar

Pupa (chrysalis)

When the caterpillar is fully fed, it crawls away into reed beds to moult to the pupal stage. Attaching its hindquarters to a silk pad on a stem, it weaves a silk girdle around its middle before moulting for the last time, giving rise to a pupa. Depending on the environment, the pupa may be green, if surrounded by leaves, or greyish brown, if on tree branches.

1. Trace the three pupa padding shapes from the skeleton outline on to the paper side of paper-backed fusible web, then fuse to the yellow felt. Cut out the shapes. Using gold sewing thread, apply the padding to the background fabric with small stab stitches, applying the smallest shape first.

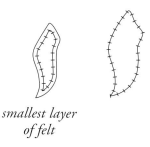

smallest layer of felt

2. Trace the pupa leather template onto a Post-it note (the sticky end under the tracing). Cut out the paper template and check against the padding for size (it needs to cover the felt padding) before sticking the template to the gold side of the kid leather. Carefully cut out the leather shape around the template.

Note: I coloured the gold kid with an olive green Copic marking pen to give a green tinge. This is optional.

pupa markings

3. Using nylon thread in a size 12 sharps needle, apply the leather over the felt padding with small stab stitches, first working securing stitches at the corners and sides, then all the way round, nudging the edge of the leather towards the felt with a nailfile or fingers as you go.

4. With gold/black metallic thread in a size 9 milliners needle, work seven couching stitches over the lower surface of the pupa to form the segment lines. Work a long chain stitch at the top of the pupa.

5. With white opal couching thread in a size 1 milliners needle, work two stitches, as shown, to form the 'silk girdle'.

completed pupa

BUTTERFLY (IMAGO)

Inside the protective case of the pupa, an amazing transformation takes place. The former larval tissues are broken down, and the new tissues of the future butterfly are formed. When the butterfly first emerges from the pupa, its wings are soft and crumpled. It moves to a place where the wings can hand downwards, and sits still while blood pumps through the wing veins to stiffen and flatten the wings. Once the wings are dry, the butterfly flies off in search of a mate.

Work the butterfly using the instructions, and detached wing outlines, provided for the Swallowtail Butterfly in the Specimen Box, pages 116–123.

Swallowtail Butterfly, *Papilio machaon*

Fig. 1: egg

Fig. 2: young larva

Figs 3 and 4: larva

Fig. 5 pupa

Figs 6 and 7: adult butterfly

Fig. 8: osmeterium *(forked process behind caterpillar's head from which it can emit a disgusting odour)*

Fig. 9: cremaster *(pupal hook-like attachment)*

Plant: Wild carrot *(Daucus carrota)*

Scientific Name

The lower edge of the stitched rectangle around the design is used to position the guidelines for stitching the scientific name of the butterfly, *Papilio machaon*. Adding the name is optional.

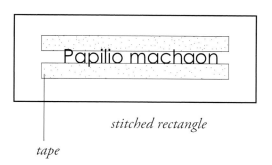

stitched rectangle

tape

Requirements

- grey-green rayon machine thread (scientific name): *Madeira Rayon No. 40 col. 1062*
- heavyweight (110 gsm) tracing paper
- translucent removable tape *(e.g. Scotch Removable Magic Tape)*

1. Trace the guidelines and scientific name onto a small rectangle of tracing paper. This will be used as a template when stitching the name to the background.

2. Apply rows of Magic Tape, 3.5 mm apart, to the background fabric to form the guidelines for the name. The letters will be stitched in the space between the two rows of tape (lifting the end of the upper tape to stitch the first letter P).

3. Place the tracing paper over the over the taped guidelines, lining up the traced lines with the taped lines. Secure the tracing to the left side edge with masking tape, allowing the tracing to be flipped up and down to help with placement of letters when stitching.

4. Using one strand of grey-green rayon thread in a sharps needle, stitch the letters, in the space between the rows of tape, with tiny back stitches, using the traced outline as a guide (aim to work five back stitches for the downward stroke of the letters).

5. Finally, remove the stitched rectangle.

completed butterfly

Bramble Garland &
Emerald Moth

This embroidered panel was inspired by two beautiful hand-coloured engravings—one depicting of the life cycle of the Large Emerald Moth, *Geometra papilionaria,* and the other showing the Blackberry, *Rubus fruticosus—* published in the eighteenth century in Amsterdam by Jan Christiaan Sepp.

Worked on cream silk dupion in stumpwork and surface embroidery, this design features a garland of blackberry flowers, with detached petals and buds, surface embroidered leaves, and raised berries, in various stages of ripeness, worked in French knots and beads. Nestled within the foliage are the stages of the life cycle of the Large Emerald Moth—beaded eggs, a looper caterpillar, a pupa worked in padded bronze snakeskin, and a moth with raised detached wings.

Blackberry, Rubus fruticosus

The **Blackberry**, Rubus fruticosus, also known as Bramble (a word meaning impenetrable scrub), is a rambling, perennial shrub that grows as a tangle of dense, arching, thorny stems. A member of the Rosaceae (rose) family, the bramble is a very common plant in hedgerows and woods, where it is a food source for many caterpillars, birds and some grazing animals, such as deer. Growing wild throughout much of the world, it is considered an invasive weed in many countries.

The blackberry plant has compound leaves of three to five leaflets, with flowers of white or pale pink produced in late spring and early summer. The flowers ripen to a black or dark purple fruit, known as a 'blackberry'. In strict botanical terms, however, the fruit is not a true berry, but rather an aggregate fruit comprised of numerous small drupelets (individual fruit). The blackberry tends to be red during its unripe ('green') phase, leading to the old expression that 'blackberries are red when they are green'. Ripe, ripening and unripe berries often appear on the same plant.

Blackberry, *Rubus fruticosus*

As blackberries produce an abundance of fruit in late autumn, it can be assumed that they have been eaten by humans for many thousands of years (there is forensic evidence from the Iron Age Haraldskær Woman indicating that she consumed blackberries some 2500 years ago). The soft fruit is popular for use in desserts, jams, seedless jellies and sometimes wine. A tea, which has a light blackberry-like flavour, can be made by steeping the leaves. Good nectar producers, blackberry shrubs bearing flowers yield a medium to dark fruity honey.

Diagrams Actual Size

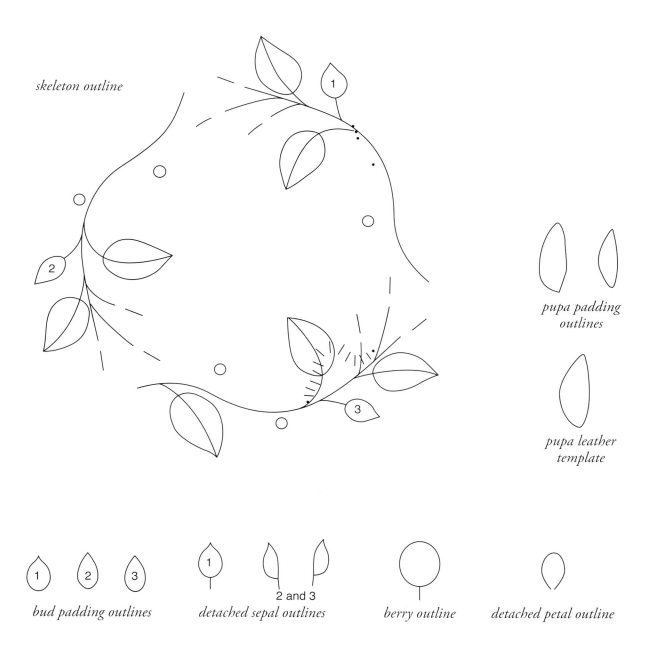

skeleton outline

1

2

3

pupa padding
outlines

pupa leather
template

bud padding outlines

detached sepal outlines

2 and 3

berry outline

detached petal outline

Large Emerald Moth, *Geometra papilionaria*

Large Emerald Moth, Geometra papilionaria

Among lepidopterans, green wings are something of an exception, but among geometrids, there are many green species. The largest of these, the **Large Emerald Moth**, Geometra papilionaria, has delicate blue-green wings crossed with faint wavy lines.

The Large Emerald Moth belongs to a large family, the Geometridae, whose caterpillars have characteristic looping movements. Unlike most caterpillars, those of the geometers have legs at each end but none in the middle, hence their method of crawling entails the arching of the body into a loop then extending forward as if the distance spanned, hence the family name Geometridae, which means 'earth-measuring'. The caterpillars are also known as loopers or inch-worms.

OVERALL REQUIREMENTS

....

This is the complete list of requirements for this embroidery. For ease of use, the requirements of each individual element are repeated under its heading—for example, Blackberry requirements, Emerald Moth requirements.

cream silk dupion background fabric:
  32 cm (13 in) square
quilter's muslin (or calico) backing fabric:
  35 cm (13 in) square
tracing paper *(I use GLAD Bake/baking parchment)*

quilter's muslin: *five 20 cm (8 in) squares*
red cotton fabric (homespun): *15 cm (6 in) square*
dark purple cotton fabric (homespun):
  15 cm (6 in) square
bronze snakeskin or kid leather:
  2.5 cm (1 in) square
white felt: *5 x 8 cm (2 x 3 in)*
yellow felt: *5 x 8 cm (2 x 3 in)*
paper-backed fusible web: *two (5 x 8 cm (2 x 3 in))*
light coloured tracing/carbon paper (e.g. Clover
Charcopy): *5 x 8 cm (2 x 3 in)*

25 cm (10 in) embroidery hoop or stretcher bars
13 cm (5 in) embroidery hoop
10 cm (4 in) embroidery hoop

needles
crewel/embroidery sizes 3–10
milliners/straw sizes 1 and 9
sharps sizes 10 and 12
tapestry size 26 or 28
chenille size 18
sharp yarn darners sizes 14–18
embroidery equipment *(see page 264)*

3 mm blue/purple glass bead
  (Hot Spotz SBXL-449)
Mill Hill seed bead 2003 *(peach)*
Mill Hill seed bead 2013 *(red)*
Mill Hill seed bead 2031 *(lime)*
Mill Hill antique beads 3025 *(purple)*
Mill Hill antique beads 3038 *(ginger)*
Mill Hill petite beads 42028 *(ginger)*

33 gauge white covered wire (flower petals):
  twenty-five 9 cm (3½ in) lengths
33 gauge white covered wire (bud sepals):
  five 9 cm (3½ in) lengths
33 gauge white covered wire (moth):
  four 10 cm (4 in) lengths

OVERALL REQUIREMENTS (CONTINUED)

....

THREAD *Note: DMC colour equivalents are close but not always an exact match for the Soie d'Alger and Cifonda colours used.*

dark rust stranded thread (stems):
  Soie d'Alger 2626 or DMC 918
dark green/gold stranded thread (stems):
  Soie d'Alger 2225 or DMC 730
dark olive stranded thread (leaves):
  Soie d'Alger 2145 or DMC 580
medium olive stranded thread (leaves):
  Soie d'Alger 2144 or DMC 581
light olive stranded thread (leaves):
  Soie d'Alger 2143 or DMC 166
pale lime stranded thread (sepals):
  Soie d'Alger 2221 or DMC 3819

white stranded thread (flowers):
  Soie d'Alger Blanc or DMC Blanc
pale pink stranded thread (flowers):
  Soie d'Alger 3041 or DMC 819
light green/gold stranded thread (flowers):
  Soie d'Alger 2223 or DMC 734

very dark purple stranded thread (berries):
  Soie d'Alger 3326 or DMC 939
dark purple stranded thread (berries):
  Soie d'Alger 3316 or DMC (not an exact match)
medium purple stranded thread (berries):
  Soie d'Alger 5116 or DMC 154
dark red stranded thread (berries):
  Soie d'Alger 945 or DMC 304
medium red stranded thread (berries):
  Soie d'Alger 2916 or DMC 3831
dark coral stranded thread (berries):
  Soie d'Alger 2915 or DMC 3712

medium coral stranded thread (berries):
  Soie d'Alger 2914 or DMC 760
light coral stranded thread (berries):
  Soie d'Alger 2942 or DMC 761

dark jade stranded thread (caterpillar): *DMC 987*
medium jade stranded thread (caterpillar):
  DMC 988
light jade stranded thread (caterpillar): *DMC 165*
medium rust stranded thread (caterpillar):
  DMC 920

white stranded thread (moth):
  Cifonda Art Silk White or DMC Blanc
very pale green stranded thread (moth):
  Cifonda Art Silk 491 or DMC 3813
light green stranded thread (moth):
  Cifonda Art Silk 492 or DMC 503
medium green stranded thread (moth):
  Cifonda Art Silk 493 or DMC 502
dark green stranded thread (moth):
  Cifonda Art Silk 494 or DMC 501
light gold stranded thread (moth):
  Cifonda Art Silk 48 or DMC 729
medium gold stranded thread (moth):
  Soie d'Alger 3815 or DMC 167
ecru stranded thread: *DMC Ecru*

brown/black metallic thread (pupa):
  Kreinik Cord 201c
variegated dark green/gold chenille thread
  (butterfly): *col. Fire*
nylon clear thread:
  Madeira Monofil 60 col. 1001

Preparation

1. Mount the silk background fabric and the cotton backing into the 25 cm (10 in) embroidery hoop or frame. The fabrics need to be kept very taut.

2. Cut a 15 cm (6 in) square from thin card or paper. Place the square template on the silk dupion (checking that it is aligned with the straight grain of the fabric) and insert a fine needle at each corner point. Remove the template. Using fine silk or rayon machine thread in a sharps needle, make long stitches from each corner point to form a stitched square on the background fabric. This will be used as a reference grid when transferring the skeleton design outline.

3. Using a fine lead pencil, trace the skeleton outline and square outline of the design onto tracing paper. Turn the tracing paper over and draw over the skeleton outline only—not the square.

4. Turn the tracing back to the right side and attach to the silk with small strips of masking tape on each side (check that the traced square is aligned with the stitched square).

5. Place a tracing board (or small book) inside the back of the hoop for support, then transfer the design by tracing over the outline with a tracing pen or stylus.

Note: Take care to use the minimum amount of lead when tracing. If your outlines are too dark, gently press the traced outlines with pieces of masking tape or Magic Tape to remove any excess graphite.

ORDER OF WORK

1. STEMS
2. BACKGROUND LEAVES
3. BACKGROUND BUD PETALS
4. BERRIES
5. EGGS
6. CATERPILLAR
7. PUPA
8. FLOWERS AND BUDS
9. MOTH

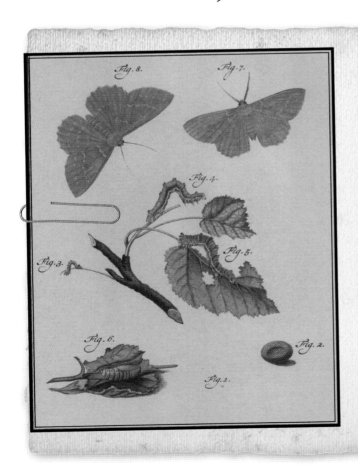

Large Emerald Moth,
Geometra papilionaria

Fig. 1: egg

Fig. 2: egg enlarged to show detail

Figs 3: young larva

Fig. 4 & 5: larva

Figs 6: pupa

Fig. 7: male adult moth

Fig. 8: female adult moth

Plant: Birch *(Bertula sp)*

METHOD: BLACKBERRY

Also known as Bramble, the blackberry is a rambling shrub that grows as a tangle of arching, thorny stems. Flowers of white or pale pink are produced in late spring and early summer, ripening to a black or dark purple fruit.

REQUIREMENTS

quilter's muslin: *four 20 cm (8 in) squares*

red cotton fabric (homespun): *15 cm (6 in) square*

dark purple cotton fabric (homespun): *15 cm (6 in) square*

white felt: *5 x 8 cm (2 x 3 in)*

paper-backed fusible web: *5 x 8 cm (2 x 3 in)*

light coloured tracing/carbon paper (e.g. Clover Charcopy):
  5 x 8 cm (2 x 3 in)

Mill Hill seed bead 2003 *(peach)*

Mill Hill seed bead 2013 *(red)*

Mill Hill seed bead 2031 *(citron)*

Mill Hill antique beads 3025 *(purple)*

Mill Hill petite beads 42028 *(ginger)*

33 gauge white covered wire (flower petals):
  twenty-five 9 cm (3½ in) lengths

33 gauge white covered wire (bud sepals):
  five 9 cm (3½ in) lengths

THREAD REQUIREMENTS

dark rust stranded thread:
Soie d'Alger 2626 or DMC 918

dark green/gold stranded thread:
Soie d'Alger 2225 or DMC 730

dark olive stranded thread:
Soie d'Alger 2145 or DMC 580

medium olive stranded thread:
Soie d'Alger 2144 or DMC 581

light olive stranded thread:
Soie d'Alger 2143 or DMC 166

pale lime stranded thread:
Soie d'Alger 2221 or DMC 3819

white stranded thread:
Soie d'Alger Blanc or DMC Blanc

pale pink stranded thread:
Soie d'Alger 3041 or DMC 819

light green/gold stranded thread:
Soie d'Alger 2223 or DMC 734

very dark purple stranded thread:
Soie d'Alger 3326 or DMC 939

dark purple stranded thread:
Soie d'Alger 3316 or DMC (not an exact match)

medium purple stranded thread:
Soie d'Alger 5116 or DMC 154

dark red stranded thread:
Soie d'Alger 945 or DMC 304

medium red stranded thread:
Soie d'Alger 2916 or DMC 3831

dark coral stranded thread:
Soie d'Alger 2915 or DMC 3712

medium coral stranded thread:
Soie d'Alger 2914 or DMC 760

light coral stranded thread:
Soie d'Alger 2942 or DMC 761

nylon clear thread:
Madeira Monofil 60 col. 1001

fine silk or rayon tacking thread

STEMS

The stems are embroidered in stem stitch with dark green/gold and dark rust threads. Work all rows of stem stitch with 2 strands of thread in a size 8 crewel needle. The garland is made up of three sprigs of blackberry, each worked in the same manner.

1. Starting at the base of a sprig, with one strand each of dark green/gold and dark rust thread, work a row of stem stitch along the main stem line to the base of the right side berry, then work the middle berry stem.

2. Using 2 strands of dark green/gold thread, work a second row of stem stitch (on the left side of the first row) along the main stem line to the base of the left side berry.

3. Work the remaining two sprigs in the same way to complete the garland.

Note: The leaf and bud stems are worked at a later stage.

LEAVES

The leaves are worked in padded buttonhole stitch with one strand of thread in a size 10 crewel needle. Vary the leaves with the shades of thread used— dark olive, medium olive and light olive.

Dark Leaf

1. Work the central vein in split stitch with light olive thread.

2. Work the stem in stem stitch with one strand of dark olive thread.

3. Using dark olive thread, work a row of small back stitches around the leaf outline, then work straight padding stitches within the outline.

4. With dark olive thread, embroider each side of the leaf with long buttonhole stitches (worked at an angle), starting at the base of the leaf and enclosing the back stitch outline. Insert the needle slightly under the central vein (to avoid a gap).

Medium-dark Leaf

1. Work the central vein in split stitch with light olive thread.

2. Work the stem in stem stitch with dark olive or medium olive thread.

3. Using dark olive thread, outline one side of the leaf with a row of small back stitches, then work straight padding stitches within the stitched outline. With medium olive thread, outline the remaining side of the leaf with a row of small back stitches, then work padding stitches within this outline.

stem outline

leaf stitch guide

completed medium-dark leaf

4. Embroider each side of the leaf with long buttonhole stitches (worked at an angle and enclosing the outline), using dark olive thread on one side and medium olive thread on the other side.

Using the appropriate threads, and the methods above, embroider two leaves in dark olive thread, two leaves using dark and medium olive threads, two leaves in medium olive thread, two leaves with medium and light olive threads and one leaf in light olive thread.

Buds

Trace bud padding shapes 1, 2 and 3 on to paper-backed fusible web then fuse to white felt. Carefully cut out the shapes.

Bud 1

1. Using one strand of pale lime thread, apply the felt bud padding (web side up) to the background fabric with stab stitches.

2. Cover the bud padding with long buttonhole stitches (like satin stitch), working the ridge of the buttonhole across the top edge of the shape.

bud stitch guide

Buds 2 & 3

1. Using white thread, apply the felt bud padding to the background fabric with stab stitches. Cover the bud padding with long buttonhole stitches, working the ridge of the buttonhole across the top edge of the shape.

Detached Sepals

1. Mount a square of muslin into a 10 cm (4 in) hoop and trace the five detached sepal outlines—one sepal 1 outline, and two pairs of side sepal outlines (for buds 2 and 3).

wire placement

2. Using one strand of pale lime thread, couch wire around the sepal outline, leaving two tails of wire at the base that touch but do not cross. Buttonhole stitch the wire to the muslin. Work a row of split stitch around the inside edge of the wire, then a few padding stitches inside the sepal.

 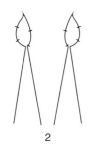 

1   2   3

3. Embroider the sepal in satin stitch, enclosing the split stitch and working the stitches towards the base of the sepal. Cut out the sepals and shape slightly.

xxxxxxxxx

To Complete the Buds

1. Using a yarn darner, insert the wire tails of sepal 1 through to the back at the base of the background bud 1. Bend the wire tails behind the embroidered sepal and secure with a few stitches. Do not trim until the bud is finished.

2. For bud 2, insert the wire tails of both side sepals through one hole at the base of the background bud. Bend the wire tails behind the embroidered bud and secure with a few stitches. Do not trim until the bud is finished. Repeat for bud 3.

3. Using one strand of light olive thread, work the bud stem in stem stitch. Work several satin stitches over the stem, below the bud, to form a base (and cover the wire insertion point). Shape the sepals and trim the wire tails.

completed buds 1 & 2

FLOWERS

The blackberry flowers require twenty-five detached petals—fifteen white and ten pale pink petals. To avoid soiling the pale edges of the petals with a traced lead pencil outline, the wires are bent into a petal shape first, before applying to the muslin. Use tweezers, and the detached petal outline as a template, to bend the wires into the required petal shapes. Work all the petals on two or three hoops of muslin and keep aside until required.

completed bud 3

1. Mount a square of muslin into a 13 cm (5 in) hoop. Shape a 9 cm (3½ in) length of wire around the detached petal outline, leaving two tails of wire at the base that touch but do not cross.

2. With one strand of white thread in a size 10 crewel needle, couch the shaped wire to the muslin. Then stitch the wire to the muslin with small, close buttonhole stitches, incorporating the couching stitches and working the buttonhole ridge on the outside edge of the petal.

petal stitch guide

3. Work a row of long and short buttonhole stitch inside the top edge of the petal (close to the wire), then embroider the petal in long and short stitch, working all stitches towards the base of the petal. Work fifteen white petals and ten pale pink petals.

To Complete the Flower

1. Carefully cut out the petals, close to the buttonholed edge and avoiding the wire tails.

2. Make five evenly spaced pencil dots around the circle outline. Using a yarn darner, insert the wire tails of five detached petals through the five dots. Bend the wires behind the petals and secure to the backing fabric with small stitches using ecru thread. Do not cut the wires until the flower is finished.

3. With 2 strands of light green/gold thread in a size 9 milliners needle, work a circle of ten Turkey knots inside the circle outline—two knots at the base of each petal—leaving a small space in the centre. Keep the tails of the Turkey knots quite long (5 cm/2 in) to make the centre easier to manage (the knots are really close together).

4. With one strand of pale lime thread, stitch a lime seed bead in the centre space. Work two stitches through the bead, taking care not to catch the Turkey knots.

5. Cut the loops of the Turkey knots then comb the threads into a bundle (like a tassel) above the surface of the petals. Holding the bundle firmly, cut straight across the threads, just above the bead (about 3 mm above the surface of the fabric). Take care to hold the blades of the scissors parallel to the background. Shape the petals then trim the wires.

petal insertion points

completed flowers

Blackberries

Blackberries range greatly in colour, from dark black-purples, to luscious rich reds and pale greenish pinks. Work three of each colour and apply at the ends of the stems, using the photograph as a guide to placement.

Purple Berries

1. Mount a square of dark purple cotton fabric into a small hoop. Using a coloured tracing (carbon) paper, trace three berry outlines, including the stem line.

2. Using 6 strands of thread in a size 1 milliners needle, fill the berry outlines with French knots (one wrap), working knots in very dark purple, dark purple and medium purple threads.

3. With one strand of dark purple thread in a size 10 crewel needle, work a row of running stitch around the berry, about 1 mm away from the edge of the knots. Start and end the running stitch at the stem line, leaving two tails of thread on the front.

4. Cut out the shape, about 1.5 mm away from the running stitch, avoiding the tails of thread. Pull the tails of thread up to form a berry shape then tie off (the gathered edges are now beneath the shape).

5. Thread the tails into a needle and insert about 2 mm above the end of the stem (check the position and reinsert the needle if necessary). Pull the tails of thread firmly and hold behind the stem with masking tape.

6. With one strand of dark purple thread (the tail of the gathering thread can be used), apply the berry with small invisible stab stitches, bringing the needle out from under the berry and taking a small stitch into the fabric between the French knots. First work four stitches (north, south, east and west), then continue around the edge.

7. Using the same thread, stitch two or three purple beads between the French knots, taking the needle through to the back each time (take care not to flatten the surface of the berry). Shape the fruit with your fingers.

running stitch guide

shaped berry

completed purple & red berries

RED BERRIES

1. Mount a square of red cotton fabric into a small hoop. Trace three berry outlines, including the stem line.

2. Using 6 strands of thread, fill the berry outlines with French knots, working knots in dark red and medium red threads. Complete as for the purple berries, substituting red threads and red beads.

PINK BERRIES

1. Mount a square of quilter's muslin into a small hoop. Trace three berry outlines, including the stem line.

2. Using 6 strands of thread, fill the berry outlines with French knots, working knots in dark coral, medium coral and light coral threads. Complete as for the purple berries, substituting coral threads and pink beads.

SEPALS

Work three sepals at the base of each berry in needleweaving (see needleweaving diagram on page 274 of the Stitch Glossary), working the sepals of some berries with pale lime thread and others in light olive thread.

1. Using one strand of pale lime (or light olive) thread in a size 10 crewel needle, bring the needle out at the base of the berry then insert again approximately 2 mm away, leaving a loop about 4 mm in length. Work a second loop, exactly the same as the first, to make the loop double. Pass a length of scrap thread through the loop to enable it to be held under tension while working the needleweaving.

2. Bring the needle out again at the base of the berry and change to a tapestry needle. Holding the loop under tension with the scrap thread, slide the needle through the centre of the loop, alternately from right and left, to fill the loop with needleweaving, keeping the tension firm and even. Remove the scrap thread and insert the needle through to the back, slightly shorter than the length woven, thus causing the sepal to curve slightly. Work two more sepals, one on each side of the first.

*completed pink
& red berries
with sepals*

METHOD: LARGE EMERALD MOTH

This embroidered panel features the stages of the life cycle of the Large Emerald Moth—
ovum (egg), larva (caterpillar), chrysalis (pupa) and imago (moth).

REQUIREMENTS

quilter's muslin:
20 cm (8 in) square

bronze snakeskin or kid leather:
2.5 cm (1 in) square

yellow felt:
5 x 8 cm (2 x 3 in)

paper-backed fusible web:
5 x 8 cm (2 x 3 in)

3 mm blue/purple glass bead
(Hot Spotz SBXL-449)

Mill Hill antique beads 3038 *(ginger)*

Mill Hill petite beads 42028 *(ginger)*

33 gauge white covered wire:
four 10 cm (4 in) lengths

dark jade stranded thread:
DMC 987

medium jade stranded thread:
DMC 988

light jade stranded thread:
DMC 165

medium rust stranded thread:
DMC 920

white stranded thread:
Cifonda Art Silk White or DMC Blanc

very pale green stranded thread:
Cifonda Art Silk 491 or DMC 3813

light green stranded thread:
Cifonda Art Silk 492 or DMC 503

medium green stranded thread:
Cifonda Art Silk 493 or DMC 502

dark green stranded thread:
Cifonda Art Silk 494 or DMC 501

light gold stranded thread:
Cifonda Art Silk 48 or DMC 729

medium gold stranded thread:
Soie d'Alger 3815 or DMC 167

ecru stranded thread:
DMC Ecru

brown/black metallic thread:
Kreinik Cord 201c

variegated dark green/gold chenille thread:
col. Fire

nylon clear thread:
Madeira Monofil 60 col. 1001

completed eggs

EGG (OVUM)

The female moth lays eggs on the leaves of the host plant. As they develop they change in colour from white, to greenish yellow and then brownish pink.

With one strand of nylon thread in a size 12 sharps needle, stitch from 5 to 7 petite ginger beads on the surface of one of the bramble leaves, for the eggs of the moth.

CATERPILLAR (LARVA)

Unlike most caterpillars, those of the Large Emerald Moth have legs at each end but none in the middle, hence their method of crawling entails the arching of the body into a loop then extending forward as if measuring the distance spanned. These caterpillars are also known as loopers or inch-worms.

1. A caterpillar has thirteen segments plus a head. On the skeleton outline, the caterpillar body is indicated by twelve straight lines and a dot at each end. With one strand of medium jade thread in a size 10 crewel needle, work a row of backstitch around the body as follows:

backstitch guide

- Starting at the tail dot, and using the straight stitches as a guide, work thirteen backstitches along the lower curved edge, ending at the head dot.
- Work a row of thirteen backstitches across the top curved edge, using the straight lines as a guide.

2. With 6 strands of medium jade thread, doubled, in a chenille needle, make two long 'looped' stitches inside the backstitched outline to pad the caterpillar (hold the tails out of the way at the back with masking tape—they will be trimmed when the caterpillar is finished). Using one strand of medium jade thread, work twelve couching stitches over the padding, using the backstitches as a guide to placement. As the caterpillar will be worked in raised stem stitch, do not pull these stitches too tight.

3. Stitch a ginger antique bead at the end of the padding for the head, the hole in the bead parallel to the stem.

4. With jade thread (see below) in a tapestry needle, work rows of raised stem stitch over the couching stitches to cover the caterpillar, working short rows almost every alternate row (to allow for the tapering head and tail), and taking the needle through the head bead on most full rows. Starting at the lower edge, work the rows in the colours as follows:

- Three rows in dark jade.
- One row in light jade.
- Two rows in dark jade.
- Three rows in medium jade.
- Two rows in dark jade.

*caterpillar leg &
spike placement*

5. Using 2 strands of dark green thread in a size 3 milliners needle, work the legs in French knots (one wrap) in the positions marked on the diagram (five legs). Using tweezers, gently squeeze the legs to define their shape.

6. With one strand of rust thread in a sharps needle, work spikes into the top edge of the caterpillar, working two straight stitches at each position as shown.

*completed
caterpillar*

PUPA (CHRYSALIS)

When the caterpillar is fully fed, it crawls away to pupate on the ground in a rudimentary cocoon spun in the leaf litter at the base of the food plant.

1. Trace the two padding shapes onto the paper side of paper-backed fusible web, then fuse to the yellow felt. Cut out the shapes. Using ecru thread, apply the padding to the background fabric (over the stem and part of the leaf) with small stab stitches, applying the smaller shape first.

pupa padding

2. Trace the pupa leather template onto a Post-it note (position the tracing over the sticky end). Cut out the paper template and check against the padding for size before sticking the template to the bronze side of the snakeskin (or kid leather). Carefully cut out the snakeskin shape around the template.

pupa segment lines.

completed pupa

3. Using nylon thread in a size 12 sharps needle, apply the snakeskin over the felt padding with small stab stitches, first working securing stitches at the corners and sides, then all the way around, nudging the edge of the snakeskin towards the felt with a nailfile (or fingers) as you go.

4. With brown/black metallic thread in a size 9 milliners needle, work eight couching stitches over the surface of the pupa to suggest segment lines.

Moth (imago)

Inside the protective case of the pupa, an amazing transformation takes place. All the parts of the caterpillar's body are chemically broken down into their various components, which then develop to make the body and wings of the adult moth. When the moth first emerges from the pupa, its wings are soft and crumpled. It sits still while blood pumps through the wing veins to stiffen and flatten the wings. Once the wings are dry, the moth is able to fly off to the nearest foliage to feed.

Work the moth using the instructions, and detached wing outlines, provided for the Large Emerald Moth in the Specimen Box, page 62–67.

completed moth

Dog Rose &
Grape Hyacinth

Worked on a background of ivory satin, this project features a
pale pink Dog Rose, *Rosa canina*, with detached petals; leaves, both detached
and embroidered on the background; Grape Hyacinths, *Muscari armeniacum*,
worked with frosted glass beads in several shades of blue, and a yellow butterfly
with raised wings. The finished embroidery may be framed, inserted into
a paperweight, or mounted into the lid of a gilt trinket box.
The original design, oval in shape, was worked with cotton threads.
A circular version has been worked in silks.

246

Diagrams Actual Size

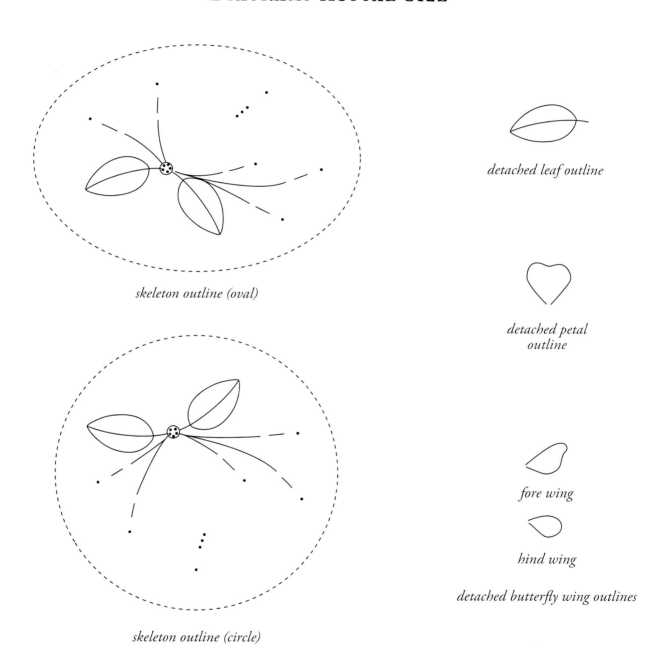

skeleton outline (oval)

skeleton outline (circle)

detached leaf outline

detached petal
outline

fore wing

hind wing

detached butterfly wing outlines

Dog Rose, *Rosa canina*

Dog Rose, Rosa canina

The **Dog Rose**, Rosa canina, is a scrambling species which commonly
inhabits the English hedgerows and blooms in summer. It is also the
stylised rose of medieval heraldry, still in use today. The fragrant
flowers are usually pale pink, but can vary between deep pink and
white. The dark green to blue-green leaves have single- or double-
toothed saw-edges which, when bruised, also have a delicious fragrance.
In autumn, the Dog Rose produces conspicuous scarlet hips, sometimes
known as dragon's eyes. These are edible and high in vitamin C, and are
often used to make rose-hip syrup, tea, jellies and other preserves. It
is believed that the botanic name, Rosa canina, may have its origins in
the use of the root of the Dog Rose in the treatment of bites from rabid
dogs in the eighteenth and nineteenth centuries.

Grape Hyacinth, *Muscari armeniacum*

Grape Hyacinth, Muscari armeniacum

Grape Hyacinths, Muscari armeniacum, are
spring-flowering, short-stemmed bulbs, with spikes
of flowers 10-15 cm (4-6 in) in height in varying
shades of cobalt-blue, purple or white. They are
so named for their clusters of small, bell-shaped
flowers that look like bunches of upside-down
grapes. They have a lovely fragrance.

OVERALL REQUIREMENTS

....

This is the complete list of requirements for this embroidery. For ease of use, the requirements of each individual element are repeated under its heading—for example, Rose requirements, Butterfly requirements. Note: DMC colour equivalents are close but not always an exact match for the Soie d'Alger and Cifonda colours used.

---

ivory satin background fabric: *20 cm (8 in) square*

quilter's muslin: *four 20 cm (8 in) squares*

tracing paper
  (I use GLAD Bake/baking parchment)

---

15 cm (6 in) embroidery hoop

10 cm (4 in) embroidery hoops

---

needles

crewel/embroidery sizes 3–10

milliners/straw sizes 3–9

sharps sizes 10 and 12

sharp yarn darners sizes 14–18

embroidery equipment *(see page 264)*

---

3 mm purple/green glass bead
  (Hot Spotz SBXL-449)

Mill Hill antique beads 3061 *(dark violet blue)*

Mill Hill frosted beads 62034 *(violet blue)*

---

33 gauge white covered wire (petals and wings):
  nine 10 cm (4 in) lengths

33 gauge white covered wire (leaf):
  one 10 cm (4 in) length (colour green if desired:
  Copic G99 Olive)

---

dark green stranded thread (leaves):
  Soie d'Alger 2135 or DMC 987

medium green stranded thread (stems, leaves):
  Soie d'Alger 2134 or DMC 988

---

light green stranded thread (rose):
  Soie d'Alger 2123 or DMC 3348

dark pink stranded thread (rose):
  Soie d'Alger 1013 or DMC 3326

medium pink stranded thread (rose):
  Soie d'Alger 1012 or DMC 818

light pink stranded thread (rose):
  Soie d'Alger 1011 or DMC 819

light yellow stranded thread (rose):
  Soie d'Alger 2522 or DMC 3823

medium orange stranded thread (rose): *DMC 741*

---

violet stranded thread (hyacinth): *DMC 792*

medium yellow stranded thread (butterfly):
  Cifonda Art Silk 173 or DMC 3855

dark orange stranded thread (butterfly):
  Cifonda Art Silk 104 or DMC 3853

dark purple stranded thread (butterfly):
  Soie d'Alger 3326 or DMC 939

---

variegated metallic thread (butterfly):
  Madeira Metallic col. Astro-1

gold/black metallic thread (butterfly):
  Kreinik Cord 205c

purple/navy chenille thread (butterfly):
  col. Amber Marine

silk or rayon machine thread for stitching
  circle outline

PREPARATION

....

1. Mount the satin background fabric and cotton backing into the larger embroidery hoop. The fabrics need to be kept very taut.

2. Using a fine lead pencil, trace the skeleton outline and the circle (or oval) outline onto tracing paper (this is the right side). Turn the tracing paper over and draw over the skeleton outline only—not the circle outline.

3. Transfer the circle outline to the backing fabric by placing the tracing paper, right side down, inside the back of the hoop of fabric and tracing over the circle outline only with a tracing pen or stylus. Transfer the circle outline to the front by working a row of long running stitches around the pencil outline, using a fine silk thread. This outline will be used to centre the embroidery within the lid of a small gilt box or paperweight if desired. If the piece is to be framed, the running stitches may be removed without leaving an outline on the front.

4. Attach the tracing, right side up, to the satin in the hoop with pieces of masking tape, lining up the traced outline with the stitched outline.

5. Place a tracing board or small lid inside the back of the hoop for support, then transfer the design by tracing over the outline with a tracing pen or stylus.

Note: Take care to use the minimum amount of lead when tracing. If your outlines are too dark, gently press the traced outlines with pieces of masking tape or Magic Tape to remove any excess graphite.

METHOD: STEMS & LEAVES

The long arching stems are green to purple, browning with age and
are covered with sharp, strong, hooked spines.

REQUIREMENTS

quilter's muslin: *20 cm (8 in) square*

33 gauge white covered wire:
one 10 cm (4 in) length (colour green if desired: Copic G99 Olive)

dark green stranded thread: *Soie d'Alger 2135 or DMC 987*
medium green stranded thread: *Soie d'Alger 2134 or DMC 988*

STEMS

Embroider the stems in whipped chain stitch with 2 strands of medium green
thread, leaving a space in the centre to insert the detached rose petals.

LEAVES

The leaves are embroidered with one strand of thread in a size 10 crewel
needle.

Surface Leaves

1. Work the central vein in chain stitch with medium green thread.

2. Using dark green thread, outline the leaf in single feather stitch, starting
each side at the top of the leaf. Work one straight stitch at the tip of the leaf to
complete the outline.

3. With dark green thread, embroider the leaf, inside the outline, with padded
satin stitch, working the stitches towards the central vein.

4. Work the veins with straight stitches using medium green thread.

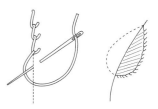

*single feather
stitch outline*

Detached Leaf

Mount a square of muslin into a 10 cm (4 in) hoop and trace the detached leaf outline (check that it is the right way up). Use a 10 cm (4 in) length of wire, coloured green if desired.

wire placement

1. Using one strand of medium green thread, couch the wire along the central vein, one end of the wire at the tip of the leaf. Overcast stitch the wire to the muslin along the central vein.

2. Using dark green thread, couch the remaining wire around the leaf outline, bending into a point at the tip and ending with a tail of wire at the base of the leaf (do not trim the wire tail). Buttonhole stitch the wire to the muslin around the outside edge of the leaf.

3. With dark green thread, work a row of split stitch close to the inside edge of the wire and on either side of the central vein (this helps avoid a white edge when working the leaf in satin stitch). Work straight padding stitches inside the wired outline.

completed surface leaf & detached leaf

4. Using dark green thread, embroider the leaf surface, inside the wire outline, with satin stitch, working the stitches towards the central vein.

5. Work the veins with straight stitches using medium green thread.

METHOD: GRAPE HYACINTH

REQUIREMENTS

Mill Hill antique beads 3061 *(dark violet blue)*

Mill Hill frosted beads 62034 *(violet blue)*

violet stranded thread (hyacinth): *DMC 792*

The grape hyacinths are worked with beads over a padding of thread. Using 6 strands of violet thread in a size 3 crewel needle, work the padding as follows:

1. Work a straight stitch between A and B, holding the tail of thread out of the way at the back with masking tape.

2. Work a detached chain stitch around the straight stitch. Work another chain stitch around this first chain stitch.

3. Work a long straight stitch, over the chain stitches, from C to D. Hold the tail of thread at the back with masking tape.

4. With one strand of violet thread, work three couching stitches across the padding (do not pull tight—just snug).

5. Using one strand of thread, apply the beads in rows over the padding, starting at the base, and working in the sequence as shown (the last single bead should cover the end of the stitch at C). Apply each row of beads with a single stitch, worked from one side of the padding to the other, then work a couching stitch between each bead. Vary the combination of beads for each flower.

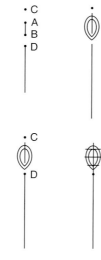

stitch placement

A
Row 6: 1 bead
Row 5: 2 beads
Row 4: 3 beads
Row 3: 4 beads
Row 2: 3 beads
D
Row 1: 2 beads

completed grape hyacinths

METHOD: DOG ROSE

....

A scrambling rose species which commonly flowers in the English hedgerow in summer.
The fragrant flowers are usually pale pink and white with the leaves a dark green to blue green.

REQUIREMENTS

quilter's muslin: *20 cm (8 in) square*

33 gauge white covered wire: *five 10 cm (4 in) lengths*

dark pink stranded thread: *Soie d'Alger 1013 or DMC 3326*
medium pink stranded thread: *Soie d'Alger 1012 or DMC 818*
light pink stranded thread: *Soie d'Alger 1011 or DMC 819*
light yellow stranded thread: *Soie d'Alger 2522 or DMC 3823*
light green stranded thread: *Soie d'Alger 2123 or DMC 3348*
medium orange stranded thread: *DMC 741*

wire placement

*buttonhole stitch
guide*

DETACHED PETALS

Mount muslin into a 10 cm (4 in) hoop and trace five petal outlines.

1. Using one strand of dark pink thread in a size 10 crewel needle, couch the wire to the muslin around the petal shape leaving two tails of wire at the base that touch but do not cross, then stitch the wire to the muslin with small, close buttonhole stitches, incorporating the couching stitches and working the buttonhole ridge on the outside edge of the petal.

2. With medium pink thread, work a row of long and short buttonhole stitch inside the top edge of the petal (close to the wire), then embroider the petal with long and short stitch, shading through light pink to light yellow in the centre. Work all stitches towards the base of the petal. Vary the shading for each petal if desired.

TO COMPLETE THE ROSE

1. Carefully cut out the petals, close to the buttonholed edge and avoiding the wire tails. Using a yarn darner, insert the tails of the five detached petals through the circle of dots (five individual holes as close to each other as possible). Bend the wires behind the petals and secure to the backing fabric with small stitches using a pale thread. Do not cut the wires until the flower is finished.

2. Shape the petals with tweezers, pushing them gently towards the centre of the flower. Fill the centre of the rose with French knots (one wrap), working the knots with 2 strands of light green thread in a size 9 milliners needle. To work the stamens at the base of each petal, work French knots with one strand of medium orange thread (in a size 10 sharps needle), carefully taking the needle through the petals to the back.

Note: These French knots could be worked before the detached petals are cut out.

Shape the petals with tweezers then trim the wires.

3. Carefully cut out the detached leaf and shape slightly. Using a yarn darner, insert the wire tail under the detached petals. Secure the wire tail to the back then trim.

petal insertion points

completed rose flower

Method: Butterfly

··

A yellow butterfly is known as a symbol of transformation due to its impressive process of *metamorphosis. It symbolises energy & growth, rebirth, evolution, commemoration, time and soul.*

Requirements

quilter's muslin: *20 cm (8 in) square*

3 mm purple/green glass bead *(Hot Spotz SBXL-449)*
33 gauge white covered wire: *four 10 cm (4 in) lengths*

medium yellow stranded thread: *Cifonda Art Silk 173 or DMC 3855*
dark orange stranded thread: *Cifonda Art Silk 104 or DMC 3853*
dark purple stranded thread: *Soie d'Alger 3326 or DMC 939*
variegated metallic thread: *Madeira Metallic col. Astro-1*
gold/black metallic thread: *Kreinik Cord 205c*
purple/navy chenille thread: *col. Amber Marine*
nylon clear thread: *Madeira Monofil 60 col. 1001*

*wire shaping &
vein stitch guide*

Detached Wings

Mount muslin into a 10 cm (4 in) hoop and trace two front and two back wing outlines.

1. Using one strand of medium yellow thread in a size 10 sharps needle, couch the wire to the muslin around the wing outline, leaving two tails of wire at the base that touch but do not cross, then buttonhole stitch the wire to the muslin. Work a row of long and short buttonhole stitch inside the top edge of the wing (close to the wire), then embroider the remaining wing in long and short stitch. Work all stitches towards the base of the wing.

2. With one strand of variegated metallic thread in the sharps needle, work veins in the wings with fly stitches. Embroider spots between the veins with French knots (one wrap), using one strand of dark orange thread.

To Complete the Butterfly

1. Carefully cut out the wings and apply by inserting the wire tails through the two upper dots as shown, using a yarn darner. Apply the hind wings first, inserting the wire tails through 2, then the fore wings through 1 (the fore wings slightly overlap the hind wings). Bend the wire tails under the wings and secure to the muslin backing with small stitches worked with a pale thread. Trim the wire tails when the butterfly is finished.

2. Work the thorax with one straight stitch across the centre of the wings (from 1 to 3), using chenille thread in the largest yarn darner. Make sure the chenille does not twist, and adjust the tension of the stitch as desired. Use stranded thread to secure the chenille tails to the backing fabric.

3. The abdomen is worked with a bullion knot (five or six wraps), from 4 to 3, using 7 strands of dark purple thread in the smallest yarn darner.

4. With one strand of nylon thread, apply a 3 mm bead for the head, working the stitches towards the thorax.

5. Using the gold/black thread in the sharps needle, work two straight stitches for the antennae, taking each stitch through the head bead to the back. Work a French knot at the end of each straight stitch.

wing & abdomen placement

completed butterfly

Part 5

TECHNIQUES
Equipment
& Stitch Glossary

This section contains general information about the techniques
and equipment that are referred to throughout the book.

The bibliography contains a list of specialised reference books
which can provide more detailed information if required.

The stitch glossary includes the stitches used.

Techniques

MOUNTING FABRIC INTO AN EMBROIDERY HOOP

Good quality embroidery hoops—10 cm, 12 cm, 15 cm, 20 cm and 25 cm
(4 in, 5 in, 6 in, 8 in and 10 in) diameter—are essential when working small to
medium size designs in stumpwork embroidery. Bind the inner ring of wooden
hoops with cotton tape to prevent slipping. A small screwdriver is useful to
tighten the embroidery hoop. Plastic hoops with a lip on the inner ring are also
suitable (because of the lip the inner ring does not need to be bound).

1. Place the main (background) fabric on top of the backing fabric then place
both fabrics over the inner ring of the hoop. If using a plastic hoop, make sure
that the lip-edge of the hoop is uppermost.

2. Loosen the outer ring of the hoop so that it just fits over the inner ring and
the fabrics, positioning the tension screw at the top of the hoop (12 o'clock).
Ease the outer ring down over the inner ring and fabrics.

3. To tension the fabrics in the hoop, pull the fabrics evenly and tighten the
screw, alternately, until both layers of fabric are as tight as a drum in the hoop.
If using the plastic hoop, the fabric-covered lip-edge of the inner ring should
sit just above the top edge of the outer ring. In stumpwork, the fabrics are not
removed from the hoop until the embroidery is finished.

Opposite: Japanese paper stencils, called katagami, *are exquisitely rendered textile motifs, carefully cut from
delicate paper and used for printing designs on cloth. The graceful butterfly is a traditional motif.*

TRANSFERRING A DESIGN TO FABRIC
You Will Need
- tracing paper (I use GLAD Bake/baking parchment)
- sharp HB lead pencil (or a 0.5 mm clutch/mechanical pencil)
- Clover Tracer Pen, stylus or used (empty) ball-point pen (to trace a fine line)
- masking tape (to stop tracing paper from slipping)
- tracing board, small book or circular lid (use inside the back of the hoop for support when tracing a design on to the front)

Preparation
1. Mount the background fabric (silk or satin) and a backing fabric (quilter's muslin or calico), into a hoop or square frame. The fabrics need to be kept very taut.

2. Trace the design on to the front *after* the fabrics have been mounted into the hoop to prevent distortion.

3. Do not remove the fabrics from the hoop until all the embroidery is finished, unless instructed otherwise.

Tracing the Design on to the Background Fabric
1. Trace a skeleton outline of the design onto tracing paper with a sharp lead pencil. Flip the paper over and draw over the outline on the back (do not make the lines too dark).

2. Attach the tracing, *right side up,* to the fabric in the hoop using strips of masking tape on all sides. Check that the design is on the straight grain of the fabric.

3. Place a tracing board (or lid) inside the back of the hoop for support then transfer the design by tracing over the outline with a Clover Tracer Pen, stylus or used ball-point pen.

WORKING WITH WIRE

Cake decorator's wire is used to form the detached, wired and embroidered shapes characteristic of stumpwork. I find the following gauges the most useful.

- *33-gauge covered wire* A fine wire with a tightly wrapped, thin white paper covering which can be coloured if desired. This wire is used for small detached shapes, such as butterfly wings and flower petals.
- *28-gauge uncovered wire* Uncovered wire (silver in colour) is used when a finer edge is required. Use it for small and detailed detached shapes, such as lacewing and moth wings.

To Stitch Wire to Fabric

- When stitching wire to fabric, either with overcast stitch or buttonhole stitch, make sure that the needle enters the fabric at right-angles, very close to the wire (not angled under the wire). The stitches need to be worked very close together, with an up-and-down stabbing motion, using a firm and even tension.

- If you need to renew a thread while stitching wire to fabric, secure the thread tails inside the wired shape (do not use a knot at the edge as it may be cut when cutting out the shape). If you need to renew a thread while stitching wire for a wing, you cannot secure the thread inside the wired shape. Instead, hold the tail of the old thread and the tail of the new thread under the length of wire about to be stitched. Catch both tails of thread in with the new overcast stitches.

- When working veins inside wings with metallic thread, it is safer to keep the tails of thread at the front of the wing until it has been cut out, then stitch the tails through the corner of the wing to the back. The tails of metallic thread are secured after the wing has been applied to the main fabric.

stitch

wire

fabric

cross section of fabric, wire & stitch

- Using very sharp scissors with fine points, cut out the wired shape as close to the stitching as possible (stroke the cut edge with your fingernail to reveal any stray threads). If you happen to cut a stitch, use the point of a pin to apply a minute amount of PVA glue to the cut thread. This will dry matt and clear.

To Colour Wire

White paper-covered wire may be coloured with a waterproof ink if desired. This is optional. When I colour wires I use Copic markers, which are available from art supply stores. These markers are fast-drying and refillable and come in a wide range of colours.

To Attach Wired Shapes to a Background Fabric

Detached wire shapes are applied to a background fabric by inserting the wire tails through a 'tunnel' formed by the eye of a large (size 14) sharp yarn darner needle.

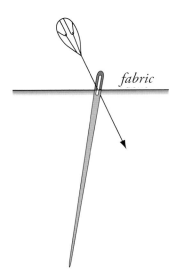

fabric

cross section of fabric, yarn darner & wired shape

1. Pierce the background fabric at the required point with the yarn darner and push it through until the eye of the needle is half-way through the fabric (this forms a 'tunnel' through to the back of the fabric).

2. Insert the wire tails into the 'tunnel' formed by the eye of the darner, through to the back of the fabric. Thread tails can also be taken through at the same time.

3. Gently pull the darner all the way through, leaving the wire tails in the hole.

4. Stitch the wire tails to the backing fabric with small stitches, preferably behind an embroidered area (make sure the securing stitches will be hidden behind embroidery or underneath a detached shape).

5. Use tweezers to shape the detached petal or wing as required then trim the wire tails. I do not cut any wire tails until the subject is finished (just in case you need to unpick and re-do). Do not let any wire tails protrude into an unembroidered area as they may show when the piece is framed.

WORKING WITH PAPER-BACKED FUSIBLE WEB

Paper-backed fusible web (also known as Vliesofix, Bondaweb and other brand names) is used to fuse or bond one material to another by applying heat with an iron. I also use paper-backed fusible web to obtain a precise design outline on felt—it is very difficult to trace a small shape on to felt and to cut it out accurately.

To Fuse a Design Outline to Felt

1. Trace the outline on to the paper side of the fusible web then fuse to the felt (fusible web/glue side down) with a medium-hot dry iron.

2. Cut out the shape along the outlines. Remove the paper before stitching the felt shape to the background fabric (e.g. flower padding).

To Fuse Sheer Fabrics for Wings

Almost any sheer, organza-like fabric or ribbon—plain, 'shot', variegated, metallic or pearlised—can be used for the upper layer of the wings. Use similar fabrics for the lower layer, or more opaque pearl, gold or copper metal organdie, to provide a lovely sheen under the sheer organzas. Use a layer of baking parchment (GLAD Bake) on either side of the fabrics to be fused to protect your iron and the ironing board.

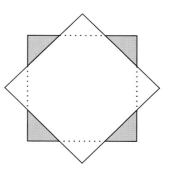

A wing 'sandwich' is made by fusing the upper and lower layers of fabric together with paper-backed fusible web as follows:

1. Fuse paper-backed fusible web to the upper layer of fabric (both cut the same size). If using ribbon as the upper layer, remove the selvedges, cut the fusible web to the same width and fuse together. Remove the backing paper.

2. Place the lower layer of fabric on the ironing board (over baking parchment). Place the upper layer of fabric, fusible web side down, over the lower layer—rotating the upper layer 45 degrees (bias grain) for a pretty effect (this also provides a more stable fabric to stitch and cut out).

3. Cover the sandwich with baking parchment and press firmly with an iron (on about nylon setting). The temperature needs to be hot enough to fuse the fabrics but not so hot as to cause bubbling. Mount the wing sandwich into a hoop while still warm for best results—the fabric needs to be kept very taut.

Equipment

THE EMBROIDERER'S WORKBOX SHOULD CONTAIN THE FOLLOWING EQUIPMENT:

- Good quality embroidery hoops—10 cm, 12 cm, 15 cm, 20 cm and 25 cm (4 in, 5 in, 6 in, 8 in and 10 in) diameter. Bind the inner ring of wooden hoops with cotton tape to prevent slipping. A small screwdriver is useful to tighten the embroidery hoops. Plastic hoops with a lip on the inner ring are also suitable.

- Slate frames in various sizes for larger embroideries

- Wooden tracing boards of various sizes: to place under hoops of fabric when tracing

- Needles

- Thimble

- Beeswax

- Fine glass-headed pins

- Embroidery scissors (small, with fine sharp points), goldwork scissors (small and strong with sharp points) and paper scissors

- Small wire-cutters or old scissors for cutting wire

- Mellor or old metal nailfile (for easing threads or leather into place)

- Assortment of tweezers (from surgical suppliers)

- Eyebrow comb (for Turkey knots)

- Tracing paper (I use Glad Bake/baking parchment)

- Fine (0.5 mm) HB lead pencil (mechanical)

- Clover tracer pen, stylus or used ball-point pen (for tracing)

- Masking tape (for tracing and to hold threads and wire tails to the back of the fabric)

- Post-it notes or 'removable' self-adhesive labels (for templates)

- Rulers—15 and 30 cm (6 and 12 in)

GLOSSARY OF PRODUCT NAMES

This list gives equivalent names for products used throughout this book which may not be available under the same name in every country.

biro	=	ballpoint pen
calico	=	muslin
clutch pencil	=	mechanical pencil
GLAD Bake	=	baking parchment
quilter's muslin	=	finely woven calico or cotton homespun
paper-backed fusible web	=	Vliesofix, Bondaweb

Stitch Glossary

This glossary contains most the stitches used in this book, in alphabetical order. For ease of explanation, some of the stitches have been illustrated with the needle entering and leaving the fabric in the same movement. When working in a hoop this is difficult (or should be if your fabric is tight enough), so the stitches have to be worked with a stabbing motion, in several stages.

BACK STITCH

This is a useful stitch for outlining a shape. Bring the needle out at 1, insert at 2 (sharing the hole made by the preceding stitch) and out again at 3. Keep the stitches small and even.

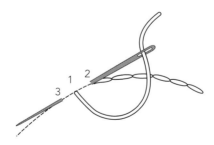

BACK STITCH, SPLIT
See Split Back Stitch

BULLION KNOTS

These require some practice to work in a hoop. Use a milliners/straw needle of the appropriate size, with the number of wraps depending on the length of the knot required. Bring the needle out at 1, insert at 2 leaving a long loop. Emerge at 1 again (not pulling the needle through yet) and wrap the thread around the needle the required number of times. Hold the wraps gently between the thumb and index finger of the left hand while pulling the needle through with the right hand. Pull quite firmly and insert again at 2, stroking the wraps into place.

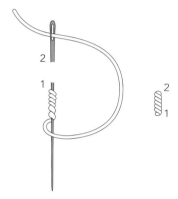

BUTTONHOLE STITCH

These stitches can be worked close together or slightly apart. Working from left to right, bring the needle out on the line to be worked at 1 and insert at 2, holding the loop of thread with the left thumb. Bring the needle up on the line to be worked at 3 (directly below 2), over the thread loop and pull through to form a looped edge. If the stitch is shortened and worked close together over wire, it forms a secure edge for cut shapes, for example, detached petals.

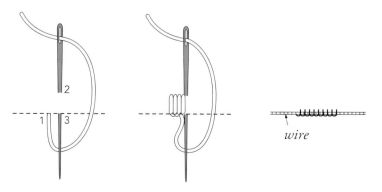

BUTTONHOLE STITCH, LONG AND SHORT

In long and short buttonhole stitch, each alternate stitch is shorter. Bring the needle out at 1, insert at 2 and up again at 3 (like an open detached chain stitch). When embroidering a shape like a petal, angle the stitches towards the centre of the flower.

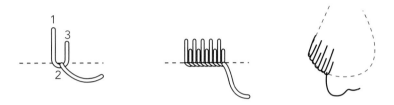

CHAIN BAND, RAISED (RAISED CHAIN STITCH)

Raised chain band (stitch) is worked with a tapestry needle over a grid of evenly spaced straight stitches worked 1.5–3 mm apart (depending on the thickness of the thread), for example, couching stitches across the abdomen of an insect.

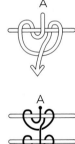

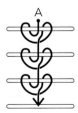

First work the grid of straight stitches then bring the needle out at A, just above the first straight stitch. Slide the needle over then under the first straight stitch coming out to the left of A. Take the needle over then under the first straight stitch again to the right of A (like a buttonhole stitch), bringing the needle through the resulting loop. Pull the thread to form a chain stitch over the first straight stitch.

Take the needle over then under the second straight stitch, coming out to the left of the previous stitch. Take the needle over then under the second straight stitch again, to the right of the previous stitch, bringing the needle through the resulting loop as before. Repeat these two movements to work a row of chain stitches over the grid of straight stitches.

CHAIN STITCH

Bring the needle out at 1 and insert it again through the same hole, holding the loop of thread with the left thumb. Bring the needle up a short distance away at 2, through the loop, and pull the thread through. Insert the needle into the same hole at 2 (inside the loop) and make a second loop, hold, and come up at 3. Repeat to work a row of chain stitch, securing the final loop with a small straight stitch.

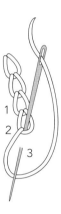

CHAIN STITCH, DETACHED (LAZY DAISY STITCH)

Detached chain stitch, also known as lazy daisy stitch, is worked in the same way as chain stitch except that each loop is secured individually with a small straight stitch. The securing stitch can be made longer if desired, for example, in a butterfly's antennae. Several detached chain stitches can be worked inside each other to pad a small shape.

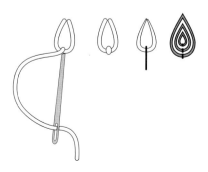

CHAIN STITCH, WHIPPED

This is a useful method for working a raised line. Work a row of chain stitch then bring the needle out slightly to one side of the final securing stitch. Using either the eye of the needle or a tapestry needle, whip the chain stitches by passing the needle under each chain loop from right to left, working back to the beginning of the row. When whipped chain stitch is used for stems, the thickness of the outline can be varied by the number of threads used.

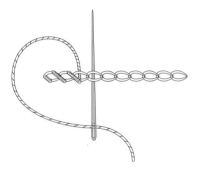

COUCHING

Couching is used to attach a thread, or bundle of threads, to a background fabric by means of small, vertical stitches worked at regular intervals. The laid thread is often thicker or more fragile than the one used for stitching. Couching stitches are also used for attaching wire to the base fabric before embroidering detached shapes.

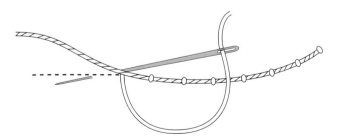

Feather Stitch

This stitch is made up of a series of loops, stitched alternately to the right and to the left, each one holding the previous loop in place. Come up on the line to be followed at 1. Insert the needle to the right at 2 and come up on the line again at 3, holding the thread under the needle with the left thumb. Repeat on the left side of the line, reversing the needle direction.

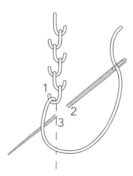

Feather Stitch, Single

Work the feather stitch loops in one direction only, either to the right or to the left. This variation is useful for working the veins in dragonfly wings.

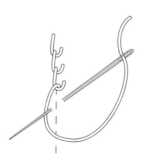

FLY STITCH

Fly stitch is actually an open detached chain stitch. Bring the needle out at 1 and insert at 2, holding the working thread with the left thumb. Bring up again at 3 and pull through over the loop. Secure the loop with either a short anchoring stitch, as for antennae, or a longer anchoring stitch as, for example, the veins in butterfly wings.

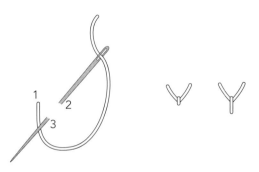

FRENCH KNOT

Using a milliners/straw needle, bring the thread through at the desired place, wrap the thread once around the point of the needle and re-insert the needle. Tighten the thread and hold taut while pulling the needle through. To increase the size of the knot use more strands of thread, although more wraps can be made if desired.

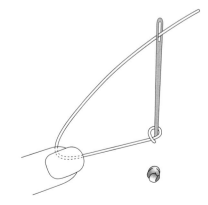

Long & Short Stitch

This stitch can be used to fill areas too large or irregular for satin stitch, or where shading is required. The first row, worked around the outline, consists of alternating long and short satin stitches (or long and short buttonhole stitch may be used). In the subsequent rows, the stitches are all of similar length, and fit into the spaces left by the preceding row. For a more realistic result when working petals, direct the stitches towards the centre of the flower. The surface will look smoother if the needle either pierces the stitches of the preceding row or enters at an angle between the stitches.

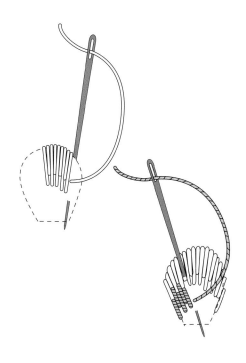

Long & Short Buttonhole Stitch

See Buttonhole Stitch, Long and Short

NEEDLEWEAVING

Needleweaving is a form of embroidery where thread in a tapestry needle is woven in and out over two or more threads attached to the background fabric. Work needleweaving over a loop to form sepals, for example, bramble berries. Use a length of scrap thread to keep the loop taut while weaving.

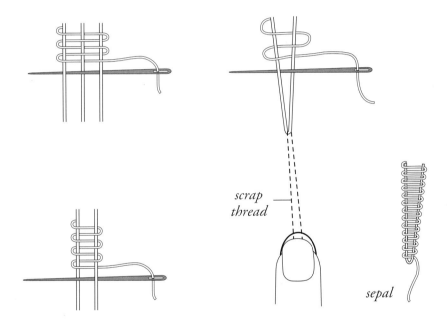

scrap thread

sepal

OUTLINE STITCH

Worked from left to right, this stitch is perfect for working both simple and complicated outlines. Worked in the same way as stem stitch, the only difference is that the working thread is kept to the left of the line being worked.

To start, bring the needle out at 1 on the line to be worked. Go down at 2, come up at 3 (to the right of the stitch) and pull the thread through. Insert the needle at 4, holding the thread above the line with the left thumb, and come up again at 2 (in the same hole made by the previous stitch) then pull the thread through. Go down at 5, hold the loop and come up again at 4, then pull the thread through. Repeat to work a narrow line.

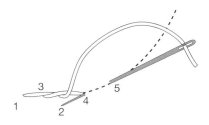

OVERCAST STITCH

This stitch is made up of tiny, vertical satin stitches, worked very close together over a laid thread or wire, resulting in a firm raised line. When worked over wire it gives a smooth, secure edge for cut shapes, for example, Green Lacewing wings. Place the wire along the line to be covered. Working from left to right with a stabbing motion, cover the wire with small straight stitches, pulling the thread firmly so that there are no loose stitches which may be cut when the shape is cut out.

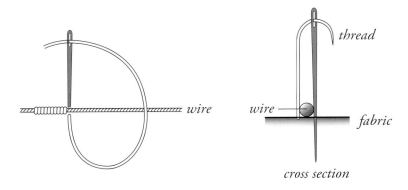

wire

thread

wire   *fabric*

cross section

PAD STITCH

Pad stitch is used as a foundation under satin stitch when a smooth, slightly raised surface is required. Padding stitches can be either straight stitches or chain stitches, worked in the opposite direction to the satin stitches. Felt can replace pad stitch for a more raised effect.

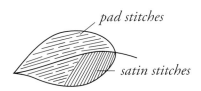

pad stitches

satin stitches

SATIN STITCH

Satin stitch is used to fill shapes such as petals or leaves. It consists of horizontal or vertical straight stitches, worked close enough together so that no fabric shows through, yet not overlapping each other. Satin stitch can be worked over a padding of felt or pad stitches. Smooth edges are easier to achieve if the shape is first outlined with split stitch (or split back stitch).

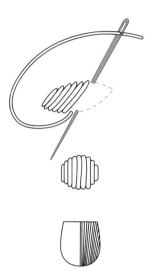

SATIN STITCH, ENCROACHING

Encroaching satin stitch is a useful method of shading. First work a row of regular satin stitch. In the second, and all subsequent rows, the head of each satin stitch is taken between the base of two stitches in the row above, so that the rows blend softly into each other—see, for example, the Chalkhill Blue Butterfly. Vary the length of the stitches to achieve more subtle shading.

SPLIT STITCH

Split stitch can be used either as an outline stitch or for smooth, solid fillings. Split stitch is worked in a similar way to stem stitch; however the point of the needle splits the preceding stitch as it is brought out of the fabric. To start, make a straight stitch along the line to be worked. Bring the needle through to the front, splitting the straight stitch with the point of the needle. Insert the needle along the line then bring through to the front again to pierce the preceding stitch. Repeat to work a narrow line of stitching, resembling fine chain stitch.

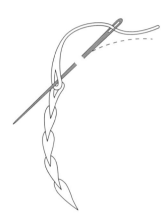

SPLIT BACK STITCH

An easier version of split stitch, especially when using one strand of thread. Commence with a backstitch. Bring the needle out at 1, insert at 2 (splitting the preceding stitch) and out again at 3. This results in a fine, smooth line, ideal for stitching intricate curves.

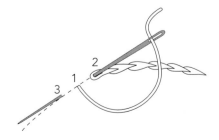

STAB STITCH

Stab stitch is used to apply leather or felt shapes to a background fabric. It consists of small straight stitches made from the background fabric over the edge of the applied shape, for example, a leather shape over felt padding. Bring the needle out at 1, and insert at 2, catching in the edge of the applied piece.

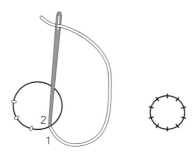

STEM STITCH

Worked from left to right, the stitches in stem stitch overlap each other to form a fine line suitable for outlines and stems. A straight (not slanted) form of stem stitch, in a stabbing motion, is ideal for stumpwork. To start, bring the needle out at 1 on the line to be worked. Go down at 2, come up at 3 and pull the thread through. Insert the needle at 4, holding the thread underneath the line with the left thumb, and come up again at 2 (sharing the hole made by the previous stitch) then pull the thread through. Go down at 5, hold the loop and come up again at 4, then pull the thread through. Repeat to work a narrow line.

STEM STITCH BAND, RAISED

Stem stitch can be worked over a foundation of couched, padding thread
to produce a raised, smooth, stem stitch band, ideal for insect bodies. Lay
a preliminary foundation of padding stitches worked with soft cotton or
stranded thread. Across this padding, at fairly regular intervals, work straight
(couching) stitches at right angles to the padding thread (do not make these
stitches too tight). Then proceed to cover the padding by working rows of
stem stitch over these straight stitches, using a tapestry needle so as not to
pierce the padding thread. All the rows of stem stitch are worked in the same
direction, starting and ending either at the one point, for example, 1, or as in
satin stitch, for example, 2.

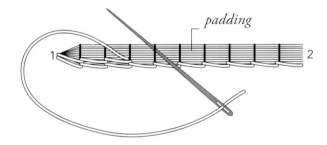

STRAIGHT STITCH

Individual straight stitches, of equal or varying length, can be stitched with
a variety of threads to achieve interesting effects, for example, insect legs in
metallic thread.

TURKEY KNOT

Turkey knots are worked then cut to produce a soft velvety pile. Although there are several ways to work Turkey knots, the following method works well for small areas.

Use 2 strands of thread in a size 9 crewel or sharps needle.Insert the needle into the fabric at 1, holding the tail of thread with the left thumb.

Come out at 2 and go down at 3 to make a small securing stitch. Bring the needle out again at 1 (piercing the securing stitch), pull the thread down and also hold with the left thumb.

For the next Turkey knot, insert the needle to the right at 4 (still holding the tails of thread). Come out at 5 and go down at 2 to make a small securing stitch. Bring the needle out again at 4 (piercing the securing stitch), pull the thread down and hold with the left thumb as before. Repeat to work a row.

Work each successive row directly above the previous row, holding all the resulting tails with the left thumb. To complete, cut all the loops, comb with an eyebrow comb, and cut the pile to the desired length. The more the pile is combed the fluffier it becomes.

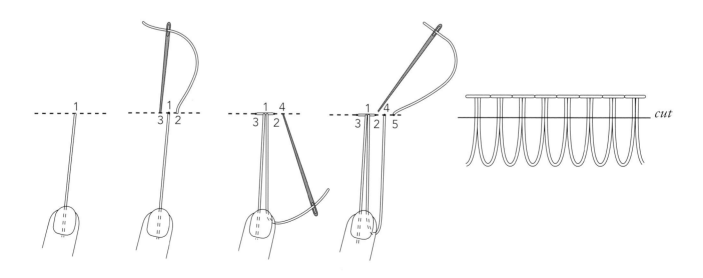

BIBLIOGRAPHY

I have referred to the following for information and inspiration.

INSECTS

Dance, S. Peter. *The Art of Natural History.* Bracken Books, London, 1989.

Field Guide to the Butterflies and other Insects of Britain. Reader's Digest, London, 1984.

Horackova, Jana. *The Illustrated Book Animal Life.* Treasure Press, London, 1980.

Laughlin, Robin Kittrell. *Backyard Bugs.* Chronicle Books, San Francisco, 1996.

MacQuitty, Miranda. *Megabugs.* Carlton Books, London, 1995.

Mansell, E. & Newman, L. Hugh. *The Complete British Butterflies in Colour.* Ebury Press, London, 1968.

Martin, W. Keble. *The Concise British Flora in Colour.* Ebury Press, London, 1965.

Monteith, Geoff. *The Butterfly Man of Kuranda.* Queensland Museum, Brisbane, 1991.

Monteith, Geoff. *The Dodd Collection of Butterfly and Insect Cases.* Queensland Museum, Brisbane, n.d.

Mound, Laurence. *Insect.* Dorling Kindersley, London, 1990.

Naumann, I.D. *Systematic and Applied Entomology*, Melbourne University Press, 1994.

Nuridsany, Claude & Pérennou, Marie. *Microcosmos.* Stewart, Tabori & Chang, New York, 1996.

Russell, Sharman Apt. *An Obsession with Butterflies.* Perseus Publishing, USA, 2003.

Sepp, Jan Christiaan. *Butterflies and Moths.* Michael Joseph Ltd, London, 1978.

Smart, Paul. *Encyclopedia of the Butterfly World.* Tiger Books, London, 1991.

Taylor, Barbara. *Pockets Butterflies and Moths.* Readers Digest (Australia), Sydney, 2010.

Urquhart, F. A. *Introducing the Insect.* F. Warne & Co., London, 1965.

Vesco, Jean-Pierre. *Butterflies.* Barnes & Noble Books, New York, 2003.

Whalley, Paul. *Butterfly and Moth.* Collins, Australia, 1988.

Whitlock, Ralph. *Insects.* Macmillan, London, 1983.

Zborowski, Paul & Storey, Ross. *Field Guide to Insects in Australia.* Reed, Sydney, 1995.

Zahradnik, Jiri. *The Illustrated Book of Insects.* Treasure Press, London, 1991.

GENERAL

Adachi, Fumie. *Japanese Design Motifs.* Dover Publications, New York, 1972.

Agile Rabbit Editions. *Art Nouveau Designs.* The Pepin Press, Amsterdam, 2000.

Appelbaum, Stanley. *Traditional Chinese Designs*, Dover Publications, New York, 1990.

Arthur, Liz. *Embroidery 1600–1700 at the Burrell Collection.* John Murray, Glasgow, 1995.

Benn, Elizabeth. *Treasures from the Embroiderers' Guild Collection.* David & Charles, 1991.

D'Addetta. *Traditional Japanese Design Motifs*, Dover Publications, New York, 1984.

Durant, Stuart. *Ornament.* The Overlook Press, New York, 1986

Fisher, Celia. *The Medieval Flower Book.* The British Library, London, 2007.

Hatje, Verlag Gerd. *Maria Sibylla Merian.* Thames & Hudson, London, 1998.

Hendrix, L. & Vignau-Wilberg, T. *Mira Calligraphiae Monumenta*, Thames & Hudson, London, 1992.

McCallum, Graham Leslie. *4000 Animal, Bird & Fish Motifs.* Batsford, London, 2005.

Mendes, Valerie. *V & A's Textile Collection 1900 to 1937.* Canopy Books, New York, 1992.

Morall, A. & Watts, M. *English Embroidery 'Twixt Art and Nature.* MMA, New York, 2009.

Nissenson, Marilyn. & Jonas, Susan. *Jeweled Bugs and Butterflies*, Harry N. Abrahams, New York, 2000.

Niwa, Motoji. *Japanese Traditional Patterns, Vol. 1*, Graphic-sha Publishing, Tokyo, 1990.

Parry, Linda. *William Morris and the Arts and Crafts Movement*, Studio Editions, London, 1989.

Rose, Augustus F. & Cirino, Antonio. *Jewelry Making and Design*, Dover Publications, New York, 1967.

Séguy, Eugene A. *Séguy's Decorative Butterflies and Insects.* Dover, New York, 1977.

Sutherland, W.G. *Stencilling for Craftsmen*, The Decorative Art Journals Co. Ltd, 1925.

Ware, D.& Stafford, M. *An Illustrated Dictionary of Ornament.* Allen & Unwin, London, 1974.

White, Palmer. *Haute Couture Embroidery.* Lacis Publications, Berkeley, 1994.

EMBROIDERY

Christie, Grace. *Samplers and Stitches*, Batsford, London, 1920.

Don, Sarah. *Traditional Embroidered Animals*, David & Charles, London, 1990.

Innes, Miranda & Perry, Clay. *Medieval Flowers.* Kyle Cathie Ltd, UK, 1997

Thomas, Mary. *Dictionary of Embroidery Stitches*, Hodder & Stoughton, London, 1934.

STUMPWORK

Nicholas, Jane. *Stumpwork Embroidery A Collection of Fruits, Flowers, Insects.* Milner, Australia, 1995.

Nicholas, Jane. *Stumpwork Embroidery Designs and Projects.* Milner, Australia, 1998.

Nicholas, Jane. *Stumpwork Dragonflies.* Milner, Australia, 2000.

Nicholas, Jane. *Stumpwork, Goldwork & Surface Embroidery Beetle Collection.* Milner, Australia, 2004.

Nicholas, Jane. *The Complete Book of Stumpwork Embroidery.* Milner, Australia, 2005.

Nicholas, Jane. *Stumpwork Medieval Flora.* Milner, Australia, 2009.

Nicholas, Jane. *Stumpwork Embroidery: Turkish, Syrian and Persian Tiles.* Milner, Australia, 2010.

PICTURE CREDITS

Endpapers, pages 4, 20, 258:
Japanese Stencil Designs, Dover Publications,
New York, 2007 (p. 31)

Pages 4, 5, 6, 7, 8, 195: *Full-Color Decorative
Butterfly Illustrations*, Dover Publications, New
York, 1997

Pages 11, 12, 16, 17, 18, 19: vintage illustrations
courtesy of Shutterstock.com

Page 13: various types of antennae, diagram of
head of butterfly, Jana Horackova, *The Illustrated
Book of Animal Life*, Treasure Press,
London, 1980

Page 15: moths, caterpillars and pupae, copper
engravings making up four small pages of
Johannes Goedart's *Metamorphosis et Historia
Insectorum*, 1663. S. Peter Dance, *The Art of
Natural History*, Bracken Books, London, 1989
(pp. 36–7)

Pages 17, 18: examples of different shapes of
lepidopteran eggs, larvae and a pupa. *The
illustrated Book of Insects*, Treasure Press,
London, 1991

Page 22: Woodcut of a butterfly by Conrad
Gessner. Sarah Don, *Traditional Embroidered
Animals*, David & Charles, London, 1990 (p. 45)

Page 23: The J. Paul Getty Museum, Los Angeles,
Ms. 20, fol. 7. *Fly, Caterpillar, Pear, and
Centipede*, Joris Hoefnagel and Georg Bocskay,
1561–1562; illumination added 1591–1596.
Watercolours, gold and silver paint, and ink on
parchment. 16.6 x 12.4 cm

Page 24: an original title page from the series on
Dutch insects by Jan Christiaan Sepp, *Butterflies
and Moths*, Michael Joseph Ltd, London, 1978

Page 25: Maria Sibylla Merian, *Two Butterflies*,
watercolour on parchment, 1706. Kurt Wettengl
(ed.), *Maria Sibylla Merian: Artist and Naturalist,
1647–1717*. Verlag: Gerd Hatje, Frankfurt and
Thames & Hudson, London, 1998 (p. 135)

Pages 27, 28: Mrs Archibald Christie, panel of
linen embroidered with coloured silks with
diamond shaped lattice with birds, plants,
flowers, berries & butterflies; English; c.1914.
© Victoria and Albert Museum, London.

Pages 28, 29, 30, 141: butterflies in Art Nouveau
design. *Art Nouveau Designs*, The Pepin Press,
Amsterdam, 2000

Page 30: stencil designs for moths and butterflies.
W.G. Sutherland, *Stencilling for Craftsmen*, The
Decorative Art Journals Co. Ltd, 1925

Page 31: Séguy's butterflies. Plates 16 and 18, E.A. Séguy, *Séguy's Decorative Butterflies and Insects*, Dover Publications, New York, 1977

Page 32: silver butterfly pendant, courtesy of Shutterstock.com

Page 33: Designing from the butterfly. A.F. Rose & A. Cirino, *Jewelry Making and Design*, Dover Publications, New York, 1967 (pp. 261, 262)

Pages 34, 36: traditional Chinese Butterfly motifs. Stanley Appelbaum, *Traditional Chinese Designs*, Dover Publications, New York, 1990 (pp. 31, 37, 38)

Page 35: traditional Japanese butterfly motifs. Graham Leslie McCallum, *4000 Animal, Bird & Fish Motifs*, Batsford, London, 2005 (p. 329)

Page 36: Japanese family crest designs. Fumie Adachi, *Japanese Design Motifs*, Dover Publications, New York, 1972 (pp. 153, 155)

Page 40: modern museum butterfly collection, courtesy of Shutterstock.com

Pages 41, 43, 44, 68: Dodd specimen case featuring *Aenetus* sp. © Queensland Museum; Dodd specimen case, *Poem Case* © Queensland Museum; Dodd specimen case, *Aenetus mirabilis* © Queensland Museum; from Dodd specimen case, *Aenetus mirabilis* © Queensland Museum

Page 50: Scarlet Tiger Moth, courtesy of Shutterstock.com

Page 57: White Ermine Moth, courtesy of Shutterstock.com

Page 62: Large Emerald Moth, courtesy of Shutterstock.com

Page 74: Longhorn Moth, courtesy of Shutterstock.com

Page 80: Lycaenidae – Chalkhill Blue Butterfly, courtesy of Shutterstock.com

Page 86: Lycaenidae – Purple-shot Copper Butterfly, courtesy of Shutterstock.com

Page 92: Morphidae – Cramer's Blue Morpho Butterfly, courtesy of Shutterstock.com

Page 98: Noctuidae – Large Yellow Underwing Butterfly, courtesy of Shutterstock.com

Page 104: Nymphalidae – Camberwell Beauty Butterfly, courtesy of Shutterstock.com

Page 110: Nymphalidae – Purple Fuchsia Butterfly, courtesy of Shutterstock.com

Page 117: Papilionidae – Swallowtail Butterfly, courtesy of Shutterstock.com

PICTURE CREDITS

Page 117: caterpillar of the Swallowtail Butterfly, courtesy of Shutterstock.com

Page 124: Pieridae – Brimstone Butterfly, courtesy of Shutterstock.com

Page 130: Saturniidae – Indian Moon Moth, courtesy of Shutterstock.com

Page 130: enormous feathered antennae of male Luna Moth, courtesy of Shutterstock.com

Page 138: Satyridae – Glasswing Butterfly, courtesy of Shutterstock.com

Page 144: Sesiidae – Hornet Moth, courtesy of Shutterstock.com

Page 156: Sphingidae – Elephant Hawkmoth, courtesy of Shutterstock.com

Page 150: Zygaenidae – Six-spot Burnet Moth, courtesy of Shutterstock.com

Pages 168, 171: Green Lacewing, courtesy of Shutterstock.com

Page 168: Large Copper Butterfly, courtesy of Shutterstock.com

Pages 173, 176: Dogwood, *Cornus cornuta*, courtesy of Shutterstock.com

Page 206: Swallowtail Butterfly, *Papilio machaon*, courtesy of Shutterstock.com; Milk Parsley, *Peucedanum palustre*, courtesy of Shutterstock.com

Page 216: Swallowtail Butterfly, *Papilio machaon*, courtesy of Shutterstock.com; caterpillar of the Swallowtail Butterfly, courtesy of Shutterstock. com; pupa of the Swallowtail Butterfly, courtesy of Shutterstock.com

Page 222: Swallowtail Butterfly, *Papilio machaon*. Jan Christiaan Sepp, *Butterflies and Moths*, Michael Joseph Ltd, London, 1978 (p. 27)

Page 226: Blackberry, *Rubus fruticosus*, courtesy of Shutterstock.com

Page 228: Large Emerald Moth, *Geometra papilionara*, courtesy of Shutterstock.com

Page 232: Large Emerald Moth, *Geometra papilionaria*. Jan Christiaan Sepp, *Butterflies and Moths*, Michael Joseph Ltd, London, 1978 (p. 199)

Page 248: Dog Rose, *Rosa canina*, courtesy of Shutterstock.com

Page 248: Grape Hyacinth, *Muscari armeniacum*, courtesy of Shutterstock.com

Embriodery Supplies
& Kit Information

The threads, beads and needlework products referred to in this book are available from Jane Nicholas Embroidery and specialist needlework shops.

A mail order service is offered by Jane Nicholas Embroidery. Visit the website and view the entire range of stumpwork kits, books and embroidery supplies including wires, fabrics, leather, beads, hoops, needles and scissors. Thread ranges include Au Ver à Soie, Cifonda, chenille, DMC, Kreinik, Madeira and YLI, and goldwork supplies. Framecraft brooches, boxes and paperweights are stocked for finishing.

Jane Nicholas Embroidery
P.O. Box 300
BOWRAL N.S.W. 2576
AUSTRALIA

Tel: +61 2 4861 1175
Mob: 0408 493 170
Fax: 0248 611 175

Email: janenic@bigpond.com
Web: www.janenicholas.com

ACKNOWLEDGEMENTS

. . . .

I would like to extend my gratitude to all those people who
continue to share their passion for stumpwork with me. Whether by
correspondence or in class, your enthusiasm provides invaluable motivation.

My wonderful family continues to provide wholehearted support and
encouragement for my work. Special thanks to John, who makes all the kits
and runs the mail order service with amazing efficiency and attention to detail.

Sincere thanks to my dear sewing friends for their companionship
and the opportunity to share ideas and cherished stitching time.

Finally, to all those involved in the production of this book at Sally Milner
Publishing—your expertise, and belief in my work, is sincerely appreciated.

Jane Nicholas 2014

ABOUT THE AUTHOR

. . . .

Jane Nicholas has been researching and working in the field
of embroidery for over twenty years. Specialising in stumpwork
and goldwork embroidery, she has written seven books and has
contributed widely to journals and magazines on the subject.

In 1999 Jane was awarded a Churchill Fellowship to further her studies
in stumpwork in the United Kingdom and in 2005 was awarded the
Order of Australia Medal (OAM), for her 'services to hand embroidery as
an artist, teacher and author'. She teaches widely in Australia, New Zealand
and the United States of America and continues to research and develop new
techniques—particularly in stumpwork. A separate, but often related,
area of her work is as a maker of artists' books and boxes.